What People Are Saying About ...
POWER TO CHANGE

"POWER TO CHANGE could be used effectively in both academic and pastoral settings. Your seminal ideas would be helpful in both sermon preparation and adult educational classes. Your theories concerning change could find a place in Pastoral Counseling courses at theological seminaries. I envision your book serving as a required text for a seminary course. In addition, I believe that the general public might find your ideas interesting and inspirational. Personal transformation is what many aspire to, and your book explains how to achieve it!"

—Dr. Francine Green, Director
Department of Social Services
Division of Mental Health and Mental Retardation
Southern Nevada Adult Mental Health Services
Las Vegas, Nevada

John Dan writes about change ... not just rearranging the chairs, but change with substance and at the spiritual core of our being. There is an old-fashioned word for this kind of change: *salvation.* Another word is *freedom.* Dan understands that this is not an easy process, but often what is impossible for us is possible for God. That's the key and that's what he means by "Second Order Change." This book can create possibilities for you.

—Chaplain Jerome Blankenship
Ordained United Methodist Clergy
Chaplain, Sunrise Hospital and Medical Center

POWER TO CHANGE ... "addresses what I see to be the very heart of our national dilemma. ... It is impossible for me to exaggerate my personal concern for the moral anarchy of our contemporary society which, I believe, derives from our abandonment of God in our thinking. God bless you, brother."

—Dr. Richard C. Halverson
Chaplain, United States Senate

"I was challenged and rewarded by the truth of statements such as this in the writing of Mr. Dan: 'It takes a prodigal experience to produce a fertile soil condition that will receive the seeds of truth.' I have found that often the experiences of life of greatest challenge need a reflective exploration to be further understood. The writing of Mr. Dan, as well as the deep truth about the pain of the change, can be a productive tool in that reflective process. The union of spirituality and psychology is called for, as we as a Christian and a healing community strive for greater personal freedrom. May this book be a vehicle for 'Thy Kingdom Come.'"

—Michael Thompson, M.S.W., C.S.A.C.

I have known Rev. John Dan for over thirty years, and it is a joy for me to recommend his book, *POWER TO CHANGE*. It is a book that reflects many years of research and practical ministry. Because of the book's central thesis, content and approach, I strongly believe it will find a wide market among Christian workers who are interested in mental, spiritual and social wholeness, and will also make a valuable contribution to evangelism.

—Dr. Bill Thomas
Associate Evangelist
Luis Palau Evangelistic Association

"Power to Change" must have a great market in the field of psychology and psychiatry. The thrilling part of the book is the fact that Jesus, only, affects the power to change in our lives. And He gives the power of the Holy Spirit to one who will believe in Him. May [Power To Change] give the impetus to unbelievers, particularly those who are really into the workings of the mind, to seek the true meaning of life — Jesus Christ, who said, "I have come that they might have life — abundant!

—Dale Evans Rogers

One of the refreshing experiences for me in recent months was spending time with the manuscript of *Power To Change* by John Dan. I know John personally and deeply respect him and his spiritual journey. His early roots in Hollywood led to a dramatic change in his own life. Graduate degrees along with work and life experiences in counseling and ministry, where he was a part of life changes in others, all are blended in this marvelous book, *Power To Change*. I highly recommend it to counselors and pastors alike. Younger pastors will especially be helped with the experience and insight and clarity of expression that John Dan has built into this text.

—Kenneth Kliever
Region Minister
American Baptist Churches of Arizona and So. Nevada

"Rev. Dan's commitment to those individuals who are less fortunate comes through clearly in his new work, *Power To Change.* His many years of counseling people with mental illness affects his philosophical and theological outlook, and the result is a synthesis of philosophical advice and just plain common sense. The book makes good reading for anyone interested in the power of the mind."

—Ann Marie Smith
President, Alliance for the Mentally Ill of Nevada

I found *Power To Change* a helpful guide for all Christians and non-Christians to better understand the way of salvation. Truly a useful and thoughtful book to be read and re-read.

—John Hinkle, Ph.D.
Clinical Psychologist

John Dan is an active marriage and family therapist in the Las Vegas area. He brings a long time understanding of people and their problems to his research and writing. Most important of all, he undergirds his philosophy of hope and help with Biblical principles ... I feel that he is on the right track offering some genuine help to understanding the source for the true power to change.

—Gene Appel
Senior Minister, Central Christian Church, Las Vegas, Nevada

POWER TO CHANGE

A Christian Psychotherapist's Examination of the Dynamics of Change

by John Dan, M. Div., M.A.

PUBLISHING

8635 W. Sahara Ave., Ste. 459 ❦ The Lakes ❦ NV 89117

The author wishes to thank the following sources for permission to quote and/or refer to material:

Change: Principles of Problem Formation and Problem Resolution by Paul Watzlawick, John H. Weakland and Richard Fisch. Reprinted by permission of W.W. Norton & Company, Inc., copyright © 1974 by W.W. Norton & Company, Inc.

Reality Therapy: A New Approach to Psychiatry by Glasser, William M. Copyright © 1965 by William Glasser, Inc. Reprinted by permission of HarperCollins Publishers, Inc.

Philosophical Investigations by Wittgenstein, Ludwig, translated by G.E.M. Anscombe. Copyright © 1953, 1981 by Macmillan College Publishing Company, Inc. Reprinted by permission of Macmillan Publishing Company.

Why I Am Not A Christian by Bertrand, Russell. Copyright © 1957 by George Allen & Unwin, Ltd. Copyright © renewed 1985 by George Allen & Unwin, Ltd. Reprinted by permission of Simon & Schuster, Inc.

Transactional Analysis of Psychotherapy by Eric Berne, M.D. Copyright © 1961 by Grove Press, Inc. Used by permission of Random House, Inc.

The Unity of the Bible by H.H. Rowley. Copyright © 1957 by H.H. Rowley and published by Meridian Books, Inc. Reprinted by permission of Lutterworth Press, Cambridge, England.

On Death and Dying by Elizabeth Kubler-Ross, M.D. Copyright © 1962. Reprinted by permission of Macmillan Publishing Company.

I'm OK, You're OK by Harris, Thomas, M.D. Copyright © 1967 by Harper & Row. Reprinted by permission of HarperCollins Publishers.

Born to Win by James, Muriel and Jongeward, Dorothy. Copyright © 1971 and published by Signet Classics, the New American Library, Inc. Used by permission of Addison-Wesley Publishing Company, Inc., Reading, Massachusetts.

Except for author's paraphrases, most Bible verses used in **Power to Change** were taken from *The Living Bible*, copyright © 1971. Used by permission of Tyndale House Publishers, Inc., Wheaton, Illinois 60189. All Rights reserved.

Cover and Text Design by Norine V. Grzesik-Rathbone
Design Ing by Norine V. • 2485 W. Wigwam Ave., Ste. 39 • Las Vegas, NV 89123

Published by Eden Publishing

FIRST EDITION / Trade Paperback ISBN 1-884898-01-7

FIRST EDITION / Hardback ISBN 1-884898-00-9

Library of Congress Cataloging-in-Publication Data
Catalog Card Number 94-70391

> *Power to Change*
> Includes bibliographical references.

TABLE OF CONTENTS

PREFACE

Psychological and spiritual concepts are often perceived as diametrically opposed and, indeed, incompatible. Mistrust of the psychological discoveries of Freud, Adler, Jung, and a great many other social scientists by members of the religious community, and conversely by behavioral scientists toward the spiritual, is tied to two basic problems:

1) There is a kind of party line concensus in the social scientist's personal ideology that rules out the spiritual and thereby often prevents him from viewing his work in the scientific and psychological realms objectively and openly. This stance too often creates a great deal of unnecessary suspicion, thereby widening the chasm and preventing the Church and the behavioral scientist from utilizing much useful data to increase a better understanding of the nuts and bolts of the mystery of change, which the Holy Spirit works to bring about within the human psyche.

One of the most prevalent difficulties is that man can never wholly understand the mind of God and His dealings with His creation. Because "we see now through a veil only dimly," many in the Christian world feel it is almost heresy even to desire or seek to go deeper into the mysteries of God.

However, I find it unacceptable in an age when science is advancing so rapidly and vying for the minds and hearts of men that the Church has not kept pace and worked with equal diligence to "rightly divide the word of truth," without fear that such exploration of the cosmos within might lead us astray. It is not necessary to isolate spiritual truth and health from other aspects of experience in order to remain faithful to the life-transforming message of the Gospel of our Lord Jesus Christ. In fact, compartmentalized Christianity is responsible for the weakened condition of the Church body, for fragmentation is the natural result of not being able to incorporate and integrate all segments of the human experience into a harmonious whole.

Therefore, it is healthy and necessary to consider the world around and within ourselves without fear, if we are to live effectively. This is the great quest to which every person aspires, be he or she Christian or otherwise. If this were not so, there would not be so many desperate and sometimes dangerous pursuits through pleasure, peace, self-improvement and other make-over attempts. Needless to say, until the Church has the courage to examine and translate into the modern idiom what the world is clamoring for, it will remain isolated from those who need its message the most. Never before has the western world been on such a crazed search for spiritual completeness, as evidenced by widespread self indulgence in drugs, sex, eastern cults, witchcraft, and the like.

2) The Church needs to stop thinking of itself as "other," standing on the sidelines, watching all this human tragedy.

Instead, it must admit that these elements are on its own doorstep, and often sitting in the pews under the cloak of respectability on Sunday mornings, but dropping its guise elsewhere.

The solution lies not in chastisement and further ostracism, but—and this is not the same as embracing evil—the Church must remove its head from the sand and see that even secular social scientists have been moving for decades in a parallel (if not fully enlightened) direction alongside the Gospel. In other words, they have come to recognize some of the same facts about the nature of man, his needs, the dual conflict within man (carnal and spiritual), and characteristics of the Trinity in man's psychological make-up. The revelation of God in the Bible came first, and one could say that over the past hundred years psychiatrists and social scientists have been coming to many of the same conclusions through their research. The Church should have been at the forefront, encouraging instead of trying to suppress this effort, in my opinion.

At any rate, each generation of the Church must learn to address those eternal truths by using the tools at hand. Playwrights and authors have been restating the same truths and ideas for centuries, and yet, by contrast, the Church has often been fearful of innovation, whether in the areas of music, new approaches to evangelism, such as mass media in its early years, and even use of language, such as, which version of the Bible is authentic, properly sanctified, and, of course, in the field of psychology.

Of course, the Church is wise to consider what it does sanction, for its message must remain faithful and uncontaminated. Nevertheless, its leadership needs to look without fear at contributions made by others which will enhance the Christian's understanding of his or her faith, and how to implement his or her faith more boldly and fully into every aspect of daily living. Anything less is to live a subnormal Christian life!

Thirty years ago, I was living just such an empty existence. As an educated man with two professional degrees, I had traveled the world and had a measure of success as an actor; I had friends and was well thought of by my peers. But nothing in a seemingly full life seemed to rid me of that gnawing gut feeling that I was just going through the motions and that there had to be more to life than what I was experiencing. I wanted to be a new man inside. For the first time in my life, I recognized that the problem was within: I didn't like the deception and corruption I knew was present within me. Even though I was not a Christian (yet), I questioned in a clumsy prayer whether it was possible that there was a God present in the lonely confines of my room. The prospect of praying to the wind or having my prayers bounce off the four walls seemed a ridiculous exercise in futility. However, no one was around to laugh at my fumbling attempt to make contact with the invisible God, about whom I knew practically nothing, so I was free to drop my usual self-sufficient act.

I had never heard that the Bible talks about being "born again" or becoming a "new creation in Christ." The sum total of my religious background as a child was a vacation Bible school in an Indianapolis settlement house for immigrants' kids and a stint as an altar boy, which ended when I had a beef with a Rumanian Orthodox priest and told him to "go to hell." None of this exposure to "religion" stuck with me as an adult; I was as secular as any of today's Yuppies, out for a good time and all the material toys I could lay my hands on. For years I had experienced the confusion and isolation of living and working in a superficial world that deceives and devalues human life. Now I realized that something was desperately wrong with my life. In fact, the remark, "Stop the world, I want to get off," reflected rather accurately how I felt at that low point in my life.

In retrospect, the scene there in my room was not without its comical aspects. Kneeling for the first time in my adult life, I found myself at eye-level with a bookcase of mostly neglected volumes, including a dusty Douay version of the Bible, which I had bought at a Catholic retreat I'd attended five years prior, more to humor a well meaning friend than because I felt any particular need or interest. In all the time since, I had never opened the Bible, let alone read it.

As I thumbed slowly through its pages, I came across a passage where Jesus was asked how a person comes to God. His answer astounded me: "I am the way, the truth and the life: No man comes to the Father but by Me." (John l4:6). My initial reaction was crude: I thought, "This Jesus is either a liar, a total fruitcake, or...He's God!" Of those possibilities, my slight acquaintance with the facts about Jesus' life lent credence to his words.

Glancing back to the previous chapter of John's Gospel, I read about Jesus washing Peter's feet at the Last Supper. From attending a neighborhood vacation Bible school as a young boy, I could identify with Peter—frequently impulsive, putting his foot in his mouth, a braggart, and full of human frailties. To me, it seemed more appropriate that Peter should have been washing Jesus' feet, but just the opposite was taking place. I sensed the Spirit of God telling me, "You're like Peter, and I love you, *as is.*" This realization of *unconditional love* was the beginning for me of a new birth and a new life of discovery in Christ.

This book is the product of this continuing discovery. It contains my observations as a Christian psychologist of how the Christian faith works spiritually, psychologically, and emotionally, as gleaned from my own personal life experiences, as well as from my work with hundreds of people who have come to me with their problems over the past twenty-eight years. My work has been conducted in a variety of clinical settings, including my work as a psychologist and program director in mental health centers; as a Baptist pastor of several churches; as a hospital and prison chaplain; and as director of an alcoholic rehabilitation program. My academic and clinical training span the fields of behavioral sciences and theology. I am also licensed to practice as a marriage, family and child therapist in the states of California and Nevada.

As a final note, I wish to stress that nothing written in this book is to be taken as a new gospel or a substitute for the Gospel. There is absolutely no intention on my part to add to or take away from the Gospel. I would be the first to say that the truth of the Gospel is intact and unchangeable. However, many people, who are psychologically, spiritually and emotionally confused, are referred to me daily for help; these have Catholic, Protestant, and Jewish backgrounds, as well as no religious orientation at all. I have found in my clinical practice that the combination of psychotherapeutic techniques and spiritual truth has helped dispel confusion and barriers to wholeness that culture, prior conditioning, and half-truths have often created. In doing this, I use the vernacular of the day as much as possible, to overcome the confusion religious jargon often presents to the modern mind.

The primary purpose of this book is to clarify and demonstrate how the Gospel works to bring about the dynamics of change, so that more people will gain a better understanding of the spiritual, psychological and emotional processes depicted in the Bible. It is my hope and prayer that many will find their way out of the morass of oppressive confusion into the truth and uncontaminated life to be realized only through God's Son, Jesus Christ.

—*John Dan*
Las Vegas, Nevada
February 1994

POWER TO CHANGE

CHAPTER 1. FACING THE TRUTH SQUARELY

We live in a world of rapid cosmetic changes of form without substance. From the dawn of history to the present, we can see that dramatic changes have taken place. Scientific and technological advances have rapidly changed the face of social structures and lifestyles. After the dust of past and current changes clears, the oppressions and distortions of life remain in tact; essentially, nothing has changed, or changes make conditions worse, or at best changes are cosmetic.

As you and I pursue the business of living, we sense an essential need deep within the core of our being, which promises fulfillment but painfully eludes and frustrates most of us. We are involved in a quest, whether we realize it or not, for verification of basic truths about ourselves, the world we live in, and the God who created us. Without this Truth, the quality of our lives becomes oppressive and burdensome, often meaningless.

From the condition of the world, it is obvious that there is something within the makeup of all human beings that prevents us from living in a healthy, harmonious way with each other. Every one of us, regardless of our station in life, cultural or national origin, religious or philosophical beliefs, or political alliances, has some flaw or contamination within our makeup.

These characteristics seem to cripple or adversely

effect each of us in some way, as individuals and in our relationships with others. People in positions of great power and responsibility have these flaws and contaminations, as well as people who are considered to be the least in social structures of all cultures. No one is exempt.

Many of us mask our flaws cleverly. We function very well in the world and are regarded as successful. We appear to be outwardly attractive and models to be emulated. On the other hand, other people function less successfully and do not appear to be as attractive or healthy. These people probably make up the bulk of the shaky foundation of world societies. There are others who function marginally. Life for these people is economically, emotionally and socially oppressive. A significant number of people do not live in harmony with other members of society and prey upon their fellow man. These people are often isolated from society and placed in prison. Some of them, in extreme cases, end up forfeiting their lives.

There is also a significant group of people who break down emotionally, psychologically and spiritually. Some, who become a danger to themselves or others, are locked in psychiatric wards. Others seek some form of therapeutic help on an outpatient basis. These people come from all walks of life, cultural backgrounds, religious affiliations, and all strata of the social spectrum.

It is apparent that the emotional, psychological and spiritual condition of all human beings is not healthy. "Healthy" can be defined as having no flaws or contamination within the human makeup. Illness or contamination exists in some form or to some degree within the emotional, psychological and spiritual makeup of all human beings. To be healthy in all three areas in this world is not "normal." Illness and contamination is normal. "Normal" is determined by what the average actual condition of a social group is. In fact, anyone would be hard pressed to find a completely healthy person in all these three areas.

That the unhealthy human make-up prevents change with substance from taking place within any social structure, regardless of size and composition, soon becomes obvious. Not only are changes prevented, but adversely unhealthy conditions are maintained and perpetuated within the human make-up and social relationships. To understand how human conditions are maintained, perpetuated and prevented from changing, and how changes with substance take place, it's important to examine five basic issues that shed light:

1. How do human beings and social groups function?

2. What is in the emotional, psychological and spiritual makeup of all human beings and social groups that makes them unhealthy?

3. How did it all become unhealthy?

4. How do individuals and social groups continue to remain unchanged and unhealthy?

5. What must occur in order to make changes with substance in individuals and social groups?

Nearly two thousand years ago, a man named Jesus was on trial in the palace courtyard of the Roman Governor of Judea. Governor Pilate was the presiding judge who conducted His trial and ordered Him crucified. During a portion of the interview, Pilate said to Jesus, "Your own people and their chief priests brought you here. Why? What have you done?"

Jesus answered, "I am not an earthly being. If I were, my followers would have fought when I was arrested by the Jewish leaders. My kingdom is not of this world."

Pilate asked, "But you are a king then?"

Jesus replied, "I was born for that purpose. And I came to bring truth to the world. All who love the truth are my followers."*1*

Pilate was thoughtful for a moment, and as he went out onto the balcony to tell the crowd that Jesus was not guilty of any crime, he muttered, "What is truth?"*2*

This question is etched into the very depths of every human being. Yet as you and I pursue the business of living, truth eludes us and is shrouded in a kind of fog or maze that produces within our lives a quality of life that is oppressive and burdensome. Pilate knew that Jesus was not guilty, yet he ordered His execution. He knew what was true and right. He struggled within himself to do the right thing and let Jesus go.

But he did the opposite of what he knew was true.

St. Paul observed the strong pull of this tendency within himself: "I don't understand myself at all, for I really want to do what is right, but I can't. I do what I don't want to do—what I hate. I know perfectly well that what I am doing is wrong, and my bad conscience proves that I agree with these laws I am breaking. But I can't help myself, because I'm no longer doing it. It is sin inside me that is stronger than I am and makes me do these evil things."*3*

Both of these men experienced the double bind of "damned if you do and damned if you don't." There is more truth than fiction in the old cliche that "the road to hell is paved with good intentions." It can be safely said that everyone of us tends to fall far short of carrying out

10

our good intentions. We all notice this pull within ourselves and have probably expressed St. Paul's sentiments: "No matter what way I turn, I can't make myself do good. Even when I want to, I can't. When I try not to do wrong, I do it anyway."*4*

Instead of taking responsibility and choosing to free an innocent man from erroneous charges, Pilate caved into political pressure and ordered Jesus' execution.

To pursue this further, we might ask:

1. What do Pilate and St. Paul have in common in their makeup?

2. What did St. Paul have that Pilate did not?

In the courtyard interview, Jesus acknowledged to Pilate that his kingdom was not of this world. He told Pilate He was born to be a King where truth rules, and He came to bring the truth to this world. All who love the truth are His followers.

This somehow went over Pilate's head. He recognized that Jesus was not guilty. His eyes were open to see that much data.

St. Paul also acknowledged that he knew what was right, and, like Pilate, Paul found he did not act on the truth. Instead they both acted on the opposite of truth. They both found themselves acting on lies and distortions. Jesus told Pilate His followers loved truth and acted on it. But both Pilate and St. Paul had something within their makeup that overruled the truth they knew. They both knowingly acted on lies and distortions. This, then, is the crux of the matter: *There is something universal within the human makeup that screens out truth and lets lies and distortions govern human will and actions.* Pilate, with a fatalistic sense of resignation, speculated on the question, "What is truth?"*5* From his actions, one could surmise that his question implied to him that "there is no such thing as truth; it's all lies. Why bother?"

In contrast, St. Paul asked not "What is truth?" but exclaimed, "What a terrible predicament I'm in!" Then he asked not "what" but "Who will free me from my slavery to this deadly lower nature?"*6*

Pilate was resigned to his fate, whereas St. Paul knew the answer: "Thank God! It has been done by Jesus Christ our Lord. He has set me free."*7*

Pilate saw the One Who is the Truth standing before him, yet failed to recognize and embrace the Truth as relevant to his own life. By contrast, St. Paul met the same Truth on the Damascus road and came to know the Truth that set him free.*8* Two men saw the same Truth. One responded and was set free from his oppressive blindness and double-bind. The other remained a prisoner to darkness and continued down the path of confusion and alienation. St. Paul was able to change and shape his life, based on clearness of Truth and light. Pilate reacted to mob pressure and buried himself deeper in darkness of lies and distortions.

St. Paul and Pilate represent the two major ways of dealing with the human condition. Within the contrast between their responses, the answers to the five issues raised earlier can be found, as well as how and why some human beings emerge from the prison of lies and distortions and come to know the Truth experientially, while others, like Pilate, remain lost in confusion and despair, reacting to the pressures of life, tossed about like a leaf in the wind.

In modern times, terms and ideas of mental illness and mental health have surfaced and become part of the philosophical fabric of most of the western world. During the twentieth century a great deal of energy, time and money has been expended in coping with issues of mental illness and health. Professionals have been trained and have emerged from all sorts of disciplines to address and cope with this problem. Strides have been made within the ranks of these professions to understand and learn the "hows" and "whats" that make human beings tick and how to treat emotional, psychological and spiritual illness with some degree of effectiveness.

Social scientists have studied and done extensive research into the institutions and functioning of human society. No one discipline has the corner on the market. None has fully learned the "hows" and "whats," much less gained an expertise sufficiently effective to warrant exclusion of other behavioral scientists. Rather, the answer lies in cultivating a more open spirit of inquiry on the part of all within the helping professions, including the clergy.

Regrettably often the views and attitudes of members of the treatment profession have created stumbling blocks in treating mental illness and promoting mental health. Such exclusivism tends to raise barriers and impede progress. This is regrettable and often destructive. Everyone can learn from others. I myself have learned from others whose views or methods I do not personally embrace and have used what has value in my practice as a therapist and minister, without compromising my own personal convictions.

A major dichotomy unfortunately exists between treatment approaches to mental illness and promotion of mental health. This is polarized into what can be characterized as the "secular" and "spiritual" points of view. Each group tends to stand at opposite poles, discounting each other and unwilling to listen and learn from each other.

A case in point: I entered training in the field of psychotherapy with a theological background, was viewed as suspect by both camps, and at times have experienced some harassment. Over the years I have discovered that people in the mental health field tend to regard mental illness and health as the province of those trained in the so-called traditional "secular setting," and to view the "spiritual" as irrelevant.

Conversely, people from the so-called "spiritual community" view the knowledge of psychology and studies in human behavior with suspicion, as if it were the tool of the devil and not to be trusted. For instance, I once heard, in a radio broadcast, a well known, respected Bay Area minister condemn Transactional Analysis as diabolical and to be avoided like the Plague by all Christians.

Suspicion is not without some justification on each side, for neither really knows and understands the other. There are those in the secular field who are downright hostile to the spiritual. Many caricaturize the spiritual as some form of magical voodoo or fanatical fundamentalistic legalism. Unfortunately, there is much in the religious-spiritual world that is unhealthy and even a source of mental illness.

In my own practice I have occasionally had to undo the damage of some well meaning pastors, who generally lacked an understanding about how human beings function, even though they may have been doctrinally sound. Consequently, some people in their congregations find themselves pounded into deeper pits of emotional, psychological and spiritual despair. The tendency is to apply or quote Scriptures to the hurting person, with a legalistic application and a condemning, rejecting attitude.

On the other side of the coin, many secular therapists have done damage to their clients by discounting their beliefs and values. Some even attack the client with the same kind of legalistic, rejecting attitude. In fact, the secular therapist is trained to ignore and disregard a person's beliefs or values. Many do not even consider that there is a spiritual dimension within human beings. Therapists-in-training are often held in derision by supervisors and other colleagues if they hold any spiritual or religious views. Any therapist or agent-for-change in the helping professions, who denies the spiritual dimension within a human being or is hostile to it, does the client a disservice. This attitude is as ludicrous as denying a person has a liver simply because you cannot see it, or being hostile because a person does have a liver.

No effective inroads or progress will ever be made in alleviating mental illness or promoting mental health until those involved in the field recognize the existence and reality of the spiritual dimension within themselves and the people they endeavor to help. All attempts in history, by any society, to deny and extinguish the spiritual within people have always ended up devaluing and exploiting people within its membership. This denial is a blinding deception. For a therapist to deny the spiritual and discount the values a client presents to them is a gross violation of sound therapeutic principles.

It sabotages therapy before it begins by not accepting the client and, in effect, rejecting the client. Certainly distorted religious beliefs and values are often the genesis of the emotional and psychological dysfunction a therapist must treat. Dealing with the spiritual dimension in therapy does not mean proselytizing or religious manipulation.

15

Wise therapists, who are themselves healthy in the spiritual, psychological and emotional dimensions, can go a long way by helping their clients to see what is unhealthy and distorted in their beliefs and values. They can help clients keep what is healthy and replace the unhealthy with healthy beliefs and values.

The spiritual-religious community must be open to understanding how human beings function and how they themselves may be a hindrance, thus promoting illness rather than health. They need to understand that a person who is spiritually healthy is psychologically and emotionally healthy. The converse is also true: A psychologically and emotionally healthy person is also spiritually healthy. It is also true that a spiritually unhealthy person is psychologically and emotionally unhealthy, and the converse is equally true.

One of the purposes of this book is to demonstrate that the psychological, emotional and spiritual do go together, and sound therapy is best achieved through the healthy integration of all three areas.

Individuals and societies will never change and find their way into psychological, emotional and spiritual health unless they are able to shed the bondage of lies and distortions that seem to blind and oppress them. Jesus tells the world only those who know the "truth" shall be set free to live.*9* All truth must be examined for what it is, if anyone is to know the truth and learn from the truth. It is unimportant and irrelevant to speculate on "what is truth?" The only thing that matters and sets us all free is when we "know the truth," and know what truth "is" and "isn't." One thing truth "isn't" is "lies and distortions." Truth, then, really deals with "what is." Truth is "what is"!

Over the past thirty years, I have come to recognize

that the behavioral sciences have uncovered a great deal of important data about "what makes human beings tick." Among other things, I intend to demonstrate that much of the knowledge found in the behavioral sciences does not conflict with faith and the spiritual nature of human beings, as is so often supposed in both religious and behavioral science circles. Furthermore, it is possible to achieve a bonding of faith and spirit with the psychological and emotional makeup of all human beings.

This bonding of the spiritual, emotional and psychological has helped lead many whom I have seen in therapy out of the same confusion and despair that oppressed Pilate and St. Paul years ago.

Many writings from different schools of thought contribute to the understanding of men and women and their spiritual nature. The writings of Paul Watzlawick, John Weakland and Richard Fisch (WWF) in the field of dynamics of change, Sigmund Freud, Eric Berne, and those writers who developed the Trinitarian psychological makeup of human beings shed a great deal of light and understanding on how human beings can change from the unhealthy to the healthy, and what takes place within the human makeup that enables them to do so.

The behavioral sciences actually shed light on the spiritual nature of all people, as characterized in the Bible. The writing and concepts of WWF, Freud and Berne, and the Trinitarian terms of Parent (Super-Ego), Adult (Ego), Child (Id) and the four properties in Galois' "Theory of Groups," in practice, are the clearest way to address and shed light on the five issues raised about the spiritual, psychological and emotional makeup of all human beings and the effects on society and change.

Dr. Watzlawick and his associates wrote the book *Change.* They give a clear understanding in their book of how people and social groups remain stuck and never change and what needs to take place for people and groups to get unstuck and change.

Freud and particularly the writers who have amplified on the Trinitarian concepts developed by Berne, give the lay person an understandable picture of the psychological and spiritual makeup within all human beings by using the concept of Parent-Adult-Child. The interrelationship and interaction between the Trinitarian concepts of Super-Ego, Ego, Id, and the Parent, Adult and Child clarify the psychological, emotional and spiritual dynamics that take place within all people. PAC, or Super Ego, Ego, and Id, as the psychological structure is really the reflection of the Image of God and also the spiritual structure within human nature, as characterized in the Bible as Father, Spirit, and Son. Therefore, an unhealthy PAC (or Super-Ego, Ego, Id) is a distortion of this Image and is characterized as the sinfulness of human nature in the Bible; whereas a healthy Parent (Super-Ego), Adult (Ego) and Child (Id) reflects the undistorted Image of God.

Understanding the nature of change as described by Watzlawick and his associates, along with the Trinitarian psychological-spiritual dynamics of Freud and Berne, enables us to see more clearly what makes human nature and social groups unhealthy, and what it takes to make individuals and groups healthy. This enables us to see the bond between the psychological and spiritual, and the effects of the psychological upon the spiritual, and the spiritual upon the psychological. It brings into focus the nature and ingredients of faith in God, as portrayed in the Bible, and the effects this has on the psychological, spiritual and emotional health of a person and his relationship to other people.

Healthy societies are made up of human beings who are psychologically, spiritually and emotionally healthy. To see, know and act upon the truth is a psychological and spiritual imperative, if individuals within society are to be healthy. This imperative cuts across all social, cultural, political, religious, national and economic lines, and ties in with the biblical theme from beginning to end. Through the eyes of an undistorted, clear faith, processed through a healthy Adult-Ego thinking function, men and women can discover "truth and reality" and be led out of despair and darkness.

That truth and reality finds its source in the God of Abraham, Isaac and Jacob, Who is ultimately focused and experienced in God's Son Jesus Christ, the only agent of change with substance. His life and work paves the way for all people to be reconciled to God-Creator and to each other. He does this by restoring an undistorted Image of God within human nature.

This is the biblically stated goal and purpose of salvation, whereby spiritual and psychological health can be experienced. Through this faith process, using the Faith faculty of a healthy Adult-Ego, all people can be set free from the oppression of their deceptive, distorted nature. Freedom from deception paves the way for discovery of truth and life, as revealed and given in Jesus Christ.

I have found the application of Watzlawick's and the Trinitarian dynamic principles of Freud and Berne useful in my endeavors as a Christian and a therapist to demonstrate how God made it possible for all human beings to be reconciled to Him and know Him as the source of truth; how the saving work in the death and resurrection of Christ decontaminates the Trinitarian human nature and impregnates it with the life and truth of God. From this view, we can see how living out the salvation process restores and enlarges the Trinitarian psychological and spiritual Image of God within human nature. This in turn works to bring about a metamorphosis of healthy changes in the relationships between members of social groups.

Hopefully this book will not only help make the truth about ourselves and our inner dynamics clearer, but will also help the reader come to experience this process personally.

POWER TO CHANGE

CHAPTER II. GALOIS' FOUR PROPERTIES GOVERN INDIVIDUAL AND SOCIAL BEHAVIORS

William Shakespeare wrote, "All the world's a stage, and all the men and women merely players. They have their exits and their entrances, and one man in his time plays many parts."*1*

Throughout history, life's many large and small dramas have been played out in every nook and cranny of the globe, all part of a greater world drama. All dramas have casts of human members, who interact with each other and play out life scripts with all their plots and subplots. All scripts mirror the emotional condition of every cast member and social condition within the life drama of social groups.

Dramas on the world stage are ongoing, filled with continual action and motion; they are never static. Each drama journeys through hills and valleys, experiences life's high and low tides, its sorrows and joys. Life dramas in social groups may span generations. New cast members are born; old members exit permanently from the scene when their life roles come to an end.

What takes place between cast members may be viewed as the life drama of all social groups. Common characteristics inhabit all cast members; common themes run through the scripts of all life dramas, reflecting social conditions and determining the outcome of both individual and group dramas.

In the nineteenth century, Evariste Galois, the French mathematician, developed an imaginative branch of mathematics. He introduced the term "group" in his "Theory of Groups." Galois' theory gives insight into what takes place and governs human behavior and social relationships in human dramas.

According to the theory, a "group" has the following four properties:

1. It is composed of members who are alike in one common characteristic. They can be numbers, objects, concepts, events, or anything else that has a common denominator, as long as the outcome of any combination of two or more members is itself a member of the group. For instance, the numbers '1' through '12' on the face of a clock are members of a group representing hours. Any combination of two or more members is again a member of the group (9 A.M. plus ten hours is 7 P.M.). No matter what combination of subtraction or addition is used, the result will be the hours of the clock.

The common characteristic that identifies the game of football, for instance, is that it's made up of twenty-two players, divided equally into two teams. The players are dressed in uniforms that are alike in every aspect, except the colors, which distinguish the teams. No matter how many players, or in what combination, the coach substitutes during the game, there are never more than twenty-two players on the playing field during the game.

2. A group contains an identity member in combination with another member that maintains this other member's identity. For example, the identity member in 5 + 0 - 5 is zero. It is one (5 X I = 5), when the combination rule is multiplication.

Each player's position is an identity member, which in combination with other players in their positions, maintains the identity of the other players as football players, and members of a team in the game. Second base is a position identified in baseball and is never a position identified in football. Regardless of the position of a football player, his behavior on the field will never change the fact that he is playing by the rules of football and not baseball.

3. Another property of a group is that no matter how you conceive its varying sequences, the outcome of the combination remains the same. For example, make four moves of a unit of one inch in the direction of each of the four cardinal points. Regardless of the sequence (north first, then east or west, or whatever), the result after the fourth move will be a return to the starting point. *(See Figure 1 below.)*

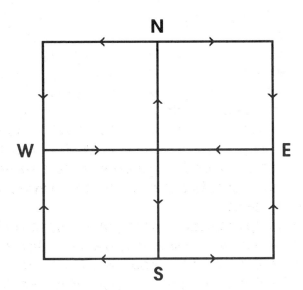

Fig. 1

The same would happen if eight moves of a one inch unit are made in the direction of eight cardinal points. Regardless of the sequence (north, northeast or northwest, etc.), the result after eight moves will be a return to the starting point. Results will always be the same, no matter how you increase the progression and moves.

The game rules of football always maintain the game as football. Any combination of moves by the players within these rules always maintains the game. When the players' moves are within the rules of football, they will always be playing football and not some other game. They will not behave like baseball players in a football game.

4. Every member of the group has its reciprocal or opposite. For example, where the combination rule is addition, 5 + (-5) = 0. There are always twenty-two group members or players in the game of football. The group is divided into two teams of eleven players each. Football, like all sports is adversarial, or a contest in values; and the game is played to win by each team. When one team is on the offense, the other is opposing on defense. Thus, each member of the team has an opposite or reciprocal opposing it. Reciprocals or opposites may be either adversarial or complementary in nature. In each example, we find that, on one hand, the combination produces a marked change, but the result is itself a member of the group.*2*

Galois' four properties govern not only mathematical groupings but also human behavior and the interaction and structures within and between social groups. These properties help focus in, like a TV camera, to see what common characteristics inhabit all human members of any social group.

They also enable us to see the common themes running through the life scripts of all social group members and the group collectively:

1. The *universal common denominator* running through all social groups is its composition of human members. Regardless of number, mix of gender or age, all cast members of social drama groups are human beings. All human members are endowed with a Trinitarian psychological and spiritual makeup.

2. The *identity members* that maintain and perpetuate the individual and social conditions within all social groups and between social structures are the themes, mindsets, beliefs, views, and ideas embraced by group members. The *identity members* shape the plots and subplots of the group's life script.

3. *Rules* govern the behavior of group members and the social interaction between group members and relationships with other social structures. *Rules* include laws, culture and customs within social groups. *Rules* carry out plots and subplots of the life script the individuals and the group live out.

4. As the script is played out, *reciprocal* relationships emerge between the membership of groups and between social groups that are either adversarial or complementary, or may be a combination of both.

Understanding how Galois' four properties work in shaping individuals and relationships between social group members and between social groups sets the stage for examining and seeing how individual and social change do or do not work and function. This helps us see how our life scripts and life dramas play themselves out in a healthy or unhealthy way.

POWER TO CHANGE

CHAPTER III. TWO KINDS OF CHANGE.

"The things I would do, I don't do." — St. Paul.

1. First Order Change
2. Second Order Change

1. FIRST ORDER CHANGE

There is an old French proverb that says, "The more something changes, the more it remains the same." This is more than a witticism. It is a phenomenon that really takes place in our daily lives. No doubt you have asked yourself, "What is going on? No matter how hard I try to change, I never change. I'm like St. Paul. I keep doing the opposite of what I want. I find myself doing the same thing over and over, even though I am aware it may be wrong or not in my best interest. I keep trying to make something work that will never work, like trying to make square pegs fit into round holes."*1*

This phenomenon governs both individual and group behavior. From early history, Herculean and often heroic efforts have been made to effect change with substance in individual and social conditions. Governments have spent enormous sums of money on programs designed to bring about change and resolve individual and social problems. Few, if any, of these endeavors can be cited as contributing to substantial changes or improvement in the individual and social conditions they are meant to help. In fact, these endeavors frequently make the social conditions worse and perpetuate the conditions.

Two questions need to be addressed when we keep observing that individuals, families, governments, and all social groups, regardless of composition, persist in responding to life and problems in repetitive ways that create problems; make problems worse; and keep problems going:

1. How do undesirable conditions or situations keep persisting without change or radical improvement?

2. What is required to make changes with substance or, more precisely, what needs to happen if change with substance is to take place? Watzlawick and his associates observed in their investigations that over the centuries many theories of persistence or change were formulated, but none of the theories of persistence and change have ever been put together. In addressing this problem, Watzlawick and associates drew on theories from the field of mathematical logic: (l) The Theory of Groups and (2) The Theory of Logical Types.*2*

The four properties of Galois' Theory of Groups were outlined in the previous chapter. We observed that all individual and social behaviors are governed by the prevailing conditions that exist within these four properties. There is nothing within the makeup of group members and the system itself that can transform itself and change the prevailing conditions within the four properties. WWF refer to all efforts of change from within a group system as a First Order Change or System.*3*

In a *First Order Change or System,* the characteristics of Galois' four properties maintain a predictable operative individual and social system that never changes, regardless of individual and group effort. It can be observed that every human being has vulnerabilities and flaws within his/her psychological-spiritual makeup. These flaws and vulnerabilities are the key factors interacting with the characteristics of the four properties that shape the unhealthy human and social conditions within all groups and between social groups. The human flaws effect the characteristics of the four properties, and, at the same time, the characteristics of the four properties effect the human makeup of all group members.

The *universal common denominator* in a First Order Human Social System is the *flawed psychological and spiritual makeup* of every group member. This common denominator is universally imbedded in all members of any social group, regardless of gender composition, number of members, or geographic location. These flawed conditions lead group members to embrace an *identity member* of *distorted beliefs and views of life. Rules* of *power, control and conformity* to the group social system evolve from distorted beliefs and views.

These rules take the form of *self-defeating and destructive life scripts* for the individual members and the group social system. Laws, regulations, customs, and cultural constraints are at work to govern individual and group behavior and interactions. The presence and combination of the first three unhealthy properties lead to *adversarial reciprocals and relationships* between group members and among the community of social groups around the world.

Since Galois' four properties operate and govern individual and group behavior, any efforts toward change within a *First Order System* end up maintaining the existing system and human condition. Corrective solutions are taken that never work; they create more problems, make them worse, and keep the problems going.

Many attempted corrective solutions seem, on the surface, to be a reasonable way to bring about change and improvement in the human condition. They are attempted in every area of individual and social group endeavor—politics, economics, religion, social changes, etc. Some corrective approaches deny or avoid problems; others have magical approaches and expectations; or, if something isn't working, doing more of the same might achieve the desired result.

Alcoholism has always been a serious social problem from the dawn of history. Repeated efforts to curb this deadly social problem by placing legal and moral restrictions on the consumption of alcohol have never eliminated the problem. *More-of-the-same solutions,* typical within the framework of *First Order System,* were carried to the ultimate in the 1920s by passing a Constitutional Amendment prohibiting the manufacture, sale and use of alcohol.

The cure turned out to be worse than the disease. Alcoholism rose. Special law enforcement agencies were needed to track down emerging bootleggers. Extreme corruption rapidly developed, reaching its tentacles into every strata of the social fabric. Action was taken that not only increased the problem of alcoholism, but created problems that never existed before, and thus kept the problem going.

Prohibition was set aside when it proved to be an unworkable solution. Abandoning an unworkable solution permits the freedom to explore more realistic solutions to the basic underlying problem.

Another unworkable and more common solution often used to deal with a difficult situation is to deny that there is a problem. We are all familiar with the expression, "putting your head in the sand," or, "If you don't look, it will go away." For most people denial or avoidance of problems serves the need to maintain an acceptable social facade. Out of this need is born the open secret that "nobody is to know that everybody else knows." This is often known as the "family myth;" in political circles, it becomes the "party line." In this kind of solution, action is necessary, but none is taken. Maintaining individual life scripts and group rules, customs and traditions takes precedence over healthy changes.

People often expect utopian, magical solutions that are ideal and perfect in nature, rather than accepting things "the way they are." This often leads to disappointment and, at times, even devastation. To many, Utopia conveys the idea of some kind of ideal environment or circumstance. However, *Utopia means "never was."* The word was introduced to pun ideas about what is generally thought of as an ideal. In a utopian kind of solution, the expectation is unreasonable and unattainable; it expects reality to conform to ideal beliefs. An example of how action taken at the wrong level brings an impasse is to connect the nine dots shown in Figure 2 by drawing four straight lines without lifting the pencil off the paper and without retracing. Before you read on, take a piece of paper and try to solve the problem on the next page before turning to the solution shown in *Figure 3.*

Nine Dot Exercise

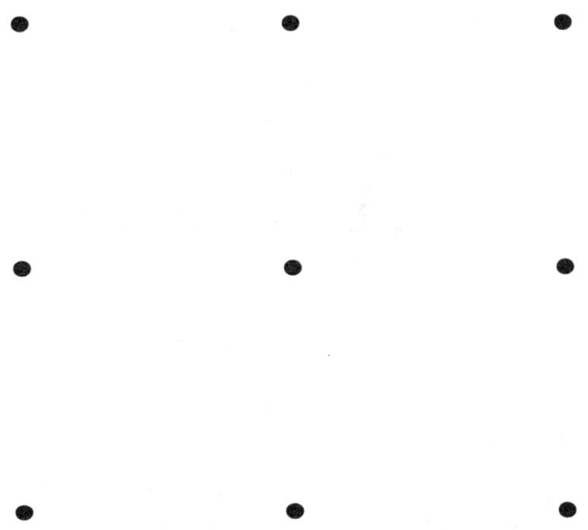

Instructions:
Draw four straight lines and go
through each dot without taking
the pen or pencil off the paper.

Fig. 2 (nine dot)

If you are like many who feel frustrated, don't fret! In my experience, it seems that about 999 out of 1,000 make the same assumption. The dots compose a square, and most people assume the solution must be found within this self-imposed boundary. The failure is not in the impossibility of the task, but in the assumptions made in the attempted solution, and in its self-imposed limitations. A problem is created in this solution because no matter which combination or order of four lines you try, there will always be one unconnected dot.

Nine Dot Solution

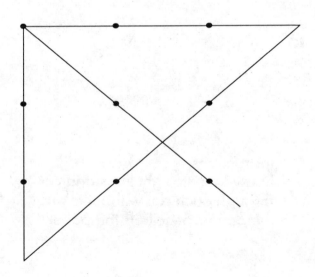

Fig. 3 (solution to nine dot)

It probably becomes apparent to you how many times you have found yourself in a bind. No matter how logically or calmly you tried to find a solution, you ended up going around in circles. In other words, you have been attempting First Order Changes. The solution to the nine dot problem is found not in the nine dots, but in the assumptions made about the dots. Most people never examine assumptions they make about life and tenaciously hold onto them. It is unlikely anyone will ever find his way out of oppression and frustration without being willing to discard unworkable assumptions about solving his/her life's problems. Tragically, and sometimes comically, most solutions to conflicts between people or groups of people are attempted at the level of First Order Change.

Nine dot types of solutions are prime examples of mindsets that exist in *First Order System.* From the unhealthy human and social conditions, we can safely conclude that *First Order System is deeply entrenched in the social fabric around the world.* The odds for any substantive change in First Order System are highly improbable, if not impossible. In fact, many times the therapist, psychiatrist, minister, or others in the helping professions may be attempting First Order Change, when, in fact, they desire to effect Second Order Change.

As the nine dot figure demonstrates, the attempted solution was a First Order Change, whereas a Second Order Change was needed to solve it. Sometimes it is important to distinquish between something being what people call a "difficulty" and a problem that persists, when attempting a solution. A "difficulty" is usually an undesirable state or condition that can be resolved by commonsense action—usually of the First Order Change.

For example, if it's cold, turn on the heat. If it's hot, turn on the air conditioner. At times, people attempt Second Order Change when a First Order Change solution would be appropriate. The attempted action in this kind of solution is taken at the unworkable level.

There are also solutions taken that produce paradoxes. This creates an impasse and an untenable solution of "damned if you do, damned if you don't." In its extreme, this results in "crazy making." Dictatorships tend to impose paradoxes. They are not content with mere compliance to commonsense laws like most democracies. Dictators like Hitler wanted to change people's thoughts, values and outlooks. Mere compliance or lip service was considered passive resistance, and a sign of hostility. It's like saying, "You must not only put up with the coercion, you must also want it and like it." A fiction that is often dear to educators and parents is the claim that "school is fun" or "should be fun." However, in actuality, this doesn't seem to be the experience of a great many students. This could lead the student who doesn't experience school as "fun" to ask something like, "What's wrong with me? I must be stupid. I don't see how school is fun."

When my youngest son Peter was in the fifth grade, my wife and I received a note from his teacher, asking for a conference, because he wasn't handing in his school work. When we arrived, the prinicipal told us this teacher was his finest and most experienced. After talking with the teacher and the prinicipal for a few minutes, it became apparent why Peter wasn't handing in his school work. The teacher kept asking me and my wife questions like, "Why do you suppose I asked him to do that?" This lovely young lady seemed stunned when I abruptly interrupted and told her, "For the past five minutes, you've been asking me to guess your mind. I don't know what's in your mind unless you tell me. I suspect you ask your students to do the same. I suggest you tell them or instruct them in specific terms as to what you want or expect from them." When I checked with my son a week later, he understood the assignments and was turning them in. In this teaching situation, the teacher was essentially communicating, "I expect you to do your assignment, but you've got to guess what it is." Unfortunately, this is not a rare and isolated incident in human relationships. In paradoxes, conflicting solutions are attempted, producing conflicting results that lead to confusion and, thus, to an impasse.

Nine dot types of solutions are prime examples of mindsets that exist in *First Order System.* From the unhealthy human and social conditions, we can safely conclude that *First Order System* is *deeply entrenched in the social fabric around the world.* The odds for any substantive change in First Order System is highly improbable, if not impossible. In fact, many times the therapist, psychiatrist, minister, or others in the helping professions may be attempting First Order Changes, when, in fact, they desire to effect Second Order Change.

2. SECOND ORDER CHANGE

The Theory of Logical Types addresses the second question, "What is required to change?" This theory was developed in large part by Alfred Whitehead and Bertrand Russell in their writings, *Principia Mathematica.*[4]

As in the Theory of Groups, the components of the totality or group are called members, while the totality itself is called a "class," rather than a "group." For example, mankind is a class of all individuals but is not itself an individual. Another example: The Republican Party is a class made up of a number of individuals, but the Republican Party is not an individual.

The Theory of Logical Types, in essence, is not concerned with what goes on inside a class,*5* that is, between its members. The Theory gives a frame of reference for considering the relationship between member and class, and the peculiar metamorphosis which is in the nature of shifts from one logical level to the next higher. It is somewhat like shifting gears in an automobile. The shift is from out of the range of lower gears into the whole new range of the higher gears. This shift is never made by the lower gears or from within the lower gears. It is made from a mechanism from without the system in an automatic transmission, and by the driver of the car in the clutch-driven car. W-W-F refer to this as *Second Order Change or System.*

By accepting the basic distinction between the two theories, you can begin to see that there are *two different types of change: One that occurs within a given system, which itself remains unchanged; the other occurs from without the system and changes the system itself.*

A person having a nightmare can do many things in the dream, but no change in any of his behaviors will ever terminate his nightmare. This is a First Order Change. The only way out of the dream is to wake up, or change to an altogether different state. This type of change is a Second Order Change. This is a change of change, and as WWF point out, the very phenomenon whose existence Aristotle categorically denied.*6*

For a Second Order Change to occur, the focus

must shift from efforts within the system to an agent or frame of reference from without the system. This must all be new and different from the modus operandus within a First Order System.

As long as the universal common denominator of all social groups is flawed psychologically and spiritually, the characteristics of the other three properties continue to be shaped and maintained in an unhealthy condition. All efforts to bring about change in human conditions have been primarily focused on three of the four properties: the identity members, rules, and reciprocals. This focus attempts to change outward human and social conditions. As in the case of Prohibition, this focus makes conditions worse and never brings about healthy changes.

Mental health agencies, practitioners and others concerned with healthy changes have learned a great deal about how the flawed psychological human makeup works. Some treatments can be provided that help group members reduce stress and learn to cope and function in life more effectively. All of this is helpful, but human conditions overall still remain unchanged and unhealthy.

Attention in First Order Change is primarily devoted to fixing and adjusting the psychological human makeup and outer social conditions. Little or no attention is devoted to the spiritual dimension within the human makeup and social structure. The spiritual dimension is relegated primarily to religious activities that are generally viewed as irrelevant and a pain in the neck to the social structure. Strong forces within a First Order System deny or totally distort the nature of a healthy spiritual dimension. This hostile opposition has generally worked to render the spiritual inoperative or ineffective in matters of healthy human and social changes.

In Second Order Change someone or something outside the First Order System intervenes in a way that brings about a transformation in the four properties that govern the system and the human members living out the life scripts within a system. Transformation is a metamorphic process that works to totally replace flaws and unhealthy conditions within the human and social systems with a healthy flawlessness. Without the intervention of the spiritual dimension, a Second Order Change is impossible. Essentially all group members within a First Order System are impotent and without personal life power. Their flawed psychological and spiritual makeup cuts them off from the life forces and power resident in the spiritual dimension of life.

Only an intervention that incorporates the spiritual dimension with its life-giving force can bring about a transforming Second Order Change. A healthy spiritual life force must impregnate and permeate the flawed psychological-spiritual makeup of group members, in order to set in motion the metamorphic process toward a healthy, flawless human makeup. The *universal common denominator* is transformed from unhealthy to healthy human group members. Group members with a healthy human makeup set in motion and extend the transforming process to the other three properties.

The *identity member* is transformed from distorted beliefs and views to healthy beliefs and clear views which embrace truth and genuineness. The *identity member* is brought out of fog and darkness into light. Light allows beliefs and views to be focused and congruent with human and spiritual realities of truth and genuineness. Undistorted beliefs and clear views of truth and genuineness lead to a transformation of rules and life scripts governed by *unconditional love.* Unconditional love transforms an oppressive human environment into one that nurtures and empowers the development of the human uniqueness of every group member. *Adversarial reciprocals* are transformed into *complementary relationships* that free people to relate and interact in ways that are mutually beneficial to all group members.

In a nutshell, a Second Order Change works to transform an unhealthy, powerless *First Order System* into a healthy, powerful *Second Order System.*

With our inborn video cameras we can zoom in on individuals and groups throughout the world, whose lives bear evidence that healthy psychological-spiritual and social changes have taken place. These spiritually transformed members and groups are yeast, leavening and permeating the social loaf in a Second Order Change. A complete Second Order Change and System will only transpire in proportion to a significant increase in the intervention by the spiritual dimension in the drama of human affairs. Otherwise, the light remains dim and eventually fades out.

Back in 1974 or 1975, Dr. Watzlawick conducted a seminar on "Change" in Las Vegas. During a coffee break, I asked him if a conversion experience to Christ, or the "born again" experience depicted by Jesus, would be considered a Second Order Change. He reflected a moment, then agreed that these experiences would be considered a Second Order Change.

In First Order Change, we discover that *problems which people or nations have lie not in the fact of having problems but in how people or nations attempt to solve these problems.* Most of the western world, if not the entire world, reflects the Aristotilian mind when searching for solutions. A lot of energy is expended trying to understand why we have the problem. We ask a lot of questions and then expend a lifetime of energy, only to discover that we are asking unnecessary questions in the first place, and for which there probably are no answers. The Aristotilian assumption is that if we know "Why," than we can change.

Recently a woman who had been in and out of therapy for the past twenty years was in a great deal of distress. Her alcoholic and abusive husband had made an about-face three weeks earlier. He was now treating her decently and generously. He bought her a new car and gave her a substantial amount of money. The more decent his behavior, the more she became suspicious and confused, trying to figure out "why" he changed and what this meant. She seemed to be rocked by my suggestion that she might experience less distress if she just accepted and let herself enjoy this good turn in fortune, rather than figuring out "why" he changed. Then, "it was as if the light turned on," she said to me. "When I first started in therapy twenty years ago, my therapist told me that I had to understand 'why' I was emotionally ill and 'what caused it' before I could change. Do you mean to tell me he lied?" My retort was, "Probably, but not intentionally. He may not have known any better at the time."

What seemed to be helpful to this woman was that I had introduced a Second Order Change. The situation was reframed and redefined to take the focus from searching for a cause or reason, so she could see that it was more to her benefit to "accept" what was happening and enjoy it. To ask "why" is not scientific, as is often supposed. More will be dealt with later about the unproductiveness of asking "why?"

Essentially, in a Second Order Change, the boundaries and limitations imposed by assumptions in the First Order System are removed. This enables us to discover "what is" and find workable solutions that fit the facts and apply to our own life situations. This is essentially what happens in any therapy that works, regardless of what techniques may be used or the discipline the therapist has been trained in. For example, Dr. Milton Erickson was brilliant in using Second Order Change by reframing it in his work in hypnosis.

After identifying the principles of problem formation and resolution, WWF suggest a four step procedure to implement the practice of change:

1. A clear definition of the problem in concrete terms. This means the translating of vaguely stated problems into concrete terms that permit the crucial separation of problems from pseudo-problems.

2. An investigation of the solutions attempted so far. A careful exploration of these attempted solutions shows what kind of changes and solutions have been attempted. Then you can avoid repeating these unworkable solutions. In this way, you know and realize what has maintained the situation and where to apply the change and discover a workable solution.

3. A clear definition of the concrete change to be achieved. This removes the denial and utopian aspects that formulated the problem initially.

4. The formulation and implementation of a plan to produce this change. This will be dealt with later. Suffice it to say for now that the first three steps are necessary preliminaries that can be accomplished rather quickly.*7*

This chapter furnishes a thumbnail sketch of how

people get stuck and never change, no matter what they do to change. This is what WWF call First Order Change or System.

I have also touched on what takes place when people are able to move out of the First Order System into the Second Order Change. This is a change of Change that entirely leaves the old system and enters entirely into a new system. Understanding these two perspectives will shed light on the dynamics of the spiritual nature of human beings.

In the following chapters, we will examine "how" and "when" people are healthy or unhealthy spiritually, psychologically and emotionally, and how a spiritually empowered life-change moves a person from an unhealthy to a healthy state.

POWER TO CHANGE

CHAPTER IV: WHAT MAKES HUMAN BEINGS TICK?

1. *How Human Group Members Function*
   A. Four Life Positions
   B. Penfield's Experiment
   (Instant Replays During Live Action)

2. *How Life Experiences Shape and Distort Human Development*

3. *The Healthy Spiritual Dimension*
   (The Image of God in PAC of Man)

4. *How Original Sin Universally Distorted the Image of God*
   A. Original Game Leads to Original Sin
   (Cussedness of Man)
   B. Sin Distorts the Image of God in Human Nature

1. HOW HUMAN GROUP MEMBERS FUNCTION

So what makes us tick? What is there in human nature that brings out inconsistent and often destructive behavior?

Philosophers, theologians, poets, historians, psychologists—in fact, anyone who is thoughtful at all—seem to come up with one consistent impression: that human nature is multiple and in conflict with itself. Somerset Maugham once made an observation about himself similar to that made by St. Paul: "There are times...I recognize that I am made up of several persons, and the person that at the moment has the upper hand will inevitably give place to another."*1*

At the turn of the twentieth century, Sigmund Freud probed into this human dilemma and developed the theory that warring factions existed in the unconscious of man. These factions were identified as the "restrictive and controlling force of the Super-Ego over the instinctual drives of the Id, with the Ego acting as a referee out of enlightened self-interest."*2*

Freud's thinking dominated the field of psychiatry and psychology during the first half of this century. In l949, Eric Berne, M.D., introduced his theory of Transactional Analysis at a small seminar of six people in San Francisco. He was trained as a psychiatrist and psychoanalyst. The ideas of psychoanalysis influenced him and are evident throughout his writings, but he was bothered by its slowness, overcomplexity, and rigidity. Both Freud and Berne observed that the psychological human nature resident within all people is Trinitarian in function and character. Freud characterized the Trinitarian makeup as Super-Ego, Ego and Id. In Freud's concept the Id is characterized as the instinctual part in human nature that needs controlling.

The Super-Ego acts as a damper on the Id, somewhat like a judge that gives disapproval or approval to the Id. Freud tended to see the Super-Ego as more disapproving than approving. The Ego is the part that mediates and acts to control the Id. The Ego is essentially the human will that makes decisions and takes action. Berne characterized the psychological trinity as a Parent-Adult-Child. This characterization is more descriptive of function than ego states and is more understandable than Freud's. It is more useful and helpful to the average person in understanding how he or she functions day in and day out.

The Parent is more than a damper or source of approval or disapproval. It also functions as a nurturer, teacher, and corrector of the Child. The Parent can accept others constructively, or destructively reject them. Freud's Super-Ego tends to be more restrictive in character than the nurturing Parent. Berne's Child function can be teachable and grow, or it can be destructive and never learn. Freud's Id is vague and tends to characterize the destructive mischief maker in human nature. Freud had little, if any, emphasis on the Id as a healthy side of human nature. He tended to emphasize the need to control the Id, more than teach the Id.

Berne's Adult, unlike the Ego, functions more as a decision-maker and action-taker than a controller of the Child (Id). The human will is resident in the Adult (Ego) and has the capacity to evaluate all kinds of information and make choices. *Choice is always the cornerstone of faith and human freedom.* Without choice, there is no expression of faith, nor freedom to govern one's own destiny in life. Faith is processed through the Adult (Ego) and empowers the human will to carry out decisions.

Freud's analyses focused primarily on the destructive interaction of the spiritual and psychological within human nature. He was in tune with much of the destructiveness of religious form in human nature, but seemed oblivious to any notion that human nature could reflect, even in part, the healthy Image of God.

Berne and many of his followers seem to have a sense of the spiritual dimension in human nature. There is an underlying sense within Berne's ideas that the trinity in human nature needs to be in harmony within and function with a sense of oneness in character and substance for it to be healthy. Berne seems to have a recognition of the healthy characteristics needed in human nature that reflect the Image of God, even though he never labeled it as such.

In his writings Dr. Berne sets out to demonstrate that his theory of the Parent, Adult and Child is not the Freudian concept of Super-Ego, Ego and Id. Freud's Trinitarian concept of human nature is unclear to the average lay person. PAC is an observable phenomenon and reality. Pastimes, games and scripts are not abstractions but operational social realities in the human drama.*3*

Berne's writings, and the many who have further developed his ideas, shed a great deal of light in understanding the human and spiritual nature of man and its peculiar interaction. In fact, much of what is written in this section comes from the ideas and thoughts not only of Berne, but Thomas Harris, M.D., Muriel James, Dorothy Jongeward, and many others who have contributed to the development of Transactional Analysis.

Berne essentially defines Transactional Analysis as a method of examining the basic scientific unit—the transaction where I do something to you, and you do something back in response. The next step is determining which part of the multiple nature of each individual (Parent, Adult or Child) is predominantly responding in the transaction.*4*

PAC is a state of being and function that is produced by playbacks of recorded information from past events, involving real people, times, places, decisions, and feelings.*5*

Muriel James and Dorothy Jongeward wrote that Transactional Analysis is concerned with four kinds of analysis:

1. Structural Analysis: The analysis of individual personality.

2. Transactional Analysis: The analysis form early in the child's experience.

3. Game Analysis and Structured Time: The analysis of ulterior transactions, leading to payoffs and how people structure their lives.

4. Script Analysis: The analysis of specific life dramas that persons compulsively play out.*6*

The main concern of this book's theme is met by taking a look at the structural analysis of individual personality. This is a method of analyzing a person's thoughts, feelings, and behavior, based upon the phenomena of ego function states--Parent, Adult and Child.

Parent Ego Function State contains the attitudes and behaviors derived primarily from parental or other external sources. Outwardly it is often expressed toward others in critical, prejudiced, and nurturing behaviors. Inwardly, it is expressed as old parental messages which continue to influence the inner Child.

Adult Ego Function State has nothing to do with age. This is the thinking function that deals with reality "as is" and gathers objective information. It is organized, adaptable, intelligent, and functions by testing reality and estimating probabilities. Within the human will as part of the Adult function, decisions and actions can be taken, based upon evaluations that sort out objective from distorted information.

Child Ego Function State is where all feelings come from. It contains all impulses that come naturally to an infant, including the recording of early childhood experience and response. It also defines itself and others, and expresses "old" (archaic) behavior from childhood.

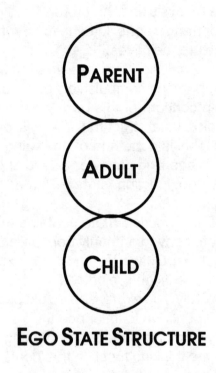

EGO STATE STRUCTURE

Fig. 4

A. FOUR LIFE POSITIONS

Dr. Tom Harris observed that by the time a child is two to three years of age, he has decided on one of four life positions.7 Dr. Harris used the term "OK." For the purpose of this book, the term "value" is more descriptive and accurate, and will be used in lieu of "OK."

1. *"I don't value me (not OK)--I value you (you're OK)."* Dr. Harris believes that there is an overwhelming accumulation of evidence that the "I don't value me," or "not OK" feelings take form early in the child's experience. The basis of man's struggle is not sex, as Freud asserted, but rather feelings of inferiority and a sense of not measuring up. The child, in his early experience, lacks the information from a nurturing parent and the development of his Adult assessment faculty. The child accepts the judgments from a Parent figure, which at first are communicated to him verbally and non-verbally.

2. *"I value me—I don't value you."* If a Child experiences parental brutality over an extended period of time, it often concludes that the only one who has value is itself, and that Parent, who was valued, is found to be of no value. He develops toughness, and his inner Parent gives him permission to be tough and cruel. In extreme forms, this is often the early history of criminals. Oftentimes, these people develop into judgmental and critical people who are concerned with power and control over others. This inner Parent devalues the Child in others.

3. *"I don't value me—I don't value you."* By the end of the first year, a Child begins to walk and finds that it's not being picked up and stroked as much. Many times a sense of extreme abandonment develops within the Child. This may continue without relief throughout

adulthood. The Child may conclude that no one is of value, and begins to give up. This person tends to develop a sense of hopelessness and often ends up in a mental institution in a state of extreme withdrawal and regressive behavior. He has experienced extreme deprivation of strokes or love. The individual in this position stops using his Adult faculties in relationships with others and is often extremely difficult to reach.

4. *"I value me — I value you."* This fourth position is the position of one who develops into a healthy human being. This individual has the Adult faculties working with no or minimum contaminations from the other ego function states. In this state, a person is expressing a healthy faith; examines the facts and realities; gives assessment and evaluation; makes decisions; and takes responsibility and control over his own life. Irrational feelings are expressed in the first three life positions, emanating from early contaminated material and undeveloped Adult faculty.

Dr. Harris observed that *people do not drift into the healthy life position:* "It is a decision we make. In this respect, it is like a conversion experience. We cannot decide on the fourth position without a great deal more information than most persons have available to them about circumstances surrounding the original positions decided on so early in life."*8*

B. PENFIELD'S EXPERIMENT
(Instant Replays During Live Action)

About the time Berne was introducing his theory of the observable phenomena of PAC, Dr. Wilder Penfield, a neurosurgeon from McGill University in Montreal, gave additional verification of Berne's observations. In 1952 Penfield presented and published a paper on his findings.*9* Over a period of several years, Penfield conducted a series of experiments while performing brain surgery, in treating patients with focal epilepsy. He touched the temporal cortex of the patient's brain with a weak electric current transmitted through a galvanic probe. In each case, the patient was under local anesthetic, fully conscious and able to talk with Penfield. He found that the electrode stimulated recollections clearly derived from the patient's memory. When the electrode was withdrawn, the experiment stopped, and would repeat itself as the electrode was reapplied.

Penfield drew some significant conclusions:

1. The response to the electrode was involuntary, evoking a single recollection, not a mixture or a generalization.

2. Past events and feelings associated with the events were recorded in detail.

3. Penfield further concluded that events and feelings are inextricably locked together in the brain so that one cannot be evoked without the other.

4. The brain functions as a high fidelity audio and visual tape recorder. It tapes and records every experience from the time of birth, possibly even before birth.

5. The recordings are in sequence and continuous. The thread of continuity in the recollections seems to be time.

6. People can exist in two states at the same time. The patient knew he was talking with Penfield, and at the same time was seeing the Seven-Up Bottling Company and the Harrison Bakery. The patient was in the experience and outside of it at the same time, observing it.

7. Recorded experiences and feelings are avail-

able for replay today in as vivid a form as in instant audio-video replay of a particular action in a football game. *10*

Recalling and reliving past experiences and feelings that have nothing to do with the present is what colors the nature of today's transactions. People not only remember what they saw and felt in the past, but experience being there and feeling the same way in the present. This could be called "instant replays during live action." Sports TV viewers are used to viewing instant replay *after* live action, but would be confused if instant replay took place during live action. This phenomenon is experienced by all of us more than we realize.

I personally experienced this phenomenon when I first entered clinical training. As part of my training, I was required to participate in group therapy. After several sessions, the group therapist, Mary Jane, confronted me with a startling fact, that she experienced me as hostile toward her. Of course, I vehemently denied this on the grounds that I had only recently meet her. However, I stewed about this, as for several weeks I became increasingly irritable and a pain in the neck to my family. Finally, my misery became so unbearable that I was forced to deal with this in the group.

Forunately Mary Jane was a skilled therapist and able to help me work through my irrationality. Through her intervention, I came to realize that I wasn't experiencing myself as a grown man but as a twelve-year-old boy being humilated by my seventh grade teacher, Miss O'Malley (not her real name).

Miss O'Malley was an Irish spinster school teacher who wore her flaming red hair in a severe bun. She had a fiery temper that frequently exploded, followed by a volley of erasers thrown at the kids in her class. I thought most of them were thrown at me. As my rage mounted, the crowning humiliation occurred: Miss O'Malley arbitrarily vetoed my election as president of the music club in front of the entire class. It was like being castrated.

As a twelve-year-old boy, I lacked the maturity and sophistication to cope with such a poweful teacher. My sense of frustration was overwhelming. I felt damned if I fought back, and damned if I didn't fight.

As I worked through my feelings within the group, I came to realize that Mary Jane bore a striking resemblance to Miss O'Malley. Her physical and facial features and especially her red hair worn in a bun had triggered an instant replay of rage.

Very skillfully, Mary Jane helped me engage my Adult so I could sort out the past from the present and put things into perspective. As a result, I discovered that Mary Jane was a very nice person and realized that Miss O'Malley was a good teacher, on the whole. I also acknowledged that I wasn't exactly an angel in those days. [Now, on occasion, when my wife pins her hair up and I start to object, she humorously reminds me that she isn't Miss O'Mally either!]

Penfield's findings are observable evidence that these biological studies support and help explain the observable evidence in human behavior as described by St. Paul. These findings, along with those of Watzlawick and his associates, as well as Berne and Harris, give a clear view of how human group members function psychologically and spiritually. This enables us to see what transpires when human beings discover and begin to live by faith in God.

2. HOW LIFE EXPERIENCES SHAPE AND DISTORT HUMAN DEVELOPMENT

"I know I am contaminated through and through, so far as my old nature is concerned." —St. Paul

All human group members are alike in the fact that each person has a Parent (Super-Ego), Adult (Ego), and Child (Id) ego function. PAC (or Super-Ego-ego-Id) is really human nature (or psychological make-up) within every person. PAC is more descriptive of the functions of human nature than the Freudian Trinitarian concept, and will be used to refer to the psychological, spiritual make-up during the remainder of this book.

Each of us develops uniquely. We differ in the content that has been recorded in our PAC, and in the functioning of it. At birth the infant's Parent and Adult ego function states are not developed. By the time a child is a year old, we see evidence of the Parent and Adult functions taking shape. These recordings are the unique experiences of each of us and determine how our PAC functions.

Dr. Tom Harris once asked a sixteen-year-old girl what PAC meant to her. After a long silence her reply was, "It means that we are all made up of three parts, and we'd better get them separated, or we're in trouble."*11* When separated (see Figure 4), each member function of PAC is free of interference and contamination from other Trinitarian members. Each function contributes uniquely to the harmonious oneness of a healthy Trinitarian function. We would all live with each other in a healthy and trouble-free manner, if every group member's Trinitarian make-up functioned congruently.

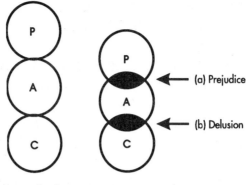

A. Ideal   B. Contaminated

Graph from Thomas Harris' *I'M OKAY, YOU'RE OKAY*,
page 82. Used by permission of HarperCollins

Figs. 5A and 5B

However, this is not the case with any of us. Our PAC circles overlap (see Figure 5b). The overlapped circles are contaminations of the Adult functions by the unexamined ideas, beliefs and feelings from the Parent and Child functions. Ideas and beliefs from the Parent (a) are externalized as true. Prejudicial, rigid beliefs and assumptions develop in the Parent, such as "a woman's place is in the home." This develops early in childhood, when the fear of parental rebuke shuts down inquiry into certain subjects. *Essentially the Child is told not to think or question.*

The Child is contaminating the Adult in the (b) overlap. Odd Child feelings are inappropriately externalized in the present. The contamination of the Adult by the Child often takes form in delusions and hallucinations.

Delusions are grounded in fear. To a small child, the world may appear to be awful and overwhelming. A grown-up who experienced parental brutality and abuse may, under stress, trigger off similar fears that fabricate logical ideas and beliefs to support his delusion.

In hallucination, a recorded experience from the past is experienced as real, and a person hears voices that existed in a past reality. This phenomenon is produced by extreme stress. The content of the voices is generally described as words of threat, rejection, criticism, or violence. The more bizarre the verbal and physical abuse experienced as a child, the more bizarre will be the probable hallucination. A significant number of people have an heredity factor that makes them vulnerable to various kinds of thought disorders. Medications are used in these cases to help restore the circuits of the neuroleptic receptors within the brain. Restoration of clearer thinking by use of medication and reduction of stress facilitates a condition whereby people may correct their lives' debilitating issues.

Another disorder is exclusion, where an excluding Parent locks out the Child, or an excluding Child blocks out the Parent. Many of us know people who are workaholics. They are all business and never seem to have fun. This person typically has a Parent-contaminated Adult with a blocked-out Child (see Figure 6).

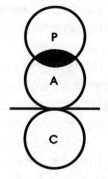

Graph from Thomas Harris' *I'M OKAY, YOU'RE OKAY*, page 127. Used by permission of HarperCollins Publishers, Inc.

Parent contaminated Adult
with a blocked out Child

Fig. 6

The all work and no play person is not much fun to be around. He puts a strain on his family and friends. This person probably has had very little happiness recorded in the Child. A person who seems to be without a conscience is often a serious problem to society. This person has a Child-contaminated Adult with a blocked-out Parent (see Figure 7).

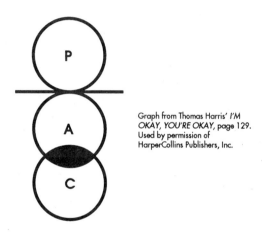

Graph from Thomas Harris' I'M OKAY, YOU'RE OKAY, page 129. Used by permission of HarperCollins Publishers, Inc.

Child contaminated Adult
with a blocked out Parent

Fig. 7

When this condition develops, the person who fulfilled the parental role was either brutal and terrifying or extremely indulgent. This person eventually assumes the "I value me — I don't value you" life position, typical of the psychopath and sociopath. This person experiences very little or no shame, remorse, or guilt. The main Adult concern of this person is not to get caught. In the case of an alcoholic, the rebellious Child blocks out the critical Parent, who is never pleased, no matter how much the Child tries to please.

A psychotic person has a decommissioned or blocked-out Adult and is out of touch with reality (Figure 8). Though the Parent and Child come on straight, the person experiences a jumbled replay of early experiences that do not make sense in the present because they did not make sense when they were recorded. The life position of this person is, "I don't value me—I don't value you."

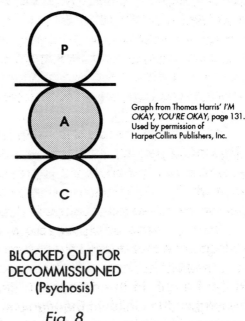

Graph from Thomas Harris' *I'M OKAY, YOU'RE OKAY*, page 131. Used by permission of HarperCollins Publishers, Inc.

BLOCKED OUT FOR
DECOMMISSIONED
(Psychosis)

Fig. 8

EXTREME MOOD SWING

A person who expresses a constant Parent, Adult or Child that excludes the other two parts, responds to circumstances in a rather fixed and predictable manner. Most of us have mood changes in response to the contribution of each part of our PAC. Most of the time, we can figure out which part is affecting us. Either the Parent is criticizing, or the Child is feeling happy over something like a toy.

There are people who periodically experience severe and unexplainable mood shifts. This condition is called Manic-Depressive or Bi-Polar Disorder. During a manic phase, a person feels an exaggerated high and euphoria—something like being on top of the world and full of powerful energy. In this condition, the Parent does not seem to have any restrictive influence over a runaway Child within the person. This person may tend to feel he can do no wrong and may become obnoxious to others. In this condition, the Adult function is impaired and extremely contaminated, often to a point where the person may need to be restrained or hospitalized.

When, for some unexplainable reason, the person sinks into a period of extreme depression, the Parent seems to return with its old oppressions of stored-up criticism. The Adult function is impaired again, and the person becomes immobilized in depression.

Both of these unexplainable and extreme mood swings are experienced by a person on a periodic and recurring basis. These are responses to old recordings in the Parent. In the depressive state, the Parent is beating up the Child. In the manic state, the Parent is cheering the Child and applauding the Child.

The manic depressive person seems to have an overbearing Parent who gives contradictory commands and permissions. This condition seems to develop within the first two years of a child's life, when he or she may become overwhelmed by the inconsistencies and contradictions of a powerful and overbearing parental figure. The little child's Adult function cannot make sense of the periodic changes in his Parent, and gives up trying to unscramble the confusion.

Some of the conditions in the Parental figure that precipitate and produce these extreme mood swings in the child are extreme and legalistic religiosity; drug addiction; alcoholism; psychosis; or the parents themselves are manic-depressives. This condition tends to run in families and, like any other emotional and spiritual problem, can only be treated by engaging and encouraging the Adult function to examine the Parent data and Child feelings. People experiencing mood disorders often have thought disorders. Chemical imbalance and drastic changes take place within the brain. Combinations of medications are often needed to stabilize both the mood and thought disorders before any cognitive or emotional therapy can help people function in life.

Another kind of contamination manifested in some people is not necessarily dysfunctional but seems to produce boring people. The recordings in the Parent and Child of these people are insipid. They were rarely punished or rewarded, and rarely, if ever, excited about anything. These people tend to be "the good kids," who rarely caused trouble and are hardly ever noticed. The Adult in these people may be somewhat emancipated but perceives reality as dull, and they rarely reach out to others.

This boredom often exists among high school and college students and adults in church settings. They are given simplistic answers and not encouraged to examine their beliefs.

The implication is that examination implies unbelief and lack of faith, rather than discovery of truth. A healthy person has an emancipated Adult function that examines objective information from both the Parent and Child function states and from the reality around them. This allows one to make sound evaluations, decisions, life discoveries and to express faith.

However, the Adult function develops later than the Parent and Child and has a difficult time catching up throughout life. The Parent and Child functions tend to dominate and automatically respond to the stimuli before the Adult function can kick in. As a result, all human beings go through life with an Adult function heavily influenced and reacting to contaminated data from their Parent and Child. This Adult function is unhealthy at best and in need of rebirth and emancipation.

3. THE HEALTHY SPIRITUAL DIMENSION
(THE IMAGE OF GOD IN PAC OF MAN)
From the unchanged conditions of the world around us, we can safely conclude that practically all interventions for change take place within the framework of a First Order System, a system which maintains the unhealthy human and social conditions; and/or makes the conditions worse; and/or perpetuates unhealthy conditions.

All First Order interventions of change exclude and ignore the spiritual dimension within human beings and the social fabric. Exclusion of the spiritual dimension ends up cutting people off from the source of life, power, light and nurturing ingredients needed to bring about a transforming change in the human and social condition. Unfortunately, powerful influences, such as literature, stage, movie and television, studiously exclude the spiritual dimension in portraying the drama of life, often treating it as inconsequential or nonexistent.

Any recognition given to the spiritual is usually a caricaturization and distortion, representative of mindsets entrenched in the First Order System.

If an unhealthy society and individuals within that society are to experience the transformation necessary to become healthy, then all who profess to be agents of change, i.e., mental health practitioners, religious counselors, social workers, political and business leaders, as well as lay people in every social strata, must open their eyes to see and learn how the healthy spiritual dimension works in the human make-up and within the social fabric.

Behavioral scientists have done extensive research and know a great deal about how unhealthy psychological human nature functions, yet very little seems to be known about what constitutes the make-up of a *healthy* emotional, psychological and spiritual human nature and how it functions. Few, it seems, among the behavioral sciences community have seriously asked themselves, *"Has human nature ever been healthy or uncontaminated?"* This is a question that must be taken seriously and deeply probed! Behavioral scientists and, indeed, all concerned people must be willing to lay aside preconceptions and examine and probe deeply this question, if an unhealthy society is to experience the transformation needed so desperately to become healthy.

Judaic-Christian values and views have spread all over the world during the past two thousand years and made some inroads into nearly every geographic area of the world. The development of the western world and its cultures has been dominated and heavily influenced by Judaic-Christian values and outlook. The primary source of these values and views has emerged from the collection of writings commonly known as the Bible. Genesis (meaning "beginnings") is the first book found in the Bible. It opens with the statement, "In the beginning God created the heavens and the earth..."*12*

The Bible is often discounted because it does not lend itself to the speculative mindset of philosophical thinking. One must always bear in mind, however, that the Biblical accounts of creation were written by Hebrews, who were not speculative in their approach to life. Hebrew writers made no assumption or speculation about God. They made no attempt to develop a philosophical base to prove the existence of God. The writers simply stated that "God is," and that He created His world. They recorded their experiences and observations of God's dealings with His creation. They accepted and stated that they "*knew* that "God is" through the empirical eyes of their faith and presented it to others for examination. The only valid way to examine and understand Biblical data is not by applying philosophical speculations of the western and eastern minds, but by viewing it from the non-speculative Hebrew mindset.

The creation story tells us that God said, "Let us make man and woman in Our image."*13* Remove a person from in front of a mirror, and his image will also disappear. The image is inextricably one with the source and cannot exist or live without the source. The image of a person in the mirror reflects the exact likeness and characteristics of the person standing before it. This is the picture the Biblical writers portrayed in Genesis 1:26, that man is created in the image of God. Their statement, "let us," also indicates the plural nature of God's personality. Moreover, Genesis begins with the interesting words, "In the beginning, God [Elohim] created the heavens and the earth."*14* The Hebrew word used for God, Elohim, is a plural word, indicating more than two. Biblical commentator Matthew Henry says it signifies "the plurality of persons in the Godhead—Father, Son and Holy Spirit."*15* Hebrew and Christian theology is emphatic that there is only one God, and there is absolutely no inference of multiple gods. Old and New Testament writings stress that God has revealed Himself as having three basic ego functions: Father-Parent (Super-Ego); Spirit-Adult (Ego); Son-Child (Id).

In the Garden we see that the first male and female were created in the Image of God, endowed with God's nature and ego functions (see Figure 9). Genesis describes the creation of human beings in God's Image as the capstone of God's glory. Wherever God is active and whatever He inhabits reflects Himself: His character and His glory. The Trinitarian Image of God (Figure 9) is the healthy spiritual dimension in the human makeup.

The Holy-Healthy Father-Parent is the ultimate creator-authority who gives unconditional love. He is the source of uncontaminated values (the Ten Commandments) and all knowledge.

He is the healthy holy nurturer and teacher. The *Spirit-Adult* is the source of life and power. This is where faith is expressed. Faith expressed in the Spirit-Adult-ego has the ability to evaluate data from the Father-Parent and Son-Child and the world around it. Faith facilitates the making of uncontaminated decisions and choices. God (the Father-Parent/Creator) made man and the earth; and God (the Spirit-Adult-ego) evaluated them as good. The Spirit-Adult is the heart of the will, where responsibility toward others and for self is exercised.

Man in an uncontaminated intimacy with GOD his Creator, as the Source of Life and Being.

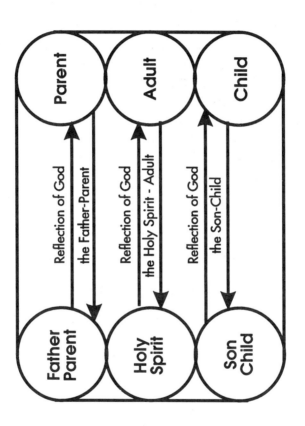

Fig. 9

The *Son-Child* is the One who responds in unconditional and uncontaminated love to the Father-Parent. The Son-Child is teachable, willing, responsive, and obedient to the Father-Parent. The Son-Child knows the heart and mind of the Father-Parent. This is filtered through the Spirit-Adult. The Son-Child is uncontaminated and innocent. There is an absence of guilt, fear and anxiety within the Son-Child. No defense of any sort is needed in this state of innocence. The Son-Child has absolute peace, certainty, and confidence in who He is and where He stands in relationship to the Father-Parent.

After creating the first man and woman in His image, God blessed and gave them instructions to multiply and have dominion over His creation. However, God also gave them this warning: "You may eat any fruit in the garden except fruit from the tree of conscience; for its fruit will open your eyes to make you aware of right and wrong, good and evil. If you eat of its fruit, you will be doomed to die."*16* This is an Adult-ego to Adult-ego transaction, which transmits uncontaminated, factual data of instructions and consequences if they failed to comply.

A popular notion held by many people is that the first couple in the Garden was doomed because they ate fruit from an apple tree. Another popular notion suggests that God dangled some kind of attractive forbidden fruit that would entice and zap them. Both of these notions and many like them are quite erroneous. Fruit is always the result or product of what a particular tree produces in due season. Fruit in this Biblical context is a picturesque way of expressing the results or consequences of a potential decision or action the people in the Garden could take.

The first male and female lived in a state of intimate fellowship and oneness with God. They were connected to God and each other. Their Trinitarian ego function and physical environment were uncontaminated. God inhabited their PAC functions and was the source of their life and being. Initially the first couple lived in a complete state of innocence and had no knowledge of good, bad or evil. They were blessed by God and instructed to multiply, fill the earth and take control of it.*17* God wanted this couple to enjoy and delight completely in the benefits His creation would produce for them.

Biblical writers also tell us that some time in God's creation, even before man was created in God's Image, the creation became contaminated by created spiritual beings who rebelled and made a power grab to be gods unto themselves.*18* This introduced a spirit of lies, deception, distortions, and power struggles into creation. St. Paul writes about creation groaning under the oppressive weight of sin.*19* Biblical writers, throughout the Scriptures, express the consistent view that God is the Spirit and Source of all Truth.*20* Satan or the devil is the spirit and source of all lies and deception. Jesus called Satan the father of lies.*21*

The warning given the couple refers to the fact that contamination of evil, lies and deception was present. The couple is warned not even to flirt with the tree of conscience. Fruit of lies and distortion produced by that tree would contaminate their Trinitarian human nature (PAC) and would infect them with a guilty conscience. This would result in squeezing out and eventually killing the healthy life that was present within them.

The word "conscience" means "to know." To know has to do with intimacy. We are intimate with those whom we know well. In their innocent state, the first couple only knew truthful, undistorted reality. Their lives reflected at that point an undistorted Image of God. If they began flirting, or in any way allowed themselves to be enticed by the distorted knowledge from the "tree of conscience," evil would infect their Trinitarian make-up, distorting the Image of God within them. They would be cut off and estranged from the Source of life and truth. Once drawn into believing lies and deceptions, their conscience would convict them of guilt. A domino effect of anxiety and fear would be set in motion within their human nature (PAC). The contamination and distortion of this Trinitarian human nature in generations following would be the dire consequence. Lies and distortions would dominate human relationships for generations to come, with no hope of change or escape without the Creator's direct intervention.

God was not being a killjoy when He warned the first couple. The warning was an act of love, similar to the love a parent has when he warns and instructs his child about potential dangers to his safety. However, from a child's perspective, such admonitions often do not appear to make sense. What he is warned about often appears harmless and even good. A child does not see the potential danger and ignores his parent's warning.

This is the point of the warning and instructions given in the Garden. At this point, the first couple was innocent. Their Trinitarian make-up was intimate with the Source of life and truth and totally uncontaminated. They had a clear, undistorted view of life. Anxiety, fear, doubt, and uncertainty of any kind were unknown to them. Inner peace and rest within their PAC was the status quo. Turmoil of any kind was unfamiliar. This couple was absolutely healthy psychologically, spiritually and emotionally. The purpose of the warning was to prevent them from jeopardizing their equilibrium and that of subsequent generations. Imagine what the condition of this world might have been if the initial healthy state within the PAC of subsequent generations had remained intact. Mind boggling, isn't it!

4. HOW ORIGINAL SIN UNIVERSALLY DISTORTED THE IMAGE OF GOD

(1) Original Game Led to Original Sin (Cussedness of Man) — Sin-Contaminated PAC = First Order Change

(2) Sin Distorts the Image of God Within Human Nature

> "It is sin inside me that is stronger than I am that makes me do these evil things." —St. Paul

Persistent attempts at First Order Change emanate from the distortion in human nature, which St. Paul observed in himself, namely, sin.**22** St. Paul also observed that all human nature is universally sinful: "All have sinned and come short of the glory of God."**23** Most people's reaction to the word "sin" (including therapists or counselors) is colored by the idea that confines it to a strictly religious connotation of condemnation. *The word "sin" in the Bible is not meant to condemn, but to describe the contaminated human condition that has always existed and been observable.* This condition is apparent to us all. The stage for Second Order Change is set only as this condition is acknowledged and accepted by the Adult function within an individual.

(1) *Original Game Led to Original Sin (Cussedness*

of Man), which in turn contaminated the PAC of the First Man and Woman!

Tom Harris made this observation: "We simply cannot argue with the endemic *cussedness of man*."[24] Harris believes it is possible from data at hand to say something new about the problem of evil and sinful human nature, which is apparent in every person. He further observes that by nature every small infant, regardless of the culture into which he or she is born, and because of his/her clearly human situation, decides on one of three contaminated life positions:

1. "I don't value me—I value you."
2. "I value me—I don't value you."
3. "I don't value me—I don't value you."

This tragedy does not become demonstrable evil until the first game is begun. The ulterior move is made toward another person to ease the burden of the "I don't value me." This first retaliatory effort demonstrates man's intrinsic 'original sin' or badness.[25]

In the Garden story of Adam and Eve, recorded in Genesis 2 and 3, we see the original game become the original sin. It is here that the first game was played out by man and woman. A game of deception contaminated the PAC of the First Couple, and sin universally infected and distorted human nature in subsequent generations. [Sin, unhealthy, and contamination are used interchangeably throughout the rest of this book. Healthy, uncontaminated, and holy are also used interchangeably.]

As the scenario unfolds in the drama that brought about the original game and original sin, another crafty creature, described as a serpent, appears on the scene. The serpent represents Satan, who is the personification of evil and deception in the universe alluded to in the warning issued by God in the Garden. The serpent first engages the woman in a conversation and subtly twists the facts and asks the question, "Really? God says you mustn't eat any of the fruit of the Garden?" This statement appears to emanate from the Adult function of the serpent, but is contaminated with distorted Parental data that had an ulterior motive to set up and hook the woman's Child function in order to manipulate it.

Eve gives an uncontaminated, clear Adult-ego response: "Of course, we may eat it. It's only the fruit from the tree at the center of the Garden that we are not to eat. God says we mustn't eat it, or even touch it, or we'll die."

Frustrated by the clear Adult response of truthful data given by the woman, the serpent becomes angry and blatantly accuses God of lying: "It's a lie! You'll not die! God knows very well that the instant you eat it, you will become like Him, for your eyes will be opened, and you'll be able to distinguish good and evil." The serpent's response is a clear example of one who is a master of deception. The statement has a Parental authoritative ring that strongly appeals to the need of instant gratification, typical of the Child ego state. "The instant you eat it, you will become like God." Her Child ego function was vulnerable to the overpowering, distorted Parental appeal of the serpent. Instant gratification (being like a powerful God) has strong appeal to a powerless Child ego function. The little Child within her blocks out the clear, uncontaminated Parental data from God. She fails to use her Adult function to process out and evaluate the deceptive data. She introduces rationalization as a form of self-justification into the human make-up: "It looks good and lovely, and it will make me wise. How can wanting to be like God do any harm?"

The first lady in the Garden totally disregarded the factual instructions and consequences given to her by God, data her Adult function had initially accepted. As the scenario continued to unfold, we see that her Child ego function prevailed, and she partook of the fruit. It was at this point that the first game was introduced. An act of rebellion and disobedience began to take place. She went on to offer and share the fruit with her male companion. Without thinking, he partook of the fruit and failed to use the evaluative processes of his Adult. He totally disregarded the warning.

From that moment, intimacy with God began to break down. They had failed to engage their Adult function to examine the deceptive data from the serpent. Light from the Spirit was screened out, causing darkness and contamination to infiltrate the Adult-ego function. They responded to the appeal made to the desires and feelings of their Child function. The serpent's lie sounded good. To be like God was rationalized as desirably good. By partaking of the fruit of good and evil, for the first time in their life experience, they began to sense their naked, vulnerable condition. Guilt and embarrassment replaced their state of innocence. Finding themselves alienated and cut off from their intimacy with God, they became involved in the first "cover-up" in human history.

As fear began to grip them, they hid from God, hoping to avoid the feared consequences and the further embarrassment of violating a trust and responsibility given them by God. Their response to God's inquiry as to their whereabouts was mankind's initial self-definition, which has infected all mankind: "I don't value me. I don't value you."

Thus, "original sin" entered the human experience. This devaluation of self and others is the genesis and source of all psychological and spiritual illness. It is a devaluation of what God created and the trademark of a sinful human nature.

When confronted by God, neither the man nor the woman took responsibility for their decision. Instead, they became defensive and placed blame on God and the serpent. The only way their "not OK" Child could justify and take the heat off itself was to shift from the "Not-OK" Child function to the "OK" Parent function state, to accuse and blame God and the serpent. They were "OK," but God and the serpent were "not OK." God and the serpent were lumped together as the "bad guys."

The Adult-ego function began to break down during this series of transactions. The original game was played out to contaminate and distort the three ego function states and became the original sin. This original sin continues to infect, infiltrate and permeate human nature. It has been passed down from generation to generation. The consequences are seen in what Dr. Harris had earlier described as the "cussedness" or meanness of human nature.

(2) *Sin Distorts the Image of God within Human Nature.* The contaminated PAC is the sinfulness of human nature. It is a distortion of God's Image within human personality, as a direct consequence of the original sin. It can be compared to the distorted and exaggerated beanpole or fat image we laugh at when we stand in front of an irregularly surfaced mirror in the fun house. The distorted image God sees reflected of Himself in the PAC functions of all human beings began when fellowship was broken in the Garden and

continues even today.

St. Paul used the Greek word *armata* for "sin."
Armata describes a person shooting at a target and
missing not only the bullseye but the target altogether.*26* Paul describes sin as falling far short of the
glory of God.*27* Missing the bullseye and falling short
have resulted in the distortion of God's Image within
man's PAC, short-circuiting God's presence and glory
within human nature. A sinful PAC is devoid of the
presence, truth, light, power and life of its Creator.

The original sin was the failure of the First Couple
simply to continue believing and trusting the truth.
Instead, they failed to use their Adult-faith faculties to
evaluate the deceiver's data and wound up calling the
Source of truth a liar. Man continues to call God a liar
every time he believes distortions and lies rather than
truth. Belief and trust in the truth of God produces and
maintains life, light and the Image of God within human
nature, whereas acting on lies produces darkness and
distorts the Image of God, finally extinguishing life
altogether. The inevitable consequences of living in
alienation from God and others is death.

POWER TO CHANGE

CHAPTER V: FIRST ORDER SYSTEM

1. Sinful PAC Perpetuates the Sickness in First Order Society
2. Grief and Death Are the End Result of First Order System

1. SINFUL PAC PERPETUATES THE SICKNESS IN FIRST ORDER SOCIETY

The persistent game of First Order Change is perpetuated by the sinful human nature of all people. No matter how anyone tries to change, he merely continues to remain in an oppressive condition, and nothing really changes. The same is true of any social system or group, simply because it is made up of people with a sinful human nature. This condition persists, because the Adult function within all human beings tends to be dominated by deceptive and distorted ideas from the Parent and Child.

Four properties in Galois' mathematical group theory were outlined and briefly discussed in Chapter I. Watzlawick and his associates drew on this theory to demonstrate the unchangeable persistence of First Order Change. Galois' four properties are indelibly etched within the very fibres of the Trinitarian, sinful human nature.

(1) *The common characteristic of the group known as the human race is its composition of human beings (male and female), who are all endowed with distorted*

PAC functions. A person remains contaminated and distorted, regardless of the changes he or she might attempt, just as the numbers 1 through 12 on a clock always remain hours. St. Paul discovered he was always governed by sin in his contaminated PAC, no matter how he tried to change. He could never free himself from the sinful PAC that caused him to miss the mark and, thus, remain a prisoner to his sinful nature.

(2) An immobilized Adult function dominated by distorted and contaminated data from the Parent and Child functions is the *identity member* that universally maintains human nature in a contaminated, distorted condition. The Adult function is not always able to accurately perceive and evaluate the reality around it. Consequently, contaminated Adult judgments are often distorted, and the decisions of the will so impaired that in extreme cases the Adult nearly ceases to function at all. A person in this condition may develop some form of neurosis or under extreme stress become psychotic.

Faith has to do with what a person believes and in whom a person believes. Faith also has power and the will to act on what is believed. Faith is the key that brings a person into an intimate relationship with God and maintains God's Image within his human nature. Faith can only be expressed when the Adult function is sufficiently healthy and emancipated from sin to sort out truth and separate it from distortion and deception. Dominance of contaminated Parent-Child ideas inhibits and immobilizes the thinking faith faculties within the Adult function toward God. Light from God is shut out, along with understanding and wisdom from the uncontaminated Father-Parent, Spirit-Adult, and Son-Child.

This condition persists, regardless of the cultural,

social, economic or religious heritage of a person. No matter how human beings interact with each other, people simply continue to remain in a sinful, unhealthy condition. *Distortions and deceptions are always the information that issues from the contaminated identity member, and is itself the identity member that maintains the distortions within human nature.* Transactions between people, as well as people toward God, are mostly dominated by distorted views based upon distorted information and mindsets. When truth is blocked out and not available to the Adult faith function, lies and deception will dominate to distort the Image of God within human nature.

The observable characteristics of the identity member seem to emerge mostly from the contaminated Child ego state, which tends to have utopian and magical expectations and beliefs. Such expectations are often seen in young people who are romantically and sexually attracted to each other. Much has been written in literature, fairy tales, musical lyrics and poetry about "falling in love," and "living happily ever after." When the Adult function in these situations is dominated by the distorted Child function, the results are often tragic and disastrous.

Throughout its development, the contaminated Child function state feels vulnerable and dependent, because it views itself as small and powerless. It sees itself as having to earn and deserve love. Therefore, the Child must become lovable and pleasing to others. The contaminated Child function is unwilling to take responsibility for itself and shifts it to others. Reality is often brutal and overwhelming, so the contaminated Child compensates and survives by denying and avoiding it. A Child manufactures its own reality and beliefs through fantasies, magical thinking, feelings of guilt, fear and anxieties.

A powerless Child spends a great deal of time defending, proving and justifying itself to the powerful, contaminated Parental figure in its own head. The figure may be the Child's own parents or other powerful, contaminated Parental figures it encounters. A Child perceives the Parent as making continual demands it cannot meet. It is always guilty, no matter how great the case before the bar of contaminated Parental justice. This Child function is driven by a need to pay for its sins and make some sort of retribution to relieve painful feelings of guilt. The payola is always self-directed in the form of some self-destructive loss. This frequently can be seen in people who seem to be perpetually victimized. However, the guilt remains, and the payola is always insufficient.

All feelings emanate from the Child ego state and are usually a response or reaction to some inward or outward stimuli or condition. Feelings can range from exhilarating joy (mountain top experience) to the sad and dreary pits of the valley.

Unhealthy feelings are also a characteristic of the identity member, emanating from the contaminated Child ego state. Fear and anxiety are typical feelings of the Child. Fear is a reaction to what is perceived by the Child as a threat of possible extinction or death. Anxiety tends to stem from a sense that someone or something, real or imagined, is threatening to control the Child within us. Through the eyes of a contaminated Child, the intensity and reality of the threat are typically blown out of proportion to the facts. This often produces a distorted sense of suspicion that can bloom into a full blown paranoia, psychosis, or develop into immobilizing forms of compulsive and/or obsessive neurosis.

Most people mistake feelings for faith and really act on feelings, rather than information that has been examined by the Adult faith faculty. This is what leads people into disastrous psychological, emotional and spiritual binds. Feelings are not information but a reaction to what is happening in a person's life experience. Most feelings are processed by a faulty Adult function or even bypass the Adult. Thus, most feelings are distorted reactions to the reality of our own life experience. It is the height of suicidal irrationality to trust feelings that distort our view of reality in making any life decision. Yet this is what most people do, day in and day out. *Contaminated feelings are one of the key characteristics of the identity members that persist and maintain the sinfulness of human nature, simply because these feelings deceive us.* This is the source of the irrational thinking so aptly described by Dr. Albert Ellis and Robert Harper in their writings on rational emotional therapy. *1*

(3) *Games and rules are the third property that governs sinful human behavior.* Games emerge primarily from a contaminated Parent concerned with having power and control over others. Authority and Parental control is maintained by issuing rules in the form of injunctions. The typical verbs used in injunctions are a combination of "shoulds," "oughts," "have to," "try harder," and "measure up." Injunctions in effect say to a Child, "Don't think or examine these commands, or any data, for that matter. You have no choice but to comply, if you want my love or approval." These injunctions appear to be true to a Child, who sees himself "without value" in his own right, and views the

Parent as having more value than himself. A contaminated Child's only sense of value comes from Parental approval.

A compliant Child wants to please and believes it will receive approval and love from this potent Parent, if he measures up. A person often spends a lifetime trying to deserve and earn this love and approval. The Child within many people keeps believing and hoping that in the end it will be rewarded.

The primary way a contaminated Parent controls a Child is by withholding love or making it conditional. If the Child measures up to the Parental standards, he will deserve Parental love and approval. However, these standards are always unattainable for a powerless and vulnerable Child. The contaminated Parent passes judgment and declares the Child guilty for failing to measure up and missing the mark (the *armata* — bullseye). The critical Parent rejects and condemns. The uncontaminated Parent accepts by giving the Child light to find its way out of darkness.

Game rules maintain the predictability and outcome of human behavior. No matter what a person does, nothing changes. Change in process, but invariance in outcome. This predictability of the unchanging change can be observed in family systems. In all families, an interesting phenomena of rules, myths and alliances among family members emerge and develop. Every family member plays a prescribed role and serves a prescribed purpose. Alliances are formed to keep a family's balance and cohesion. Certain myths and skeletons emerge within the family, but the rule within the family is for every member to pretend that none of these things exist. These denials and deceptions perpetuate a family sickness. In all families, one member tends to become the scapegoat that bears the family sickness. Family myths and alliances are propagated by the members with powerful contaminated Parent ego functions, who control the weaker members dominated by Child ego functions. These myths maintain a Parental power base within a family system. Alliances keep the weak Child sick and a scapegoat. Myths and alliances maintain the solid front that prevents any changes in the system.

One day I was explaining the dynamics of PAC and family relationships in one of my group therapy sessions when all of a sudden the light flicked on in a middle-aged woman. "Good Lord," she blurted out, "I have been bearing my family's sickness for over twenty years." She had started drinking with her husband early in the marriage and proceeded for twenty years to become an alcoholic so that he would not become one. Whenever she went on a drinking binge, her husband stayed sober, and along with the rest of the family, took care of her. She became the family "sickie" to keep the other members healthy. The husband and family became upset when she decided to disengage from that role and become a healthy, responsible person in her own right. They thought she was going crazy because she was changing. A phenomenon of homeostasis began to react within the family. In homeostasis, every member reacts and pressures the member who is disrupting the family system (rules) to remain the same and maintain a First Order System. Change is unfamiliar but also disrupting to members within a system and provokes anxiety within them. Thus, change is always resisted to reduce anxiety. This woman faced the reality that if she got well, it would upset the family, and some family member, most likely her husband, would take her place. But she made a Second Order decision not to play the family game and exposed its deceptions. Her decision had a painful but healthy effect on the family, in this case. It forced the husband and family to face the realities of their family condition. This lady deserves a great deal of admiration for her courage in exercising her healthy Adult function to assess her condition. By making a responsible decision and taking control over her life, she not only upset the family sickness but enhanced its chances for health.

The contaminated Parent plays God by making the assumption that it alone is of "value" and others are not measuring up to its standards, thus having "no value." Unexamined assumptions are made from the contaminated Parent. Legalistic rules, biases and prejudices are formed and expressed to make everything, including the Child and God, fit within its prescribed boundaries. The contaminated Parent can maintain control only if it makes all reality fit within its assumptions. The only way any reality can be distorted is by deception. Assumptions and distortions from the Parent are the primary data available to the Child. A compliant Child expends a lot of energy and thought into making a square peg fit into a round hole, when it only has distorted data available. The contaminated Parent is forever asking, "Why?" and demanding "reasons" for everything.

The compliant Child, in its "no value" state, is continually on the witness stand, answering questions. A Child feels obliged to defend and justify itself. The only concern of the prosecuting Parent is legalistic nitpicking. The prosecuting Parent is continually searching for the "speck" in the eye of the Child within others.

It remains blind to its own contaminated condition. This dynamic is prevalent in legalistic forms of religion. The predominant concern of religious legalism is to search for and highlight flaws in people. The legalistic God is a critical Parent who is continually finding fault with the compliant Child, who never measures up. A legalist only sees the "speck in his brother's eye" and is blind to the "log jam" in his own eye.*2*

Prejudices, biases and legalism are the distorted and deceptive rules of the game. The Child ego state is coerced and pressured by the contaminated Parent to fit into its distorted mold through deception. Self-deception leads the contaminated Parent to believe it is a god. It can only remain a god by intimidating games and coercion. Every game that humans play with one another is described by Eric Berne in his book, *Games People Play.3* These games are played in every conceivable human situation and relationship. Injustices and alienations among human beings are always the result of games played by people to win. Jesus continually pointed out the hypocrisy of religious games played by the Jewish religious leaders. Of course, Jesus' refusal to play the religious game led to His crucifixion.

(4) *Paradoxes and reciprocals are always adversarial in the First Order System.* Here the winner of the game becomes the loser, because he is entrapped in deception. The prize never brings the winner the expected benefits.

Games always perpetuate paradoxes or opposites, and are adversarial in nature. The sole purpose of two opponents is to cancel out the other and win. Thus, games among human beings are always contests resulting in a winner-loser, or who is right and who is wrong. It is apparent that any relationship experienced as a contest will inevitably produce estrangement, alienation, and rejection between the contestants.

Opposites develop dynamically within human beings as well as among human relationships when the contaminated Adult ego function is dysfunctional or not in control, and overridden by the contaminated Parent and Child. When the compliant Child begins to realize that it can never please the critical, controlling Parent from within and without, the rebellious Child emerges to defeat and thus free itself from the tyrannical Parent. The rebellion is either passive-aggressive, or openly aggressive and hostile in form. A Parent-Child warfare takes place within all human beings, as well as between human beings. A person becomes tense when his compliant Child tries hard to please the critical, controlling Parent. This sets in motion inner resistance that opposes the "try harder" injunction. For example, in an arm-wrestling contest, two people push against each other. Or in a tug of war, they pull away from each other. In each case, there is resistance to the other which tends to cancel out the other or create an impasse, or the one with superior strength overpowers the other. However, if one of the opponents decides not to resist and disengages from the contest, the force of the other is dissipated. The one who stops resisting is free to go on and do his thing without wasting time and energy resisting and maintaining the impasse. For instance, generally the compliant Child within a baseball player in a batting slump is pressing hard to live up to the expectations of his inner critical Parent. His hitting begins improving as his Adult function disregards the Parental injunctions, stops pressing, and relaxes. The relaxation reduces inner opposition and permits the player's batting talent to be efficiently expressed.

The adversarial nature of the contaminated PAC is universally observable in all human relationships in one form or another. As long as human relationships are locked into a contest, the participants experience alienation and estrangement from one another. People can never experience the desired intimacy between one another, or between themselves and God, as long as this condition persists.

2. GRIEF AND DEATH ARE THE END RESULT OF FIRST ORDER SYSTEM

"The wages of sin [contaminated PAC] is death."
—Romans 6:23

It is an observable fact that all human beings eventually experience death, a time when life in the body is snuffed out and all that remains is a lifeless corpse. The Old Testament writer well understood this when he wrote, "It is appointed unto man once to die."*4* In her book, *On Death and Dying,* Elizabeth Kubler-Ross writes about the human aversion to facing the reality of death:

"When we look back in time and study old cultures and people, we are impressed that death has always been distasteful to man and will probably always be. From a psychiatric point of view, this is very understandable and can perhaps best be explained by our basic knowledge that, in our unconscious, death is never possible in regard to ourselves. It is inconceivable to imagine an actual ending of our own life here on earth; and if this life of ours has to end, the ending is always attributed to a malicious intervention from the outside by someone else. In simple terms, in our unconscious mind we can only be killed; it is inconceivable to die of a natural cause or of old age. Therefore, death itself is associated with a bad act, a frightening happening something that in itself calls for retribution and punishment."*5*

In the Garden story, the couple was warned that if they partook of the tree of conscience, they would become aware of good and evil, right and wrong; and this would doom them to death. Failure to use their Adult function to examine the deceptive lie in the light of the data given them by God contaminated their PAC and distorted the Image of God within them. The contaminated PAC impaired the Adult function and locked them (and subsequently all human beings) into a First Order System. This universally sowed the seeds of death in the human spirit, from which there is no escape. All human beings locked into the death process of First Order System go through and experience at least the first four of the five stages of death and grief described by Dr. Kubler-Ross; (1) Denial and Isolation. (2) Anger. (3) Bargaining. (4) Depression. (5) Acceptance.*6*

The First Order System inevitably produces death. People living within this system end up alienated from others and estranged from their Creator and Source of life. From birth to adulthood, people crave closeness and love. Psychiatrist William Glasser postulates that a basic human need is to be loved and to give love.*7* Love produces intimacy, closeness and certainty regarding where one stands with God and others. Estrangement and alienation produce uncertainty and hostility in human beings toward God and between one another.

I recently observed my newborn grandson raising

a ruckus until his mother picked him up and cuddled him. Then he became peaceful and happy. Numerous studies demonstrate that infants flourish when given attention and body contact. Those who are deprived tend to experience severe emotional problems in their development and even eventual death.

Life within the First Order System is full of conflict. The environment is always hostile and adversarial in nature. Fear and anxieties produce various kinds of emotional dysfunctions within people locked into this system. People become tired and oppressed in the futile effort to make their lives fit within the system's framework. Human nature becomes hardened and set in cement. People seem to become less and less teachable as they grow older. Life within this contaminated system is confusing and gets so distorted that deceptions and lies become the rule rather than the exception. This confusion is like the maze we experience in the fun house at an amusement park. There is always a way out of the maze in the fun house, but there is absolutely no way out of the maze in First Order System. All sinful human nature is sealed into the system. Hopelessness and disillusionment thus grip and squeeze life out of the human spirit. Life in the First Order System eventually becomes so unbearable that extinction of life often seems preferable to the hell and misery of a life stuck in this contaminated condition.

The First Order System is characterized by continual loss in some form or another. It eventually results in the death of all human beings. All human beings are, therefore, continually going through one of the five stages of the grief process. The duration that one remains in each stage varies with the individual. Some make a continual circular route from the first through the fourth stage, and never seem to reach the fifth stage of acceptance. Others seem to get stuck in one of the stages most of their lives.

(1) *Denial of death and isolation is inevitable.* The Child within many people spends a lifetime avoiding responsibility and pain by pursuing magic and trying to gain or deserve love. Instead of love, the Child receives Parental condemnation and rejection. Our inner Child is left to fend for itself when our Adult is unable to evaluate and sort out illusion from reality. The inner Child must build its own bearable life of illusion that must deny pain and the final consequences of death. The finality of the consequences makes death distasteful to face. A great deal of money is expended on funerals and on cosmetics to give the illusion of sleep. Society is preoccupied with the cult of youth. A whole lucrative industry has emerged to support the illusion of maintaining one's youth. Vast numbers of people are caught up in the Peter Pan syndrome of not wanting to grow up.

The illusion is that "death happens to others and will magically bypass me and my loved ones." The human system goes into a shock when the illusion is dispelled. People, at this point, instead of accepting the reality of "what is," will either retreat into denial or become frustrated and angry.

(2) A contaminated inner Child becomes *frustrated* and *angry* with itself and others when its illusions are dispelled. "How come others in my life have failed to cooperate and fit into my schemes? A lot of unfinished business is still unresolved with meaningful people in my life." A great deal of this anger is also directed at God for letting us down and not cooperating with our schemes.

(3) An amazing reaction often occurs if and when the anger ever subsides: Our inner Child begins to see that its efforts are not working. However, it is not willing to take responsibility for its failures. This Child persists in perpetuating illusions, and begins to manipulate the environment by *bargaining* with others and with God. It resorts to clever negotiations and attempts to make deals it is unable to perform or keep. When a person is between a rock and a hard place, he'll often say to others or to God, "If you'll do this for me, I'll do that for you." It's like the old story of a drunk who swears to God and his wife that he'll never take another drink if he is spared the consequences of his behavior. However, regardless of the sincerity of the moment, this person soon discovers his inability to keep his end of the bargain; or that others refuse to negotiate with his irrational and often outrageous schemes.

(4) Disillusionments and disappointments begin to make inroads within the human spirit when his efforts at the bargaining table have fallen through and reached an impasse.

This soon embitters the human spirit. *Hopelessness, despair, and often total depression set in and immobilize the human spirit.* Life becomes dark. In its extreme, death and extinction seem to be the only way out.

(5) Stubborn human nature fights any change and finds it difficult, if not impossible, to accept the reality of "what is." *Acceptance is often confused by many with resignation.* However, when the eyes of faith are opened, a person can see the deadness that lies and deception have produced within his human spirit. He can see that the square pegs of life do not fit into his round holes. The prodigal experience brings a person face to face

with the emptiness of his illusions and acceptance that his life is rapidly passing by.

Acceptance frees a man to have a funeral and bury the garbage of his past. All people go through the four stages in grieving over the death of a loved one or a loss of any kind. In fact, life itself is an experience of continual loss and grief. We are always losing something. We keep getting older. We lose time, jobs, money, love, etc. Change is always a loss. The familiar gives way to the unfamiliar when change takes place. The old gives way to the new. Acceptance of the reality of death or loss, be it your own or that of a loved one, frees you to go on living. Acceptance of change frees one to learn and discover life. Seeds are sown for a Second Order Change in the stage of acceptance of life's losses.

POWER TO CHANGE

1. CAN PEOPLE CHANGE?

Can people change when, by nature, they perpetuate and are stuck in First Order System? Do people have free will to change? This has been debated among theologians and behavioral scientists over the years. There are those who hold theological views that man's destiny is predestined by God. There are also schools of thought that hold to the "cause and effect" phenomenon observed in the universe. Those schooled in Freudian thought and behavioral orientation tend to look for the cause and effect in human behavior. Freudians and determinists look into a person's past to find out "why?" What is the cause, or causes, from the past which make this person behave as he does? When carried to its ultimate, a determist concludes that a person is not free to choose, because he is programmed by past events and thus not responsible for his acts.

This seemed to be a popular theological stance among many clergy in the 1960s. I remember talking to a prominent prison chaplain, who espoused that society was responsible for shaping the criminal, and that the criminal was the casualty of a sick society. There are elements of truth peppered in that assertion that seem plausible to an indiscriminate mind. However, this presents an untenable dilemma to the discriminate person. It is an observable reality that sickness permeates society, but society is made up of human beings who all have contaminated PACs. To say society is responsible is a vague notion. It precludes identifying the specific source that is responsible for the sickness. If the responsible source can never be identified, then any attempts at change are futile, because you are dealing with a phantom.

Deterministic thinking perpetuates First Order System, simply because it perpetuates the deception that an individual can never be held responsible for his life and behavior. He is at the mercy of the gods of his current and past environment. It was the failure of the couple in the Garden to take responsibility for their decisions and actions that contaminated and infected their PACs with sin, and locked them into the First Order System.

Of course, we all experience the reality of cause and effect in our lives. In the game of billiards or pool, the cause and effect reactions are clearly observable on each ball as one strikes the other. Billiard balls caught up in the trauma of cause and effect continue to remain billiard balls subject to cause and effect. However, history demonstrates that human beings, unlike billiard balls, often grow and develop. They can become more than what they were as they experience the forces of life's traumas impinging upon them.

People are certainly affected and contaminated by past events and experiences. These events and experiences often influence and color a person's perception of the present, thereby affecting how they act or handle the present. However, human beings can contemplate, make decisions, and act to alter the effects and consequences. Unfortunately, determinism in theological, philosophical and psychiatric circles has been pressed, at times, to absurdity.

2. FREEDOM TO CHOOSE AND TO CHANGE

The goal of any psychiatric treatment and spiritual salvation is to enable a person to have the freedom to choose; the freedom to change if he wishes; the freedom to change recurring responses to his life's environment. The only way any person can acquire the freedom to choose is when he engages his Adult function. He can then begin examining data from his contaminated PAC. This examination permits him to sort out the deceptions and distortions that contaminate his PAC. At this point, a person is ready and able to evaluate the uncontaminated data at hand, draw conclusions, and see what possible choices and courses of action are open to him. A person is now free to choose, free to take whatever action he may evaluate as appropriate and beneficial to him. It follows, then, that each person is responsible for his choices and the consequences of his actions. Only as a person takes responsibility for himself and makes healthy Adult-ego assessments, does he really become free from the oppression of his sinful PAC.

3. WHAT INHIBITS AND PREVENTS CHANGE?

One of the characteristics that makes escape or

release from the First Order System and the sinful PAC difficult and nearly impossible is that it becomes an entrenched habit, familiar and predictable. A threat of any kind of change provokes anxiety within all human beings, regardless of cultural backgrounds. In fact, culture, customs, rituals, prejudices of all kinds have emerged and developed to meet the human need of certainty and predictability. *Our need of certainty and predictability is what drives all of us to expend a great deal of energy and effort to make our world fit into familiar schemes and notions.* These tenacious efforts to maintain the status quo perpetuate the First Order System. Dr. Harris made a similar observation when he wrote:

> "The Child in us demands certainty. The Child wants to know the sun will come up every morning, that mother will be there, that the bad guys will always get it in the end; but the Adult can accept the fact that there is not always certainty...When the Parent or the Child dominates, the outcome is predictable. This is one of the essential character-istics of games. There is a certain security in games. They may always turn out painfully, but it is a pain that the player has learned to handle."*1*

Efforts to change always produce conflict among human beings as well as within human beings. It can be universally observed that whenever change of any kind is attempted at any level in society or among different levels of human relationships, resistance soon emerges. Tenacious battles erupt to maintain what is familiar and traditional. Often after many years of marriage, one of the partners will begin campaigning for change or equalization in the balance of power. This will threaten and produce tremendous anxiety in the contaminated

Child of the controlling spouse. The initial reaction of the threatened spouse is to resist and make every effort to maintain the familiar ground rules of the marriage.

The scenario that probably takes place between spouses engaged in a power struggle goes something like this: After a period of being a compliant Child, the dissatisfied spouse begins to rebel against the controlling Parent of the satisfied spouse. This spouse asks the controlling spouse to relinquish some of his or her power and control. The contaminated Child in the satisfied spouse is threatened with uncertainty when the status quo of the relationship is disrupted. This triggers the rebellious Child in the satisfied spouse to urge his controlling Parent to step up his efforts to squelch the rebellion before it gets out of hand. If the rebellious Child in the dissatisfied spouse is tenacious, it mobilizes its "OK" critical Parent to counterattack the Child of the satisfied spouse, and soon an escalating battle royal is in progress. After inflicting heavy casualties on each other, the scenario generally ends in the death of the marriage; or the stronger of the two emerges the ostensible victor; but the battle goes underground. The defeated spouse endures the so-called marriage by covertly sabotaging the victorious spouse. When the course of the marriage is run out, neither has won anything; but both have lost and wasted their time. Fortunate are couples who have developed an emancipated Adult function to engage and negotiate an equitable, mutually beneficial balance in their marriage.

The homeostasis and pecking order phenomenon of maintaining the status quo is clearly observable in all families and social groups, regardless of the cultural setting. Many times, for example, pastors of churches, to their dismay, experience the wrath of the flock when they attempt to make what appear to be, on the surface, insignificant changes, such as rearranging the order of service or moving the piano to a different location in the sanctuary.

Another factor within the First Order System that inhibits people from changing is the tenacious need of their sinful Child to justify and defend itself continually. This need for self-justification is a strange Child instinct of survival.

A contaminated Child is only familiar with the idea of conditional love with strings attached. Without love and approval, the Child is garbage, without any value in his own eyes. Someone needs to value him if he is to survive. He is compelled to defend and try to win his case before the bar of justice of the accusing, critical Parent for not measuring up. He must placate or inflict some sort of self-punishment to pay for his sins and failures to get this demigod off his back.

Rebellion is the only other alternative to survival when a Child is unable any longer to bear the accusation for not measuring up to the stringent standards of the tyrannical Parent. This person survives by shifting gears and allows his critical Parent to accuse and blame others for his condition. His Parent is always looking for a scapegoat to bear blame and responsibility. The vicious game between the contaminated Parent and Child can never end without intervention and control by the emancipated Adult function within us. Only this intervention sheds light that there is no need for self-justification. There is a Parent-God who loves us "as is" without strings attached.

Faith in this God justifies us and does away with the need for self-justification.

4. WHAT MAKES PEOPLE WANT TO CHANGE?

What are the conditions within the human spirit that eventually free a person to change? What are the conditions that impel a person to seek freedom from the oppression in his sinful human nature and the unchangeable First Order System?

The first apparent condition that impels any human being to seek change is when the pain of his oppressive condition becomes totally unbearable. This oppressiveness either whets a strong, determined desire within the human spirit to be free, or it gives in to a sense of hopelessness.

Jesus basically told a crowd of people that only those desiring and craving to be free from the oppression of their sin-contaminated PAC shall experience genuine happiness and satisfaction.*2* Only people whose hearts (PAC) are pure (sin-free and uncontaminated) shall see and re-establish intimacy with Him. This is an intimacy which sustains us all in a continual state of inner satisfaction and happiness.*3* Jesus went on to warn the crowd that their righteousness must exceed that of the Pharisees and other Jewish leaders.*4* In other words, their PAC must be pure, not contaminated like the proud, self-righteous religious leaders. Otherwise, they would all remain locked into the oppressive unchangeable First Order System.

5. THE PRODIGAL EXPERIENCE IN SECOND ORDER CHANGE

The second condition for change is when the emancipated healthy Adult engages within a person and begins to assess the heavy loss and cost to themselves. In the parable of the prodigal son, the youngest

97

son received his inheritance prior to his father's death. He went out to the big city. The bright lights and tinsel dazzled him. Feminine attention beguiled him, and friendly leeches bled him out of his inheritance. When the monetary well ran dry, the friendly ladies and fair weather friends abandoned him. His situation rapidly deteriorated, and in desperation he hired himself out to a pig farmer. After wallowing in the filth and stench of the pigpens, he finally came to his senses and engaged his Adult faculties. The prodigal assessed his degrading situation and determined that the servants working for his father had far better working conditions and received much higher pay than he. The boy finally concluded that his lot would vastly improve if he returned home and asked his father to hire him as a servant. He quickly decided to quit his job and return home. The Dad spotted him coming up the road and ran out to greet his son. As his father tearfully embraced him, the boy remorsefully told his father, "Dad, I really blew it. I'll try to make it up to you if you'll take me back as one of your hired hands."

The overjoyed Dad ignored the son's contrition. Instead the Dad instructed the foreman to prepare a party to end all parties. "My lost son has found his way home. Prepare the best food and drink, and make sure there's plenty of it. Hire the hottest band in town!"

The father walked the boy to the ranch house and had him shed his dirty old clothes and take a shower. The Dad removed the family ring from the safe and placed it on his son's finger. The ring signified that the boy was his Dad's son—a son who had all the inherited rights and privileges of a son. He then gave him a specially made coat, which signified the Dad's special favor and affection. [The old patriarch Jacob gave his son Joseph a similar kind of coat to express his favor and affection.*5]* The father observed that the boy had lost his shoes and had returned home barefoot. As a son, he was entitled to shoes, so the father gave him the best custom-made shoes money could buy.*6*

The third condition for change is when a person becomes convinced that they can change. They must see that there is a way out of their oppressive imprisonment. After assessing his condition, the prodigal son saw that the only way out of his condition was to get out of the pigsty and return to his father's house.

"Of all the people in this world," he surmised, "only Dad probably still cares about me. Hopefully he will not reject me, but accept me, at least as a servant."

Only after acting on his decision did the son discover the true nature of his father's love. He discovered acceptance and restoration to the heritage and privileges of a son's intimacy with a father. He was once again free from the oppressive pigsty and could pursue his life and realize his heritage.*7*

This is a story of love, the portrayal of reconciliation between God and man. It was the son who estranged himself from the father; but it was the father who bore the pain and loss. It was Dad, who with great joy received the boy back and gave him unconditional acceptance and love. This love, emanating from the heart of God, provides the hope and power that frees all people from their oppressive sin-contaminated PAC. This is the love that leads all human beings out of First Order System into the life of Second Order System, and brings salvation to the human spirit. *The story of the Prodigal is a portrait of the spiritual dimension required to bring about a Second Order Change.*

POWER TO CHANGE

CHAPTER VII: SECOND ORDER CHANGE AND SYSTEM
"He cancels the first system in favor of a far better one." —Hebrews 10:9

1. *"What Is" vs. "Why???" Is A Second Order Change.*
2. *Second Order Change Is the Salvation Process* (Restores the Image of God)
3. *God's Reconciling Work In the Salvation Process*
   (1) Reconciling work removes deception from the universe.
   (2) Jesus the trailblazer of faith and reconciliation
   (3) Jesus absorbs the sinful PAC and emancipates the Adult faith faculty
4. *Resurrection Completes Reconciliation*

1. "WHAT IS" vs. "WHY???" IS A SECOND ORDER CHANGE

Confucius once observed, "The way out is through the door." Then he posed the question, "Why is it that no one will use this exit?"

In contrast, philosopher Ludwig Wittgenstein once asked, "What is your aim in philosophy?" Then he proceeded to tell us his aim: "to...show the fly the way out of the fly bottle..." Confucious' question,, on the surface, appears profound and wise. But is it necessary for any of us to know "why" people do not use an exit? Even if we did know "why," would it make any difference in the outcome of whether anybody uses it or not? In fact, the aim of Confucius' statement is quite clear. However, his question is irrelevant and unnecessary. It creates a problem where none existed. It would be more relevant to follow up Confucius' observation with data that would identify the nature of the problem that might exist with the door. The result of playing this kind of question out to its end will be confusion and oppression, soon gravitating to a sense of hopelessness.

This is the very nature of First Order Change. On the other hand, Wittgenstein's statement doesn't lead into this kind of confusion. Instead, he tells us his aim. He gives us data and information about his purpose and intent.

A. *What Is Second Order Change?* To put it simply, First Order Change locks us into the problem, because the solution must solve the answers to unnecessary questions. *Second Order Change simply shows the way out.* Watzlawick and his associates make the following four observations about Second Order Change:

1. The problems people have is not the problem. The solutions attempting to answer questions and making the answers fit into prescribed or preconceived notions is the problem.

People keep trying to make square pegs fit into round holes.

2. First Order Change always appears to be based on what is assumed to be "common sense," "logical," or "scientific."

Keep trying more of the same, because it's traditional, or the way it's always been done, or it just "seems right." It's based on familiar but unexamined assumptions. Second Order Change, on the other hand, appears to be weird, unexpected, lacking common sense. It appears puzzling and paradoxical, because it doesn't fit preconceived notions or common sense familiar to First Order Change.

3. Second Order Change deals with effects and results, not causes or "why's."

4. Second Order Change reframes a solution by lifting it out of preconceived views and assumptions, and places it in a different frame of reference. It translates a situation that is based upon a person's learned injunctions of "should," "ought to," or "try" to one that permits "choice." Injunctions confine a person to the rules of First Order System. *Choice permits a person to discover and learn.* A person locked into injunctions never learns but keeps repeating the same mistaken patterns over and over again. This person is never responsible or in control of himself. A person who chooses takes responsibility for himself and is in control of himself.*1*

Most professionals engaged in changing human and social behavior focus on "causes and effects," or "why's," rather than "what is." Throughout history, those engaged in science have dogmatically subscribed to the notion that it is scientifically necessary to have explanations as a precondition for change. Watzlawick and his associates observed,

"...the myth that in order to solve a problem, one first has to understand its 'why,' is so deeply embedded in scientific thinking that any attempt to deal with the problem only in terms of its present structure and consequences is considered the height of superficiality."*2*

Philosopher-mathematician Ludwig Wittgenstein

took a strong stand in his writings against explanations and their limits:

"Explanations come to an end somewhere. But what is the meaning of the word 'fine'? Meaning does not enter here at all, only how the word 'fine' is used.*3* ... It often happens that we only become aware of the important facts if we suppress the question 'why?' and then, in the course of our investigation, these facts lead us to an answer."*4*

However, one can add to the confusion and ask "why" it is necessary to have an explanation in the first place. If someone were to ask me, "Why do you like chocolate ice cream?" I would probably never get around to eating it. Instead I'd be totally engrossed in giving an explanation. When it comes right down to it, I don't really know "why" I like chocolate ice cream. I just do! At times, I observe that others prefer vanilla or strawberry, but I don't lose much sleep over "why" they prefer those flavors. In fact, Wittgenstein, in one of his early works, touches on the idea of whether it makes any difference if we have all the answers to "why?"

"...even if all possible scientific questions were answered, the problems of life have still not been touched at all. Of course, there then is no question left, and just this is the answer. The solution of the problem is seen in the vanishing of the problem."*5*

Mathematics is the bedrock of science, but it never asks "why?" Yet it is the road, as Watzlawick points out, "to penetrating analysis and imaginative solutions."*6* Watzlawick was amazed how seldom the question "What?" is seriously asked.*7* "Why's" are mere speculations, whose purpose is to make life, or things, fit into preconceived notions, or answer unnecessary questions, and do not effect change. In fact, it hampers change and needs to be discarded. It is the discovery of the "what's?" that effect change in the Second Order System. *What were the past decisions, perceptions, ideas, injunctions, that contaminate and interfere with the person's perception of the present?* This discovery provides the impetus for change and freedom from distortion.

Second Order Change took place when the prodigal son "came to himself." The condition of his life had rapidly deteriorated to the lowest form of degradation. He was literally in the pits of a pigsty. This condition removed the blinders from his contaminated PAC and forced him to take responsibility for himself. He assessed the situation through the eyes of his Adult function and was then able to see his way out of his situation.

The prodigal discarded all of the deceptions that perpetuated and maintained him as a prisoner in the pigsty of First Order System.

Second Order Change can only occur when a person has an emancipated Adult function. With a healthy Adult, a person is able to separate and discard all distortions. Then he can see the undistorted truth that will lead him out of the clutches of First Order System. Second Order social changes can only occur when all or at least the vast majority of social group members have a healthy Adult-Ego function. Spiritually transformed group members with healthy Adult functions are more apt to interact with each other in a complementary fashion, rather than adversarial.

2. SECOND ORDER CHANGE IS THE SALVATION PROCESS THAT RESTORES THE IMAGE OF GOD.
Second Order Change is the salvation process.

God instituted this process immediately after the first couple contaminated the Image of God within their human nature. *The first goal of salvation is to cleanse and free human nature from the contamination of lies and deceptions in First Order System. The second and ultimate goal of salvation is to restore an undistorted Image of God within the individual's PAC.* Salvation begins with a rebirth and the emancipation of the Adult faith faculties. Rebirth and salvation begin for all of us by seeing through the eyes of a prodigal experience. Light from God's Spirit illuminates the contaminated condition within our PAC and the pigsty of deception and distortions in First Order world system. This light also reveals to us God's provisions and resources for decontaminating our PAC and the way out of the pigsty into the new life found in the Second Order System.

The territory becomes new and unfamiliar, once a person enters into Second Order System. He may become anxious and hesitate about going any further. The contaminated Child within us wants certainty and would rather have the familiarity of misery in First Order System than risk the unknown.

Moses encountered a great deal of resistance from the Hebrew people as he led them out of bondage in the hot Egyptian sun. Griping and murmuring rippled through the camp. His own sister instigated impeachment proceedings against him. The Hebrews knew the data: Moses was God's appointed leader. God traveling in their midst, providing everything needed to sustain their lives, was evident on a daily basis. Guidelines and instructions were given on how to survive in a hostile environment. They were being led to a choice piece of real estate promised by God, that would sustain them in abundance. They failed, however, to see the opportunity set before them.*8* Blinded by their deceptive inner Parent-Child data, they cowered in fear and craved the familiarity of their formerly oppressive life under the Egyptian First Order System.

Joshua and Caleb were among the handful who had developed an emancipated Adult function of faith and desired Second Order Change. They were the minority who examined the data and saw the opportunity and gift presented to them by God. These two men knew and had the confidence to proceed and occupy the land. The vast majority became obsessed with the problem of removing the powerful occupants of the land.*9*

Deceptive fear immobilized the faith faculties of the Hebrew people. They employed the typical First Order solution of a contaminated Child and failed to take responsibility and action. Their inner critical Parent found fault with Moses and God. The Hebrew people rebelled and avoided possible confrontation, rather than believing the data of what God was showing them. This avoidance produced and perpetuated even more misery for the Hebrew people. They were described as a hard-headed, stiff- necked people, who were unwilling to trust and learn.*10* The Hebrew people ended up going around in circles for forty years as a result. They wandered the desolate wasteland until the unbelieving generation died out and a new, more willing generation emerged to occupy the promised land. It was no coincidence that Joshua and Caleb were the leaders chosen eventually to lead the Israelites into this new land.

I have lived with my family in Southern Nevada for over two decades. I could not conceive of wandering around this arid, hostile desert in mid-August for even one day, let alone forty years! This certainly highlights the tenacity of the sinfulness of human nature.

The point of Israel's pilgrimage was that God, through Moses, was leading the nation not only out of Egyptian slavery into freedom, but also to occupy a fertile land given to them by God. God's purpose involved more than a change of externals, but also involvement in internal change, with Himself as their only God, totally occupying their hearts and minds and wills. Jesus told a group of listeners about an empty house that was all cleaned up. One day an evil spirit came by and saw that it was clean but empty. This spirit called in other evil spirits to go in and occupy the clean house; and they messed it up worse than its previous condition.11 A sound therapeutic process is seen in Israel's pilgrimage and the story of the clean house. It is not enough to be set free and cleansed from the oppressive sin-contaminated PAC of First Order System. Something or someone who is not contaminated must now occupy the cleansed vessel.

Complete salvation of the distorted Image of God in human nature is the ultimate goal of Second Order Change. The first step is to free people from the darkness of their contaminated PAC. The second step is to lead them out of the prison of First Order System into the uncontaminated, resurrected life of Second Order System. The first step is accomplished by impregnating a new, uncontaminated life within human nature. The new birth paves the way for restoration of the Image of God in human nature. This, in turn, paves the way for complete reconciliation and restoration of intimacy with God. The process of salvation is the continual decontamination of the PAC. The contaminated life is continually replaced and occupied by a new, uncontaminated life. This process renews intimacy with God, eventually restoring fully the Image of God within human nature. A person can only be filled and occupied by the uncontaminated Father-Parent, Holy Spirit-Adult, and Son-Child in his PAC as he is freed and cleansed from his sinful human nature.

The infilling of the Spirit and restoration of the Image of God is the awakening and forming of the spiritual dimension within the PAC of human beings. Social behavior is transformed in proportion to the number of group members with an awakened healthy spiritual dimension. The social interaction is transformed from adversarial to complementary. *Social behavior will always remain adversarial as long as agents for change ignore the spiritual dimension.*

3. GOD'S RECONCILING WORK IN THE SALVATION PROCESS OF SECOND ORDER CHANGE

(1) God's Reconciling Work Removes Deception from the Universe.

(2) Jesus, the Trailblazer of our faith.

(3) Jesus Absorbs the Sinful PAC and Emancipates the Adult Faith Faculty.

"Since we, God's children, are human beings made of flesh and blood...Jesus became flesh and blood, too... to die a criminal's death on a cross."
—Hebrews 2:14-15

(1) *God's Reconciling Work Removes Deception from the Universe*

A permanent reconciliation between God, all human beings, and social groups can only take place when the mighty satanic forces of darkness are eradicated. God's sovereignty can then be fully re-established in the hearts (PAC) of all human beings.

This is a therapeutically sound process. The only way to restore and maintain total emotional, psychological, and spiritual health in all human beings and social groups is to remove deception and its source. Truth can then prevail. Sin will never be able to infect God's creation and human nature again. In essence, the therapeutic program of God, as outlined and seen in the Scriptures, is to eliminate the contaminated First Order System and replace it with an uncontaminated Second Order System where God is sovereign. This is the goal and salvation process of God, as stated earlier.

The thrust of the Old and New Testament writings point to the coming of a Messiah-Savior who would (1) bruise the head of the serpent; (2) eradicate his power of deception; (3) bear the destructive consequences of human sin; (4) cleanse the heart (sin-contaminated PAC); (5) restore human beings to innocence; (6) bridge the gap of estrangement; and (7) mediate a reconciliation between God and all human beings. (8) The most important thing about all this is the end result: *It emancipates the Adult-faith function and fully restores the Image of God (uncontaminated PAC) within any human being who responds by faith to the Messiah-Savior.* This re-establishes intimacy with God and reflects His glory.

In Hebrew theology, this Messiah-Savior is characterized as an innocent Lamb of God without blemish or flaw. This innocent Lamb is to be sacrificed on the altar of God to bear and absorb the sins of the people; remove their guilt; and cleanse their sin-contaminated PAC. The sacrificial innocent Lamb accomplishes all the mediating work of the Messiah-Savior, thereby restoring the Image of God within the Trinitarian makeup of human nature.

The New Testament bears witness to the fulfillment and accomplishment of what has been foreshadowed in the Old Testament. The Good News is God's love letter to all human beings, summed up in these words:

"God loved the world so much that He gave His only [unique] Son so that anyone who believes in Him shall not perish but have eternal life. God did not send His Son into the world to condemn it, but to save it."*12*

It is obvious that the vast majority of the world does not embrace Jesus as the Savior-Messiah. "God so loved" unfortunately draws a blank response in the hearts and minds of the vast majority of people. There are as many distorted views of Jesus today as there were during His lifetime, and throughout history since. Distortions about Jesus range from His being a drunk and a whoremonger who hung around the dregs of society and engaged in immoral practices with them, to some mystical ethereal character who magically walked around in some spiritual body that wasn't flesh and blood. Many others see Jesus as another religious leader, who is no worse than the most corrupt or better than the most saintly. There are a lot of other views that are not covered here, but they are basically all a product of First Order thinking.

St. Paul wrote,

"God was in Christ, reconciling and restoring the world [all human beings and creation] to Himself, no longer counting men's [and women's] sins against them, but blotting them out."*13*

Reconciliation between God and people, or people and people, can only take place when the victim, or the one offended, forgives and bears the loss and cost of

110

the consequences resulting from the offense. For example, if a person spreads a false rumor about a friend, and this lie is believed by others, the character of that friend has been besmirched. No amount of apologies or payment of money from the perpetrator will ever eradicate the pain and damage inflicted on the victim.

Reconciliation between victim and perpetrator can only take place when the victim chooses to bear the cost himself and forgives the perpetrator. By bearing the cost and forgiving, the victim says to the guilty party, "The slate between us is clean and clear. There are no barriers between us now. You owe me nothing. You and I are friends and intimates again."

This unconditional acceptance frees the perpetrator from any guilt, debt, or sense of obligation that he has to pay the victim back. The condition of the relationship is now free of contaminated data. The perpetrator is free to return to the original state of friendship and intimacy. Reconciliation is only established and completed when the perpetrator begins to value the once lost intimate friendship and determines not to violate the relationship again.

In the Garden, God's character was slandered. He was blamed by the man and equated with the serpent as a liar. God was victimized. Even if the two people had repented and attempted to make some kind of payment for their offense, it would not have removed the effects of the perpetrated lie, and the consequences of their contaminated PAC. They could never atone or do enough penance to merit forgiveness. Only the love of the victimized God can offer His forgiving love. A love that bears the pain and cost of the estrangement. Only His love and forgiveness, *given as a free gift,* can pave the way for reconciliation between Himself and all contaminated human beings locked into First Order System.

God the Father is the One who provides His only uncontaminated Son as an innocent Sacrificial Lamb to pay for and bear the sins of the contaminated PAC of all people in His own body. It is the blood of His Son that cleanses and eradicates the contaminated PAC in all human beings and emancipates the Adult-faith function. The blood is the source and sustainer of life in all people. Only as a person by faith invites Christ to live and rule his heart (PAC), will the resurrected life and Spirit of the sacrificial Son begin permeating his PAC to forgive, cleanse and eradicate the contamination.

In all religions of the world, from the most primitive to the more sophisticated mythological gods of ancient Rome and Greece, sacrifices are offered to the gods as a sort of appeasement to get them off people's backs. This is done to lessen the oppression and to gain some sort of favor. These gods are mafioso chieftains who take payola for protection. Unfortunately God is seen in this light by a vast number who regard themselves as Christians, be they Protestant or Catholic. Payola type sacrifices never free anyone from his sinful human nature. They only bury him deeper into First Order System.

(2) *Jesus, the Trailblazer of Our Faith*

The question may be asked, "What makes Jesus the Savior- Messiah? How does He accomplish such a feat?" The writer of the book of Hebrews tells us that Jesus is the High Priest and Trailblazer of our faith who emancipates the Adult-faith function in all of us. *14*

"He did not come as an angel, but as a human

112

being—yes, a Jew. It was necessary for Jesus to be like us, His brothers, so that He could be our merciful and faithful High Priest before God, a Priest who would be both merciful to us and faithful to God in dealing with the sins (the contaminated PAC) of the people. For since He Himself has now been through suffering and temptation, He knows what it is like when we suffer and are tempted, and He is wonderfully able to help us."*15*

The writer goes on to tell us that *Jesus, the High Priest, experienced every pull and temptation of sin from First Order System. This is the pull every human being experiences. He well understands our human weakness, which is imprisoned and oppressed by our contaminated PAC, locked into First Order System. But Jesus never gave way to the pull, nor did he sin. 16*

Upon examining Biblical data, it becomes apparent that Jesus was subjected to more Abscams and entrapments by religious and political leaders of His time than the F.B.I. has ever perpetrated on criminal, political or business figures. The only reason the religious leaders brought a prostitute before Jesus was to put Him on the spot. Would Jesus ignore their religious laws in favor of mercy? In this case, as in all other incidents of entrapment, Jesus responded from His uncontaminated Adult-faith function and dealt with the data. "Hey, fellas," was his response, "if there be any of you in the crowd that is without a sinful PAC, be My guest and throw the first stone."*17*

Interestingly, the "fellas" who had probably been patrons of the lady started peeling away from the crowd, beginning with the eldest. These religious and political leaders had their spies lurking and nitpicking in the background.

Jesus started His ministry by spending forty days in the wilderness without food and water, facing the deceptions and lies from Satan. Satan, or the devil, usually conjures up the familiar picture of a grotesque figure that might be seen in a horror movie with horns protruding from his head, dressed in a red costume and carrying a menacing pitchfork. However, the Biblical idea of Satan is a picture of one who is the source of all deceptions and lies in creation. Satan often appears as a counterfeit of light and goodness. As hunger settled in, Jesus was challenged by Satan to prove Himself as the Son of God by turning stones to food and jumping off the temple roof in Jerusalem. Jesus sat through the deception and examined the data from Scripture. "Struggling for basic needs of food does not bring life; only obedience to the data from God produces life," was his reply. "It's the height of stupidity to put God to an irrational and needless test. To prove oneself is a waste of time and a fundamental tendency of a sinful PAC." [Paraphrase is mine.]

Satan immediately changed his strategy and revealed his vanity: "Power over the whole world and all of its glorious splendor is yours if you will worship me." "Only the Lord God is to be worshipped and obeyed," was the data-based reply from Jesus.*18*

Jesus had no need to prove that He was the Son of God. *He knew who He was. He once told a group of religious leaders, "...before Abraham was, I am."19* That is either the statement of a conceited and stupid man, or of someone who knows who He is and what He's talking about. Jesus knew Satan, the deceiver of the universe, could not give Him something which Satan didn't own, since God was the Creator and Owner. Satan is the overlord of First Order System and

114

sin-contaminated PAC. Jesus did not permit Himself to be sucked into the games and power struggles of First Order System. He came to lead and free all human beings from the imprisonment and oppression of the satanic stronghold of First Order System.

3. *Jesus Absorbs the Sinful PAC and Emancipates the Adult-Faith Faculty.*

Jesus absorbs the sinful PAC of all human beings, removes the contamination, and emancipates the Adult function. The data examined to this point only demonstrates the innocence of Jesus as the sacrificial, unblemished Lamb of God. The next question is *how Jesus bore the sins of all human beings within Himself to satisfy the justice of God and restore the Image of God in all human beings. How does this emancipate the Adult-faith function?* To answer this, the scenario takes us to another garden, the Garden of Gethsemane. After spending His last night with His disciples and friends, Jesus knew that events were shaping up and coming to a head. His enemies and the forces of darkness and evil were closing in for a showdown. At stake was God's creation, the offspring of a man and woman who were initially fashioned in His Image. By now, generations of offspring had been infected with a contaminated PAC by the failure of the initial male and female to use their Adult-faith function.

Jesus comes to this garden with three disciples and asks them to watch and wait, while He goes into the garden to find a place to pray. Scriptural data describes a scene where Jesus experiences excruciating agony about the cup He was about to bear and experience. His agonizing prayer was a last minute assessment to check out if there was any other possible way for all lost

and blind human beings to be released from imprisonment of First Order System. Three times He returned
to agonize in prayer, after checking with His friends and
cautioning them to remain alert and not be overpow-
ered by temptation. He pointed out that the spirit is
willing but the body is weak and encumbered with a sin-
contaminated PAC. Each time He asked His heavenly
Father if there was any other possible way to restore
the Image of God within people and return them to
intimacy with God. He knew that there was no other
way. He accepted and submitted to God's Will and
way, rather than His own.20

Abraham, the Old Testament patriarch, experienced a similar testing hundreds of years prior to this
scene when he demonstrated a willingness to sacrifice
his son Isaac. Isaac was the son promised by God and
conceived when Abraham and his wife Sarah were way
beyond the age of producing children. It was through
this son that the coming Savior-Messiah would eventually emerge on the human scene. When Sarah heard
this promise, she found it humorous and laughed at the
idea that she might once again enjoy sexual pleasures
with her husband. As a result, the son was named
Isaac, whose name means "laughter" in the Hebrew.21
His young son, while en route to the site of the altar,
asked about the sacrificial lamb. Abraham told the boy,
"The Lord will provide." Isaac believed his father, and
with an air of confidence in his father, permitted himself
to be placed on the altar of sacrifice. When Abraham
was about to slay Isaac, God withheld his hand, and
Abraham then saw an innocent lamb helplessly caught
in a thicket. God told Abraham, "Now I know you
thoroughly trust Me, and I can fulfill My will and purpose
through you."22

Viewed through the eyes of sinful PAC, this is seen as a horrendous story. From this view, many people would say, "How could God ask such a thing?" However, when the data is examined through the eyes of faith, as viewed by an emancipated Adult-Ego, the purpose of this test becomes apparent.

Scriptural data tells us that Abraham was considered an intimate friend of God.[23] Isaac was the son of promise in his old age. The Savior-Messiah could only come through the seed of one who completely believed and totally entrusted himself into the hands of God. Though Abraham exhibited feet of clay and cowardice in his younger days, he grew in faith and stature with God and man. His Adult-Ego was tested and developed through scores of years of trusting and depending on God. His faith was based on data illuminated by the Spirit of God and processed through his healthy Adult-Ego. He had a well developed, emancipated Adult-faith faculty.

It was no fluke, then, that he could size up a situation that outwardly must appear a horrifying departure from the character of God to the limited vision of those dominated by contaminated data and governed by First Order System thinking. His confidence in God's provision was not the wishful, magical thinking of a foolish, demented old man about to commit a homicidal travesty. Only a person with his prior experience with God could have developed an Adult-Ego and the faith to know with certainty that God would provide, even though he could not see *how* at the time. Had he not developed that kind of Adult-faith faculty, his contaminated PAC would have paralyzed his faith and ability to trust his Creator.

The point of the incident is that it foreshadowed and

foretold the mission of the coming Savior-Messiah. The offspring of a woman would bruise the serpent's head. I wish to stress that this story is *not* to be seen as a universal command to imitate it indiscriminately as a test of faith. It is to be viewed only as evidence of the nature and expression of a mature faith.

After the third round of prayer, Jesus settled the issue. There was no other way human beings could be set free from the imprisonment of sinful First Order System. The only way was for Him to go through with His mission and bear this sin-contamination within Himself. An intimate betrayer led the Roman soldiers to the garden. Christ was arrested and endured three mock trials. No guilt was ever found or established. The Roman governor, fearing an uprising, gave in to the mob's cries and ordered Jesus executed, even though he told the crowd, "I find no evidence of guilt in this man."*24*

When Jesus arrived at the execution site, He was promptly nailed to the cross and executed between two criminals. One of the criminals angrily scoffed at Jesus to prove He was the Son of God and bail them out. The other criminal, through his Adult-faith function, assessed and recognized that Jesus was the Savior-Messiah. He reprimanded the complaining criminal and pointed out that while they deserved their punishment, Jesus did not deserve this humiliating fate. Turning to Jesus, the repentant thief asked Him to remember Him, whereupon Jesus assured the criminal that he would be with Him in Paradise.*25*

This brief scene, played out in the midst of the darkest hour in human history, portrays the love and grace of God revealed in His Son, the Savior-Messiah. Jesus was not encumbered with His own dilemma, but was attentive to the need of the repentant criminal who had recognized he had reached the end of the line. Sadly, the other criminal was blunted by bitterness. He was unable to engage his imprisoned Adult function to receive love, grace and undeserved deliverance from his sinful PAC.

Unfortunately the vast majority of people are embittered by the same kind of irrational hostility toward Jesus. It took the gracious work of God's Spirit to illuminate the contaminated condition within the heart (PAC) of the repentant criminal. It took the power of this Spirit to emancipate his Adult function so that he could ask for and receive love and life from God. Jesus came to heal and deliver the surrounding mobs from their deadly condition of sin. He endured the overwhelming bitterness and humiliation from the pain of their rejection. He was even abandoned by His most intimate friends and found Himself alone, facing death by a humiliating crucifixion. However, these were not the factors that made Him the Sacrificial Lamb that took away the sin-contaminated PAC of all human beings.

The factor that qualified Jesus to be the Sacrificial Lamb that takes away the sin-contaminated PAC of all human beings is that "He knew no sin." 26

Human PAC was initially contaminated by deception and a belief in lies. Scriptural data tells us that it would take the offspring of a woman to eradicate the source of deception and sin. This offspring was to be the unblemished Sacrificial Lamb, whose PAC remained uncontaminated.

The Sacrificial Lamb could only be supplied by God Himself as a gift to all mankind. *This Sacrificial Lamb is God's Son, Jesus Christ,* who,"

...though He was God, did not demand and cling

to His rights as God, but laid aside His mighty power and glory...becoming like men. He humbled Himself even further, going so far as actually to die a criminal's death on a cross."*27*

"Since we, God's children, are human beings made of flesh and blood, He [Jesus] became flesh and blood, too, by being born in human form; for only as a human being could He die, and in dying, break the power of the devil who had the power of death. Only in that way, could He deliver those who, through fear of death, have been living all their lives as slaves to constant dread."*28*

Jesus never once bought into the deceptions, nor did he believe the lies perpetrated by the Abscam-like entrapments. Jesus, unlike the first couple, never flirted with the tree of conscience. He was never enticed by the lure of sin, nor did He ever become part of the fabric of First Order System of the world. His refusal to play ball with the self-serving religious establishment led to a cross. His PAC remained untarnished by sin. He alone of all human beings qualifies as God's Sacrificial Lamb to take away the sins of the world. Unwittingly the system itself carried out the finale of the drama that began in the Garden. The system had no idea that it was executing God's unblemished Sacrificial Lamb and paving the way for Him to absorb the sins of the world, thereby reconciling people back to Himself.

God can only reconcile estranged people back to Himself as their sinful human nature is absorbed into the body of the unblemished Sacrificial Lamb He provided. Only as the contaminated PAC is run through the pure, cleansing blood of the Lamb can the uncontaminated life of God be poured back into the newly cleansed human nature. Blood in the Bible is always the cleansing agent and transmitter of life. Without viewing and believing through the eyes of faith that this process takes place as a loving act of the Creator, there can never be true reconciliation and salvation. St. Paul wrote,

"He [Jesus] who knew no sin was made sin. For God took the sinless Christ and poured into Him our sins. Then in exchange, God poured His life [the uncontaminated PAC of Christ] into us."*29*

The writer of Hebrews tells us:

"...Jesus suffered death for us. Yes, because of God's great kindness, Jesus tasted death for everyone in all the world. And it was right and proper that God, who made everything for His own glory, should allow Jesus to suffer, for in doing this, He was bringing vast multitudes of God's people to heaven; for His suffering made Jesus a perfect Leader, One fit to bring them into their salvation."*30*

Jesus, who knew no sin, was made sin the moment He cried out from the cross, "My God, my God, why have You forsaken me?"*31* (See Figure 10.) This was the moment Jesus dreaded in the Garden of Gethsemane. This was the moment His heavenly Father, God of all creation, turned His back on Him. God abandoned Him as the innocent Sacrifice and broke off the eternal intimacy Jesus had enjoyed with His heavenly Father. At that moment, the Image of God and oneness with God were withdrawn. For the first time ever, Jesus experienced the terrible estrangement from God we all experience. He Who was without sin and intimate with the Source of life was now cast off from life and knew death. He knew firsthand the excruciating oppression of a contaminated PAC, the blind-

Christ's Reconciling Work On The Cross

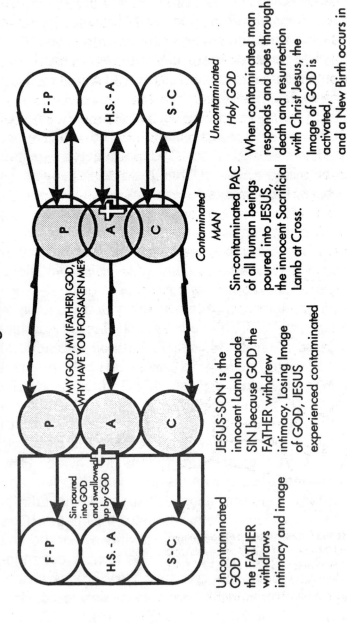

Uncontaminated GOD
the FATHER withdraws intimacy and image

Sin poured into GOD and swallowed up by GOD

MY GOD, MY (FATHER) GOD, WHY HAVE YOU FORSAKEN ME?

JESUS-SON is the innocent Lamb made SIN because GOD the FATHER withdrew intimacy. Losing Image of GOD, JESUS experienced contaminated

Contaminated MAN

Sin-contaminated PAC of all human beings poured into JESUS, the innocent Sacrificial Lamb at Cross.

Uncontaminated Holy GOD

When contaminated man responds and goes through death and resurrection with Christ Jesus, the Image of GOD is activated, and a New Birth occurs in man or woman.

Fig. 10

122

ing darkness and lifelessness of First Order System. At that moment, the floodgates of His uncontaminated PAC were opened. The sin-contaminated PAC of all humanity was poured and absorbed into His uncontaminated PAC. (See Figure 10.) At that moment on the cross, the exit door from the contaminated First Order System was opened, so that the resurrected life of Christ could permeate and transform the First Order System into a Second Order System. It is the cross that stands in the center of the Adult-faith function to emancipate it from the death of a contaminated PAC. Through this cross, the door is opened into new life. (See Figure 11.)

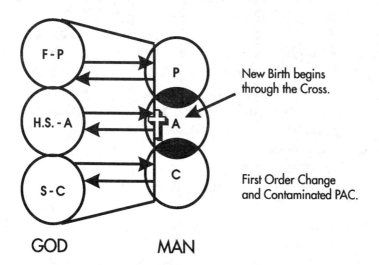

New Birth begins through the Cross.

First Order Change and Contaminated PAC.

GOD MAN

Second Order uncontaminated Image and Intimacy with GOD are established when a person is born of GOD'S SPIRIT as he/she responds by faith and receives Christ into his/her PAC.

Fig. 11

Without the work of reconciliation between God and all human beings, there will never be reconciliation between members of social groups and between social groups. Social behavior will always remain adversarial. Only the work of reconciliation can transform individual and social group behavior into complementary interaction.

4. RESURRECTION COMPLETES RECONCILIATION
"But the fact is that Christ did actually
rise from the dead."
—I Corinthians 15:20

The scenario for reconciliation is still not complete, even though God, as the victim, bears full impact and consequences of the sin-contaminated PAC for all human beings within Himself. The death and burial of Jesus renders the contaminated PAC and First Order System dead and inoperative within all who receive God's offer by faith. Jesus' death accomplishes the release from First Order System imprisonment and the cross is the exit.

However, the scenario for reconciliation cannot be completed without the resurrection of Christ. Reconciliation between God and a person is not complete until God's Image is restored and His sovereign rule established within the PAC of that person. (See Figure 12) This Image and sovereign rule is restored and established within, the resurrected, uncontaminated PAC of a person, not within the contaminated old nature. The old contaminated nature is buried with Christ, starting a process of metamorphosis that absorbs the sinful condition of human nature and transforms it. The uncontaminated PAC is then resurrected with Christ, to reflect the Image of God.

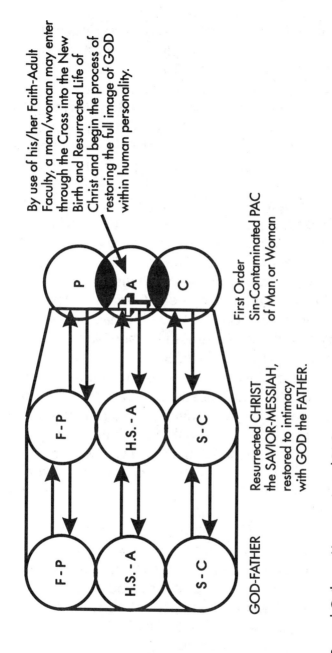

By use of his/her Faith-Adult Faculty, a man/woman may enter through the Cross into the New Birth and Resurrected Life of Christ and begin the process of restoring the full image of GOD within human personality.

First Order
Sin-Contaminated PAC
of Man or Woman

Resurrected CHRIST
the SAVIOR-MESSIAH,
restored to intimacy
with GOD the FATHER.

GOD-FATHER

Second-Order — Uncontaminated PAC

Fig. 12

125

A butterfly is the only evidence we have that a metamorphosis has taken place when a caterpillar envelops itself in a cocoon. The resurrection of Christ is the only transforming evidence upon which we can base our faith: Scripture states that "God was in Christ, reconciling you and me unto Himself."*32* Reconciliation between God and man cannot take place when the data base that provides evidence for the resurrection event is unreliable.

St. Thomas was one of those disciples who might have been from Missouri. The report from his fellow disciples that Jesus had risen from the dead and was seen alive sounded like a psychotic hallucination to this skeptic. He was present when Jesus called Lazarus out of the tomb after being dead four days. Nevertheless, he insisted, "Unless I see the nail holes in his hands and put my fingers in them, and place my hand in his side, I will not believe."*33*

Eight days later Jesus appeared to Thomas and his comrades. "Thomas," Jesus commanded, "Put your fingers in the holes in my hands and thrust your hand in my side." Confronted with the overwhelming evidence, Thomas' faith faculty finally clicked in. With reverence and awe, Thomas dropped to his knees before Jesus and humbly worshipped: "My Lord and my God!" Jesus gently admonished Thomas for doubting the veracity of the witness and evidence from his fellow disciples: "You have believed because you were given first hand evidence. Blessed are those who do not have the first hand evidence you have and yet believe the witness and testimony about me in generations to come" [paraphrase is mine].*34*

There is no life or truth available to decontaminate the PAC and restore the image of God without the resurrection. There is no reconciliation between God and people unless the Image of God is being restored within them. No Second Order Change or salvation process takes place without the resurrection, reconciliation and restoration of the Image of God. The status quo of First Order System prevails, and everyone remains stuck in the vise of death.

Unless the resurrection of Christ happened, historically, the Christian faith is without substance. It's no better, no worse than any other religion in this world. It would only be a figment of one's imagination, not to be taken seriously. Everything written thus far would then be merely worthless speculation and would not change anything or make any difference. St. Paul emphatically tells us that we remain imprisoned to our sin (contaminated PAC) unless Jesus has been resurrected:

"But tell me this: Since you believed what we preach, that Christ rose from the dead, why are some of you saying that dead people will never come back to life again? For if there is no resurrection of the dead, then our preaching is useless and your faith in God is empty, worthless and hopeless. We apostles are liars, because we have said that God raised Christ from the grave, and of course that isn't true if the dead do not come back to life again. If they don't, then Christ is still dead, and you are very foolish to keep trusting God to save you, and you're still under condemnation of your sins; in that case, all Christians who died are lost! And if being a Christian is of value to us only in this life, we are the most miserable of creatures. But the fact is that Christ did rise from the dead and has become the first of millions who will come back to life again some day."*35*

The whole accomplishment of God's program for salvation hinges on whether Jesus Christ was resurrected from the dead and is alive in the heart (PAC) of people today.

The historical fact of this event has made a transforming impact on generations of people. Thomas the skeptic was privileged to experience the resurrected Christ first hand. The influence of his transformed life extended from Jerusalem into India. A number of churches were established during his lifetime and still exist, bearing his name. St. Paul was a high ranking Jewish religious leader known for persecuting early Christians. He met the risen Christ on the Damascus Road, and his transformed life was instrumental in freeing Christianity from Jewish legalism.*36* His writings dominate the New Testament, and his work established churches in Europe and subsequently the whole western world.

Martin Luther was spiritually and psychologically awakened by the "sola fida" of the resurrection to spark the Reformation. Thousands of unknown people since the resurrection have been the salt that has flavored and the light that has guided this stale, dark world of First Order System.

Every human being is faced with the responsibility of using his Adult-faith faculty to assess the available data and evidence about the death and resurrection of Jesus Christ and its consequences for his life. It is certainly foolish to believe and live by a myth.

A great deal of Biblical data attests to the fact that Jesus was raised from the dead and was seen alive by His disciples. St. Luke was a Greek physician who wrote one of the four gospels; he opens his gospel by telling us that he made a personal investigation to verify the reports about Jesus' life, death and resurrection: "Several biographies of Christ have already been written, using as their source material the reports circulating among us from the early disciples and other eyewitnesses. However, it occurred to me that it would be well to recheck all these accounts from first to last, and after thorough investigation, to pass this summary on to you, to reassure you of the truth of all you were taught."*37*

All four Gospels give accounts of Jesus being seen alive and dining with His disciples. Luke also wrote the Book of Acts in the New Testament. In the first chapter he chronicled a number of live appearances of Jesus:

"In my first letter, I told you about Jesus' life and teachings, and how He returned to heaven after giving His chosen apostles further instructions from the Holy Spirit. During the forty days after His crucifixion, He appeared to the Apostles from time to time, actually alive, and proved to them in many ways that it was really He Himself they were seeing. And on those occasions, He talked to them about the kingdom of God."*38*

During the forty day period, Jesus appealed to the disciples' Adult-faith function. The Holy Spirit had opened up their Adult function, so they could examine and understand that *the data from the writings of Moses, the prophets, and the Psalms all pointed to Jesus. This data revealed that Jesus was the coming Savior-Messiah, who had to suffer, die, and rise from the dead on the third day. This data is the Good News that there is now available forgiveness of sin and deliverance from the deadly consequences of a contaminated PAC and First Order System.*

This Good News is universally applicable to all men, women and children, regardless of their station in life, religious affiliations, national or cultural backgrounds, since all peoples are oppressed by their sinful human nature and are locked into First Order System. The Good News is that forgiveness and deliverance are freely available to all and given to those who turn to the resurrected Christ and receive Him and His gift of uncontaminated life. Spreading this Good News around the world was Jesus' final mandate to His disciples prior to ascending into heaven.*39*

POWER TO CHANGE

CHAPTER VIII. METAMORPHOSIS OF SECOND ORDER CHANGE AND SYSTEM

1. Your PAC Must Be Born Again!
    (1) New Birth Emancipates the Adult-Ego
    (2) All Social Group Members Need A New Birth
2. The Metamorphosis of A New Creation
3. The Work of the Holy Spirit Within PAC
    "Unless you are born again, you can never
        get into the kingdom of God."
                —John 3:36

1. YOUR PAC MUST BE BORN AGAIN.
(1). New Birth Emancipates the Adult-Ego

"Born again" is a phrase that has been held in derision during the past few decades. In the 1970s a United States President openly and courageously witnessed to his faith in Christ and his experience of spiritual rebirth. In a magazine interview, this President admitted that, like any other male, he too noticed and felt stimulated by the presence of attractive females, thereby inspiring many snickers and innuendoes in the press and on national television talk shows. The phrase, "born again," has been caricaturized by the media as connected with some kind of smug self-righteous religious bumptiousness. This is the perception of sophisticated skeptics, who themselves are locked into deception and denial in a sin-contaminated First Order System, and are unable to see beyond their cynicism.

In fact, this is a universal perception of anyone locked into First Order System.

One night a prominent Jewish religious leader named Nicodemus sought out Jesus for a private interview. While he acknowledged Jesus as a teacher sent from God, Jesus interrupted him and startled him with these words: "Unless you are born again, you can never enter into the kingdom of God." *1* A puzzled look crossed Nicodemus's face as he asked, "How can an old man return to his mother's womb?" Jesus went on to explain that a person is not only born by natural physical process but must be born of God's Spirit. Men can only reproduce physical life, but the Holy Spirit imparts life from heaven. Jesus told the leader not to be surprised by His statement that he must be born again. He went on to tell him, "Just as you can hear the wind but cannot tell where it comes from or where it will go, so it is with the Spirit. We do not know on whom He will next bestow this life from heaven."*2* "What do you mean?" the leader asked, as if what Jesus had said went right over his head. With a sense of astonishment in his voice, Jesus replied,

"You are a respected Jewish teacher and leader, yet you don't understand these things? I am telling what I know and have seen, yet you won't believe me. If you don't even believe me when I tell you about such things as these that happen here among men, how can you possibly believe if I tell you what is going on in heaven? For only I, the Messiah, have come to earth and will return to heaven again. And as Moses in the wilderness lifted up the bronze serpent on the pole, even so I must be lifted up on a pole, so that anyone who believes in me will have eternal life."*3*

In this interview, Jesus identified Himself as the Messiah who came down from heaven to bruise the head of the serpent. Afterwards, He would return to heaven. Many who have been born of His kingdom would join Him there. Moses was instructed by God to make a bronze image of the serpent's head and place it on a raised pole in the midst of Israel's encampment in the wilderness. The serpent's head acted as a reminder of the source of sin and contamination. The Israelites frequently complained about the hardships, and often looked back with longing to the familiarity of Egypt. The serpent's head reminded them of the Egyptian oppression. In this interview, Jesus told the religious leader that He, too, must be lifted up on a pole (cross) to combat sin. His cross would not only crush the serpent's head and eradicate the source of deceptive contamination but absorb the sinful PAC of generations to come.

The resurrected life of Christ would emerge out of the ash heap of death and is available to all. People can respond to the life and love expressed in the cross only as the clear light of God's Spirit illuminates the contaminated condition within their trinitarian psychological and spiritual make-up. The stirring of the Spirit brings a person face to face with himself and his God; generating a hunger and thirst for a new life. *This opens the way for him to receive the impregnation of the life of God within his PAC and the new birth experience that Jesus told the religious leader he and all mankind must receive.*

Nicodemus was not a bad man. By human standards, he was a good man. But he was blind and unable to understand a fundamental truth in the theology of his Hebrew religion. He viewed the words of Jesus from the limitations of First Order perception. None of what Jesus said fit into the accepted religious dogma which sustained and maintained power over the Jewish faithful. Jesus told this teacher that human life is contaminated and powerless to change without outside intervention. The Holy Spirit is the only source and giver of uncontaminated life. This life springs from the heart of God and originally formed man and woman in His own Image. It is necessary that the old contaminated nature (PAC) be eradicated so that the new, uncontaminated life can take over and establish the Second Order System. The Image of God is restored within human nature as this takes place.

Jesus goes on to admonish Nicodemus: "You can't see or understand the things of God...Your vision is limited by your contaminated PAC and governed by the blindness of First Order System. What I'm telling you seems weird to you" [paraphrase is mine].*4*

Nicodemus is not alone in his confusion. The vast majority of human beings throughout history have shared his concept of "weirdness." They remain incredulous and reject the claims of Jesus, simply because those claims don't fit into the familiar schemes of First Order System.

(2) Social group members need a new birth.

The things of God and Second Order Change cannot be understood unless one is born of God's Spirit. *New birth* is a psychological and spiritual necessity for everyone. Birth of a new life emancipates the Adult function from the domination of contaminated Parent-Child data and empowers a person to evaluate and act upon uncontaminated data from God's Spirit. Faith in God is action taken by a person whose emancipated Adult-Ego has processed and evaluated both uncontaminated and contaminated data. Faith enables a person to choose and empowers him to act upon the uncontaminated data. *Without the impregnation of a new life, a person remains dead, powerless to choose and stuck in the pits of the old life.*

Jesus concluded His explanation of the new birth by saying, "Just as you can hear the wind but can't tell where it comes from or where it will go next, so it is with the Spirit. We do not know on whom He will next bestow this life from heaven."*5* The Spirit is like the wind, moving in unexpected ways to reach in and impart new life within the contaminated PAC of a person. We are often at a loss to explain what or how it happened, but we can certainly observe the results of a new life born within the PAC. History certainly bears out that the Spirit of God moves sovereignly to bring about a spiritual awakening and revival within individuals, families, churches, communities and even nations. There seems to be an ebb and flow in history. Periods of spiritual deadness and darkness are followed by periods of awakening and light. These awakenings have no boundaries but occur in every corner of the world, crossing cultural and religious boundaries. They have touched the rich and the poor; the well bred and crude; respected citizens and the dregs of society. New birth is a gift of God, bestowed sovereignly by Him and offered to all who will receive it by faith. The disciples of Christ are reminded of their mandate to spread the Good News so that its seeds can make the soil within human nature (PAC) receptive for its impregnation.

2. THE METAMORPHOSIS OF A NEW CREATION
"Old things keep passing away. All things keep becoming new." —II Corinthians 5:17

A war not only exists between the contaminated Parent and Child but also between the new nature (uncontaminated PAC) and the old nature (contaminated PAC). The Bible calls the old nature the "first Adam" (man) and the new nature the "second Adam" (Christ). There is a continual tug between the Image of God and the distorted PAC within every person. People who have experienced the joy and life of a new birth are often perplexed when this inner tug of war begins. They often become discouraged and feel that perhaps God is displeased with them in some way. To those who have not experienced rebirth, this appears to be a hopeless and terrible predicament with no way out. However, St. Paul knew the way out, exclaiming, "Thank God! It has been done by Jesus Christ our Lord. He has set me free."[6] Through the death and resurrection of Christ, Paul not only realized that he had been set free from the slavery of his lower nature but also from the condemning consequences of his sin:

> "There is now no condemnation awaiting those who belong to Christ Jesus. For the power of the living Spirit — and this power is mine through Christ Jesus — has freed me from the vicious circle of sin and death."[7]

In a very real sense, a person becomes a "new creation" when he receives the resurrected life of Christ within his PAC.[8] This brand new life cannot and will not co-exist compatibly with the old contaminated life. The old life must go. All things within a person become new. The new PAC swallows up the old life and forms a new, resurrected life that reflects the Image of God.[9] The power of God is activated within his Adult function. At that moment, he must make a decision to stop paying attention to the pull and distortions of his contaminated PAC and allow the uncontaminated data from God to control his life, decisions and actions.

St. Paul exhorted early Christians to present their whole beings to God and not be concerned with outward form, but be transformed from within by the renewing of their minds (PAC). Concern with outward form, or the image we project, is the consuming focus of a sinful human nature. Movie stars, politicians, and all kinds of other folks are concerned with projecting a favorable image of themselves to others. To do this, one must always be concerned with covering up or disguising what is unfavorable about himself. This, of course, always requires some form of deception on the part of the one projecting the image. The Greek word used for "transformed" is "metamorphosis." Metamorphosis is an inner change of character. It is entirely new and shows no traces of old qualities of character whatsoever.

St. Paul talks about this inner change: "I am crucified with Christ and resurrected with Christ. I myself no longer live, but Christ lives in me. And the real life I now have within this body is a result of my trusting the Son of God, who loved me and gave Himself for me."*10* Paul recognized that his personality as an individual had not been obliterated. To be crucified with Christ meant that his Adult function was disregarding the continual tenacious pull of old tapes from his contaminated PAC, in the same way that a tape recorder erases old material as it records new material. *This is the same phenomenon observed in the Penfield experiments.* The new recorded data is the life of Christ Himself. In fact, God Himself is crucifying and erasing the contaminated PAC and replacing it with His

137

uncontaminated, resurrected life (PAC) in Christ. This is called the "swallowing up" process in the Bible. "Life is swallowing up death," the metamorphosis of the old creation into the new creation. *11 There is a void within the PAC of all people that can only be filled and inhabited by God as the uncontaminated Father-Parent; Spirit-Adult; and Son-Child.* St. Augustine, in his *Confessions,* recognized that man was made for intimacy with God, and until he returns to the inner rest and joy of this intimacy, he will sense a void in his life, no matter how he strives to fill it with other things. *12*

A person with a pure heart (uncontaminated PAC) actually has the Image of God formed within him and enjoys a close walk with God. Only the pure of heart are free to enjoy and discover the unlimited love and resources of God. They are free of turmoil and uncertainty, enjoying the certainty and peace given by God, which passes all understanding.

Emptiness, resulting from a realization that lies and deceptions have distorted one's view of reality, triggers a hunger and thirst for a filling of this void. Jesus once told his audience that those who actually hunger and thirst for righteousness will be satisfied. The righteousness Jesus spoke about is restoration of the Image of God and intimacy with God. A person is totally immersed with love and life when he experiences intimacy with God and reflects His Image. A healthy spirit now rules within his PAC. His Adult-faith function is empowered to respond and receive the forgiveness and cleansing offered him by God. This is all made available through the offering of the innocent Sacrificial Lamb who died on the cross and absorbs his sin-contaminated PAC. *13*

Jesus said He must fall and die like a kernel of

wheat. His death would produce many new wheat kernels in the form of a large harvest of new, uncontaminated lives (PAC).*14* A seed planted and buried in the ground dies to being a seed; a metamorphosis takes place, permitting new life and creation to spring forth in the form of a flower or a tree. Metamorphosis only takes place as a caterpillar dies to being a caterpillar. We thus observe a totally new life, a new creation in the form of a butterfly, emerging from the grave of the cocoon.

A metamorphosis actually takes place within the inner recesses of the sinful PAC of a person when the contaminated PAC and First Order System are swallowed up by the victorious resurrection of the new creation. St. Paul victoriously proclaimed, "Death (contaminated PAC) is swallowed up in victory (uncontaminated PAC)."*15* Impregnation by the Holy Spirit in the PAC sets in motion a metamorphosis that renews the mind from within and saturates the PAC with the very life of God.

No one can enter into the Kingdom of God unless he becomes like a child who is born of God's Spirit.*16* This is not the contaminated Child but the uncontaminated, teachable Child who has received the resurrected life. This Child is free to learn and grow. The uncontaminated Father-Parent also emerges from the resurrected life as the source and supplier of love, life, power, strength, wisdom and light. God the Father accepts and gives unconditional love to His Child. This is in marked contrast to the contaminated Parent who gives conditional love for the sole purpose of controlling and having power over the contaminated Child. The uncontaminated Father-Parent is concerned with teaching and shaping the life of the uncontaminated

Child. He supplies life and power necessary to maintain the Child free from the pull of his sinful PAC.

Carl Jung recognized that psychologically and emotionally all human beings need a Father-Parent within them to guide and teach their inner Child. But he also pointed out that human beings reject God as the Father-Parent they need. *17*The ultimate consequence of the sinful PAC is the rejection of God as the uncontaminated Parent who loves us "as is." People are oppressed by the obsession of deserving love and gaining the approval from a tyrannical, critical Parent. The obsessive drive to earn and deserve love only buries people deeper in the pits of despair.

New birth ushers in the resurrected life of discovery. The emancipated Adult function processes and utilizes uncontaminated data. Birth is given to an uncontaminated Child who is able and willing to learn from uncontaminated data supplied by an accepting Father-Parent. A contaminated Child, in contrast, persists in making square pegs fit into round holes and rehearsing old data. He never seems to learn anything. His continual efforts of self-justification and trying to deserve love and approval only tighten the noose of First Order System and lead to eventual death. A newborn Child maintains a sense of freshness as he responds with love and reverence to his Father-Parent and goes on to grow and develop into the likeness of Christ. A teachable Child is humbled and stripped of any pretenses. He hungers and thirsts to know the Father intimately, and continually chooses to be obedient and submissive to the will of the Father-Parent.

The will of the Father-Parent is for the Child to inherit His kingdom. God doesn't rule His kingdom with the heavy hand of a tyrant. The purpose of His rule is to teach and develop the Child so he can inherit the kingdom of God. When the Child submits to the will of God the Father-Parent, he is ruled by His love and wisdom. *18* Submission saturates the Child with the life of the Father-God and reflects His Image. The Child comes to know God the Father-Parent and His will intimately. Light and power of truth maintain this Child free from the oppressive contamination of lies and deception. Intimacy with God results in a creative life of discovery and certainty as to where one stands with God the Father-Parent.

The new creation comes under the ownership and management of God's Spirit, as He restores and forms the Image of God in the contaminated PAC. A person abiding in Christ is a branch drawing his life from the Vine. *19* Through this process, the contaminated PAC loses its grip, while the Image of God continues to grow and become more fully formed within a person. Figure 13 shows the developing stages of the new creation in Christ and the forming of the Image of God within a faithful human being:

A. New birth is the beginning stage of growth and development as the Image of God impregnates the distorted sinful PAC. Unfortunately, many do not develop beyond this stage. *20*

B. A further stage of development results as a person continues to live by faith, using his emancipated Adult-Ego. The Image of God becomes more recognizable within a person as he or she begins bearing fruit of the Spirit. Confidence and certainty become the hallmark of a relationship with God as the Father-Parent. One experiences and realizes the reality of God the Father-Parent more and more. As blinders from the emancipated Adult-Ego function con-

A. Beginning stages of growth and development as Image of GOD is established after New Birth.

B. Another stage of development that shows further growth as the Faith-Adult faculty continues to be exercised. The Image of GOD is more recognizable within a person.

C. This is a mature, ripened stage of development after years of experience exercising the Faith-Adult faculty. The Image of GOD at this stage is powerful and makes an impact on others.

D. This is the stage when all human beings who have been born again and have lived a life continually exercising their Faith-Adult will be resurrected with Christ ... clothed in a body free of sin-contaminated PAC. In this resurrected stage, the full Image of GOD is restored in the faithful person.

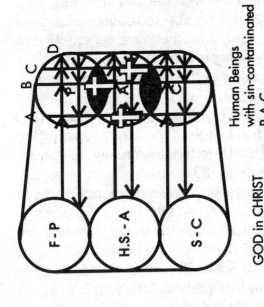

Human Beings
with sin-contaminated
P-A-C

GOD in CHRIST
Uncontaminated
F-P; H.S.-A; S-C
(PAC)

Resurrection into New life forms a new
nature and creation within an Individual.

Fig. 13

142

tinue to be removed, the revealed truth of God comes into clearer focus and allows us to see the undistorted view of the "what is" of God.

People using their Adult-Ego function bear witness to God's mercy and love as the Image of God is continually enlarged in their lives. They become a light shining in a dark, perverse world, creating a hunger and thirst in others for what they have. They become instruments and gift-bearers of life from God in His Son Jesus Christ. These are the salt flavoring a flat, taste-less world.

C. This is a mature, ripened stage of development. This becomes evident after years of experience in exercising faith, using the Adult-Ego. The Image of God at this stage is powerful and makes an impact on others. The patriarch Abraham exemplified a man with a mature emancipated Adult-Ego and ripened faith when he demonstrated his willingness to obey God, even to the point of sacrificing his only son Isaac, who was God's gift in his old age. His complete confidence that God would provide the sacrificial lamb was the result of many years of walking and using his Adult-faith function and becoming totally intimate with God the Father-Parent. This is quite a contrast to Abraham's earlier experience as a young man in Egypt, who was willing to pass his wife off as a sister so that he wouldn't offend the ruler.*21*

D. This is the final and complete stage, where the faithful in Christ will be resurrected with Christ and clothed in a body completely free of the sinful PAC. In this stage, the contaminated PAC and the sin-death of all creation will have been totally swallowed up by the life of Christ. All of creation will acknowledge Him as God and be subject to His sovereign rule, saturated

143

with His love and life. In this resurrected stage, the full Image of God has been restored in the faithful person and complete intimacy with God re-established. Second Order System has totally obliterated all sign of First Order System. Only the New Creation of Second Order Change, governed by a sovereign God in Christ, will continue to perpetuate and create infinite life, which, to our finite minds, staggers the imagination.

The metamorphosis process in Second Order Change and system is tantamount to ushering in the Kingdom of God on earth, as it is in heaven. The Second Order kingdom on earth enlarges only as the spiritual dimension is at work within the First Order System. This is the only way our world community will experience mental and spiritual health.

3. THE WORK OF THE HOLY SPIRIT WITHIN PAC
"He is the Holy Spirit, Who is the Source of all truth and leads us into all truth."
— John 14:17; 15:26.

The original Hebrew and Greek words in the Bible characterize the Spirit as the "wind." Jesus spoke of the Spirit as moving about in unexpected ways, appearing at times with great intensity and then departing into stillness.*22* Scriptural data tells us that this Spirit was active in creation from the beginning, along with the Father and the Son. He is the source and sustainer of life. This Spirit moved over the surface of the water. The Hebrew word for "move" connotes "hovering" or "brooding." The Holy Spirit hovered and brooded over creation like a hen does over her eggs, for the purpose of holding and bringing forth new life.*23* This Spirit hovered over and formed man from the dust of the earth and then breathed life into the nostrils of the first man. The words "Spirit" and "breathe" are from the same Hebrew word.

During the impregnation phase of the new birth, the Spirit breathes into the sinful PAC of a responding person, who has been estranged and dead to God.*24* The Holy Spirit swallows up the contaminated PAC in the process and begins to reproduce the Image of God within the newborn person.

The word "holy" comes from the Greek word *agios,* which means purity, and the old English word *halig,* which means health. To be in a healthy, pure condition is to be free of any contaminating elements. The opposite of health is contaminating illness. To be healthy spiritually, mentally, emotionally or physically is to be free from any contaminating illness. Jesus tells us this healthy Holy Spirit is the "source of all truth, who will teach you, as well as remind you, of everything I Myself have told you."*25*

The Holy Spirit can be likened somewhat to the airwaves beamed from the transmitter of a TV or radio station into a TV or radio in your home. A television camera "sees" the picture, and a microphone "hears" the sounds and transmits them out through a designated carrier frequency into the atmosphere. No one can see these carrier frequencies, but we do see and hear the evidence that is reproduced in the TV and radio sets. We know that TV or radio sets scattered throughout any community, receiving the same station or carrier frequency, reproduce the same sound or picture. A bank of television sets tuned to the same channel and showing the same picture is a familiar sight. So it is with the Holy Spirit as He beams the Image of God into the PAC of reborn people all over the world.

A TV or radio set doesn't reproduce the pictures or sounds on its own. It receives power from a power source outside itself. However, TV and radio sets also have a mechanism that tunes out other stations or carrier frequencies, so they will not interfere with the reproduction of the total true picture and sound. It is obviously very distracting and jarring to watch a distorted picture or listen to tinny jangling sounds of music from a set that is not properly tuned. We can appreciate and enjoy the fidelity of the pictures and sounds only when interference and distractions are removed.

After a person is born again, the Holy Spirit continues a work of fine tuning by projecting, reflecting, and reproducing the Image of the Father in the Parent, the Spirit in the Adult and the Son in the Child. This Spirit relentlessly moves into the PAC of the reborn person to continually decontaminate, occupy, saturate, and form the Image of God. This happens as the reborn person continually uses his emancipated Adult-faith function and responds to the data from the Holy Spirit.

New birth is the switch that activates and emancipates the Adult function within a person so that he can be receptive to data from the Holy Spirit. This new birth plugs a person into the Spirit just as a TV or radio set is plugged into the electric socket for its source of power. No human being has power or life within himself to change or reproduce the new birth. The Apostle John affirmed, "To all who receive Jesus, God gives power to become His children."*26* A person becomes a Child of God and a member of His family only as he receives Christ and His Spirit into his PAC. Children tend to resemble parents and siblings in human families. A newborn Child of God takes on the family likeness. The imprint of God is formed within the Child as he grows and develops. This imprint is the reflection of the Image of God.

The activated and emancipated Adult-Ego is the tuning mechanism within a reborn person that sorts out the distracting, deceptive data from his sin-contaminated PAC and from other people. As his Adult function tunes in on the data from the Holy Spirit, it tunes out the distracting instant replays from the sin-contaminated PAC. Many times people appear irrational to others, when there is no apparent evidence present in the situation to warrant their reaction. This person is often experiencing an instant replay of past experiences that may have been triggered by something in the situation of which he may have no conscious awareness. The instant replay is often intensely distracting and tends to be confusing to the person. He may be actually reliving a past experience in the present in this condition. The distraction would be similar to having an instant replay of a play that occurred several minutes earlier, being aired on the TV screen at the same time live action of a football game is taking place. As mentioned previously, this is the phenomenon discovered in Penfield's experiments.

Through therapy a young woman discovered that she experienced herself as a five-year-old girl being sexually molested by her father, whenever her husband made sexual advances toward her. During sexual intercourse she frigidly stiffened up, and the thought, "Do I have to?" ran through her head, the same thought she had as a child. Through therapy, she engaged her emancipated Adult-Ego function and was able to erase old tapes of instant replay and replace it with a healthy view that freed her up to give herself sexually. She became comfortable with her sexuality and realized that she had control over her body. She began viewing her body as a gift she made available to her husband. In the process, she was freed up to initiate and enjoy sexual activity.

The more a person uses his Adult function responsibly, the finer his tuning skills become. Fine tuning gives the Adult function clearer access to the uncontaminated data from the Holy Spirit. A finely tuned Adult processes clearer sounds and pictures of the mind and thoughts of God.

The parable about an evil spirit being kicked out of a newly cleansed but empty house makes a valuable point. The house being empty left it vulnerable for the return of seven more evil spirits. Jesus pointed out that the latter condition of the house was worse than its original condition.*27* Old contaminated data will reassert itself and overwhelm the Adult function with intensity seven times more fierce than prior to the cleansing of the PAC, if new uncontaminated data is not received and recorded within the PAC.

The new birth is impaired and there can be no experience of the resurrected life if the cleansed PAC is not filled with uncontaminated data. Fine tuning by the Adult-Ego permits data from the uncontaminated Father-Parent and Son-Child to be recorded in the PAC of a person as it erases the old data in the contaminated PAC.

The resurrected life can only be initiated and developed as the Holy Spirit occupies the PAC, cleanses and removes the contamination. The Holy Spirit beams in and forms the Image of God in a process described in the Bible as the "baptism of the Holy Spirit."*28* "Baptism" basically means an immersion in water that thoroughly soaks and saturates the immersed person.

148

A person identifies with the death of Christ on the cross when he is immersed. Immersion signifies the crucifixion and erasure of his sinful PAC. A person identifies with the resurrection of Christ as he emerges from the water. This signifies that a new resurrected, uncontaminated life has emerged to saturate and transform his PAC.

POWER TO CHANGE

CHAPTER IX. TRUTH AND GENUINENESS IN
UNDISTORTED REALITY
"You shall know the truth,
and the truth shall set you free."
—John 8:32

    1. Pilate Saw the Truth But Failed to Know the Truth.
    2. Freedom Is Knowing the One Who Is the Source of Truth.

1. PILATE SAW THE TRUTH BUT FAILED TO KNOW THE TRUTH.

    Pilate's question, "What is truth?" must be dealt with by every person, if he is to be set free from the universal slavery of his sin-contaminated PAC. Questions about truth are always speculative and raise more doubts than certainty. Before anyone can be set free by the "truth," he must know the truth and not waste time asking, "What is truth?" Jesus told his disciples at one point in His ministry, "You shall know the truth, and the truth shall set you free."*1* Pilate's question is all the more ironic, because he was interviewing the One who is the source and embodiment of truth. Just prior to this, Pilate had asked Jesus if He were a king. Jesus replied by asking Pilate if he were using the word "king" as his own recognition or just parroting the Jewish leaders. After disavowing any association with the Jewish scene, Pilate asked Jesus what He had done to the religious leaders to precipitate such a drastic crisis. Jesus assured Pilate that His kingdom was not earthly. Otherwise His followers would have fought against His arrest. Pilate seemed to recognize Jesus as a king with qualities different from worldly kings, by replying, "But you are a king then?" Jesus affirmed Pilate's recognition, "I was born for that purpose. And I came to bring the truth to the world. All who love the truth are my followers."*2* With a sense of resignation Pilate could only reply, "What is truth?"*3* He lacked the power to choose and act with integrity on the truth he saw before him.

In that brief interview, Pilate reflected the universal blindness to the truth afflicting all human beings, and to the reality of "what is" before them; moreover, they are impotent to choose and act. Even the disciples, who lived close to Jesus, failed to recognize who He was. During the few remaining hours prior to His arrest, Jesus gave His disciples extensive explanations and clarifications about Himself, God the Father, and the Holy Spirit. He warned them about persecutions that would follow so they would not be staggered.

After Judas left the meeting in the Upper Room to effect his treacherous betrayal, Jesus told Peter he could not go with Him. Peter protested his willingness to die for Him. However, Jesus knew Peter's impulsive, contaminated Child was making this boast and predicted Peter's three denials. Jesus asked His disciples to trust Him, because He was going to prepare a place for them to be with the Father. He told them they would know where He was going and how to get there. Thomas the skeptic, still not understanding, blurted out, "We don't have any idea where you are going and how can we know the way?"

Jesus gave him a straight forward answer: "I am the way, the truth and the life. No one comes to the Father except by means of Me. If you have known who I am, then you would have known who My Father is. From now on, you know Him and have seen Him."*4*

Then Philip, as though he hadn't heard or understood a word Jesus was saying, demanded, "Show us the Father and we will be satisfied." You can feel the sadness in Jesus' voice when He replied, "Don't you even yet recognize who I am, Philip, even after all this time I have been with you? Anyone who has seen Me has seen the Father!" Jesus went on to remind them to use their Adult-faith function and examine the data:

> "So why are you asking to see Him? Don't you believe that I am in the Father, and the Father is in Me? The words I say are not my own but are from My Father who lives in Me. And he does His work through Me. Just believe that I am in the Father and the Father is in Me. Or else believe it because of the mighty miracles you have seen Me do."*5*

Philip knew the data Jesus was asking him to examine. Philip seems to have been one of those disciples who never managed to recognize the significance of what was happening to him. Once Jesus challenged Philip and asked where they could buy food to feed the hungry and tired crowd of five thousand people who had been listening to Him all day in the hot sun. Philip protested, "Hey, there are no fast food restaurants around here. We have only five loaves of bread and a couple of fishes among us."*6* Philip had been present on the two occasions where Jesus fed crowds of four to five thousand people. He had the data but did not use his Adult-thinking function to recognize the significance of the drama unfolding before his very eyes. Philip was locked into his own preconceived expectations of the Savior-Messiah and the Image Jesus projected did not fit it.

Like Philip, Pilate could not break out of his mindset to apprehend Whom he was trying. He recognized Jesus as some kind of different being than the earthly ones he knew. He recognized that the religious leaders had trumped up erroneous charges and knew Jesus was totally innocent. He knew Jesus was a scapegoat and that Jesus did not fit into the game being played. Pilate the politician recognized that he was being manipulated and was caught in a political-religious squeeze play.

Jesus was an enigma. His presence exposed the oppressive corruption of the religious leaders. These leaders were extremely angry and upset when Jesus bodily threw the money changers out of the Temple in Jerusalem a few days earlier. They had developed a lucrative religious scam. At Passover faithful Jews brought their unblemished lambs to be sacrificed for the forgiveness of their sins. These lambs were first inspected for blemishes. Invariably the inspectors found some defect and would tell the faithful to purchase an "approved" lamb from the Temple stock at an inflated price. The inspectors would offer to buy the rejected lamb below market value and would place it to be sold with the approved stock. Temple lambs could not be purchased with Roman money, because it was religiously defiled. Only temple money was acceptable. This money could only be purchased through the temple money changer at a discounted exchange rate. In essence, the faithful received fifty cents of temple money for every Roman dollar exchanged.

Jesus exposed this oppressive, exploitive religious

scam. These religious and political scams were a product of a distorted trinitarian human nature, locked into the oppressive First Order System. Jesus' presence was a light and power that exposed the corrupt system and mankind's sin-contaminated nature. He posed a threat to First Order System that perpetuated the power of the religious and political leaders. The evil, satanic forces of First Order System in the universe faced the threat of exposure and annihilation with violence: The religious and political leaders' reaction emanated from a desperate need to perpetuate the First Order System. *Survival rather than change was all they understood.* Pilate became more frightened as the religious leaders continued to pressure him. He made a last ditch effort to persuade Jesus to defend Himself and take him off the hook. "Don't you realize that I have the power to release you or to crucify you?" Jesus reply took the wind out of Pilate's power play. "You would have no power at all over me, unless it were given you from above. So those who brought Me to you have the greater sin."*7*

To Pilate's credit, he wanted to be just; but he was caught in the dilemma described by Paul: "It seems to be a fact of life that when I want to do what is right, I inevitably do what is wrong...There is something deep within me, in my lower nature, that is at war with my mind and wins the fight, and makes me a slave to the sin that is still within me."*8* Pilate's desire to be fair caved in to his political instincts for survival. He was locked into First Order System of power politics. The religious leaders were politically blackmailing him. They forced his hand to choose between Caesar or Jesus. To administer justice to Jesus, Himself. Is Jesus really who He represents Himself to be?

bring his loyalty to the Roman Emperor into question. In a dramatic and politically astute move, Pilate washed his hands before the crowd telling them, "I am innocent of the blood of this good man. The responsibility is yours."*9* The frenzied mob took the bait and yelled back to Pilate, "His blood be on us and our children."*10* Pilate had successfully rationalized away his responsibility for the great injustice being perpetrated against a Man he acknowledged as good and innocent. He had successfully manipulated the irrational mob into taking responsibility for this great injustice.

The tragedy was that Pilate had some glimpses of truth but never came to know the truth Who stood before him in the flesh. His contaminated Adult-thinking function distorted the data and prevented him from making an accurate assessment. He was unable to see clearly that Jesus was the embodiment of truth. Instead, he gave in to the instinct for saving his own skin and cleverly rationalized his way out of a dangerous predicament. This prevented him from choosing and entering into the freedom of knowing the source of life and all truth.

Pilate's rationalization is characteristic of a sinful PAC. This is the same technique utilized by the male and female in the Garden of Eden, shifting responsibility from themselves to God and the serpent. All human beings have glimpses of truth but fail to use their Adult-thinking function to assess, know and choose the truth.

2. FREEDOM IS KNOWING THE ONE WHO IS THE SOURCE OF TRUTH.

It is axiomatic that only the Source of truth can reveal the truth of "what is." If this is so, then Jesus' claim, "I am the truth," must be examined seriously by everyone, regardless of cultural heritage or religious persuasion. This claim, coming from the lips of any human being, can easily be discounted as some form of emotional and psychological disturbance. This claim, however, coming from Jesus, has a different ring, which anyone concerned with knowing the truth is compelled to investigate and verify for himself. Is Jesus really who He represents Himself to be?

There was no conceit in Jesus when He told his disciples, "I am the truth!" *11* The Greek word for "truth" characterizes "genuineness." Jesus was simply saying to the whole world, "I am genuine...There is no fakery in me...I am what I represent Myself to be—God the Word made flesh."

God told Moses at the burning bush to tell the Israelites that the "I Am" was the One commissioning him to lead Israel out of Egypt. Centuries later, Jesus told a group of religious leaders, "Before your father Abraham existed, I am." *12*

The key to being set free from the bondage of lies and distortions imbedded in a sinful nature is to know the truth. *13* The word "know" as used by Jesus characterizes an intimate personal relationship. You can only know someone intimately who is transparent and willing to reveal himself "as is." Jesus is truly the epitome of genuineness, without guile or deception. His transparency gives assurance and certainty of His trustworthiness. He can be approached and known intimately by anyone. Absolute faith and confidence can only be placed in someone who is recognized and known personally to be what he represents himself to be.

Jesus, in those last few sorrowful hours with His disciples, knew that they could not fully understand or grasp all He wanted to tell them. They were more concerned that He would be leaving them than with the purpose of His impending death. As long as He was physically present with them, they would never understand or see the nature of His mission. Jesus told them outright, "The fact of the matter is that it is best for you that I go away, for if I don't the Comforter [the Holy Spirit] won't come. If I do, He will, for I will send Him to you. There is so much more I want to tell you, but you can't understand it now."*14*

The disciples could not see or understand Jesus to be the embodiment of the truth He had told them He is. They simply could not grasp it while He was still physically present with them. Jesus told the disciples that the only way they, or any other person, could know Him as the "truth" would be "when the Holy Spirit, who is the Source of truth, comes. He [the Holy Spirit] shall guide you into all truth, for He will not be presenting His own ideas but will be passing on to you what He has heard. He will tell you about the future. He shall praise Me and bring Me great honor by showing you My glory. All the Father's glory is Mine; that is what I mean when I say He will show you My glory."*15*

Jesus told the disciples that the Father, the Holy Spirit and He as the Son are congruently One. He sent the Holy Spirit, the source of all truth, from the Father. The Holy Spirit's role would be to instruct about the Son. All the Father is, the Son and the Holy Spirit is. All the Son is, the Father and the Holy Spirit is. All the Holy Spirit is, the Father and the Son is.

(See Figure 14.)

The Father characterizes the creator-authority-parenting-teaching nature of God, who is the very source of love and life.*16* The Son characterizes the creation that reflects the full glory of the Father, who inhabits His creation. The Son and creation are responsive and obedient to the Father's love and life-giving power. The Son has the Father's authority over all mankind and His creation. The Son paves the way,

1. All the FATHER *is* the son and the HOLY SPIRIT *is*.
2. All the HOLY SPIRIT *is* the FATHER and the SON *is*.
3. All the SON *is* the FATHER and the HOLY SPIRIT *is*.

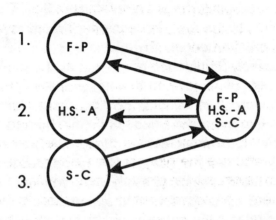

God the Father-Parent, the Son-Child, the Holy Spirit-Adult is congruently ONE.

Fig. 14

as the innocent Lamb, for all human beings to be set free from their sin-contaminated PAC, and be saved from its death-producing condition. He imparts His life to them. *17* The Son imparts to those who receive Him the glory (uncontaminated PAC) given to Him by the Father. *18* His life and glory are established within the PAC of believers and swallows up their sinful PAC. The Son is bringing them into the glorious oneness with Himself, the Father, and the Holy Spirit. *19*

All people will know that the Father sent the Son when the world sees the reality of this Oneness taking shape and completed. All will understand that the Father loves them as much as He loved the Son, whom He sent to free them from their contaminated PAC.*20* The Son wants those with redeemed, uncontaminated PAC to be intimately one with Him. These are the ones given to Him by the Father. So now they can see and be intimately united in this glory with the Son. This glory was given to the Son, because the Father loved Him before creation began.*21*

The Holy Spirit is characterized as the carrier and transmitter of the love, truth and life of the Father-Son into the creation of God.*22* The Spirit illuminates, guides and forms the Image of God in human beings. He shows forth and forms the glory of the Son in human beings who are the glory of the Father's creation.*23* Human beings are the glory of God's creation, because they were created in the full Image of God.*24* It was the Son's total obedience that brought the Father's glory to a sin-contaminated world.*25*

Pilate, the disciples, and the crowd were not able to recognize or understand Jesus as the embodiment of the truth, let alone know Him intimately as "the truth." They overlooked the fact of His authority and role in creation entirely. Only after Jesus completed His mission on the cross, was resurrected, and ascended back to the Father, did His disciples catch on. The scales from the eyes of their Adult-faith faculty were removed through the work of the Holy Spirit in their midst. Similarly, He is able to lead and guide us today into all truth and to bring us out of the bondage of our contaminated PAC.

Jesus knew that a world full of people with sinful

natures could never receive Him or the Holy Spirit. The contaminated Adult is unable to process or distinguish with clarity between contaminated and uncontaminated data. The vast majority of people do not even look for truth. Many are like Pilate and Philip, unable to recognize truth even when it's staring them in the face.*26* The world is full of people who are simply blind to their unhealthy psychological, emotional and spiritual condition.

Jesus prepared the disciples to recognize that the Holy Spirit not only leads and guides people into all truth, but "He will convince the world of its sin and of the availability of God's goodness [righteousness], of deliverance from judgment."*27* The Holy Spirit brings light into the contaminated PAC to activate and energize the seldom used Adult-faith function. The true nature of our inner condition is illuminated. X-rays and medical technology have become so sophisticated and refined that physicians can examine with precision and accuracy the interior of many organs within the body. They are able to observe the actual condition that exists through diagnostic tools at their disposal.

Recently a physician described his experience as a patient and of actually seeing the condition of some of his ailing organs.*28* I myself saw the inner workings and condition of my heart on a video screen as the physician performed an angiogram and described that I fortunately had a healthy heart. A physician confronts a patient with clinical data about his physical condition and the consequences if the condition is ignored. Diagnosis enables a patient to make a rational evaluation and a choice to submit to the prescribed treatment—or he may not, and suffer the consequences.

Often it takes a prodigal type experience to see the

pain and costly results of old contaminated data. Recognition of the sick condition of our PAC is the only way any of us comes to know and receive the truth. "Coming to oneself" frees the Adult-Ego to receive and process new, uncontaminated data and make new life discoveries and choices. The key to spiritual, psychological and emotional health lies in placing the management of one's life in the hands of the One who is the Source of truth. The Holy Spirit's job is to free one from the judgment and destructive consequences of his prior condition.

POWER TO CHANGE

CHAPTER X. SOIL CONDITIONS IN FIRST AND SECOND ORDER SYSTEMS

1. Infertile Soil Conditions of Unbelief in First Order System
2. Transition from Infertile Soil Conditions of Unbelief to Fertile Conditions of Belief
3. Fertile Soil Conditions of Belief in Second Order System

1. INFERTILE SOIL CONDITION OF UNBELIEF IN FIRST ORDER SYSTEM

"They hear but don't understand, they look but don't see!" —Is. 6:9, 10; Mt. 13:14

Intelligence and belief are often confused. According to Webster's Dictionary, "Intelligence is the ability of the mind to learn, understand, deal with the new or trying situation. It has the skilled use of reason, the ability to apply knowledge and to manipulate one's environment, the ability to think abstractly as measured by objective criteria (as tests). Intelligence is also the eternal quality of Divine Mind."

Intelligence is inherent in the PAC, and the express function of the Adult-Ego within all human beings. This is the Mind and Image of God in all people. There are many gifted and highly intelligent people who do not, or will not, perceive or believe the truth of God. Many of these individuals contribute to the development of the highly sophisticated and technologically advanced society in which we live. Great knowledge has been uncovered by many of these people. A contaminated PAC does not necessarily effect people's intelligence or ability to seek and sort out knowledge that develops technology.

Knowledge in the hands of people who do not value God and fellow human beings is monstrous. One can have a great deal of knowledge and not know the truth. Knowledge can be deceptively manipulated by unscrupulous individuals to exploit others. History and current events are replete with frightening and vivid testimony to this reality. The distinction between intelligence and belief is that intelligence deals with knowledge. Belief deals with both values and knowledge that are uncontaminated. Unbelief is really belief in deceptive, distorted value data. Unbelief confuses illusion and deception for reality and truth. Unbelief is blind and unable to see or recognize truth or reality when it is present. This was the sad condition of Governor Pilate.

The Jewish people were deeply religious. They were given the Mosaic law and teachings of the prophets. Jesus, throughout His ministry, expressed sadness over people's inability to perceive and believe the truth He was teaching and living before them. He simply illuminated for them truth from data they already knew. In fact, His own disciples were slow to catch on, to understand what He was talking about. At one point, He expressed amazement at the Roman centurion's faith and turning to the crowd, He said, "I haven't see faith like this in all the land of Israel!" *1* The prevalence of unbelief that greeted Jesus during His lifetime has universally existed throughout history.

This was aptly predicted and described by the prophet Isaiah:

"They hear but don't understand; they look but don't see! For their hearts are fat and heavy, and their ears are dull, and they have closed their eyes in sleep so they won't see and hear and understand and turn to God again and let Me heal them."*2*

The prophet describes the drastic universal consequences of sin's blindness to obvious truth. The contaminated PAC affects the Adult Ego's clarity of vision and perception of truth. Blindness to the clearness of truth leads to unbelief.

One day Jesus told the disciples a parable of a farmer sowing seeds into four different soil conditions. The first three infertile soil conditions describe the forms and expressions of unbelief that characterize the sin-contaminated PAC. The fourth described the healthy fertile soil condition of belief which characterizes the uncontaminated PAC.

"Listen! A farmer decided to sow some grain. As he scattered it across his field, some of it fell on a path, and the birds came and picked it off the hard ground and ate it. Some fell on thin soil with underlying rock. It grew up quickly enough, but soon wilted beneath the hot sun and died, because the roots had no nourishment in the shallow soil. Other seeds fell among thorns that shot up and crowded the young plants so that they produced no grain. But some of the seeds fell into good soil and yielded thirty times as much as he had planted — some of it even sixty or a hundred times as much! If you have ears, listen!"*3*

Shortly afterward, a few of the disciples asked Jesus why He used illustrations that seemed hard for them to understand. Jesus explained that only those who are receptive to spiritual truth understand the

164

illustrations. To others, parables were merely stories without meaning. He further explained that only they were permitted to understand, whereas others were not. Jesus told them how fortunate they were to have eyes and ears that saw and heard, even though at times they were slow to catch on. Many of the old prophets had longed to see and hear what they were seeing and hearing. Jesus went on to elaborate on the parable of the sowing of the seed: *4*

"The farmer I talked about is anyone who brings God's message to others, trying to plant good seed within their lives. The *hard path,* where some of the seed fell, represents the hard heart of some of those who hear God's message and don't understand it. Satan comes and snatches away the seed to make them forget it. The *shallow rocky soil* represents the hearts of those who hear the message and receive it with real joy, but they don't have much depth in their lives and the seed doesn't root very deeply. After awhile, when trouble comes, or persecution begins because of their belief, their enthusiasm fades and they drop out. The *thorny ground* represents the hearts of people who listen to the Good News and receive it, but all too quickly the attractions of this world, the delights of wealth, the search for success, and the lure of nice things come in and crowd out God's message from their hearts, so that no crop is produced. The *good soil* represents the hearts of those who truly listen and accept God's message and understand it, and then go out to bring thirty, sixty, or even a hundred others into the Kingdom." *5*

In this parable, Jesus characterized the three forms and expressions of unbelief as (a) the hard ground; (b) the rocky or shallow ground; and (c) the thorny ground.

The good soil will be discussed in the section regarding belief. All human beings have probably experienced and expressed a combination of all three forms of unbelief. Most people are dominated by one form more than the others throughout their lifetimes.

Jesus pointed out that none of these three soil conditions receive the seeds. The condition of these three soils is such that each, in the end, rejects the seeds, thereby preventing the seeds from taking root. This is a picture of the Holy Spirit, beaming truth and light into the Adult-Ego function of people whose condition can be characterized by one or more of the soils described by Jesus.

Unbelief, therefore, is a refusal and inability by the distorted Adult function to receive and consider truth presented to it. The three soil conditions described by Christ cannot process and sustain the life-giving power of light and truth. Contaminated data from the Parent and Child vie for attention and draw a dark veil over the Adult-faith function. The Adult-Ego of a person whose sinful PAC is characterized as the hard ground willfully resists and rejects the light of truth presented to it. The shell around his PAC is so hard and encapsulated that truth and light cannot penetrate into his Adult function. It lies on the surface until the rapid changes of life's circumstances blow it or pluck it away. Hard people are obtuse and blind. They are obsessed with a thirst for power and control. They remain prisoners to their distorted view of life, which invariably devalues others.

The *hard ground* in people is characterized by an alliance of their rebellious Child with the critical Parent. This alliance totally dominates and obstructs the reception of truth by their distorted Adult-Ego. The critical Parent perpetuates its deception and maintains power over others. Essentially the hard person plays god and builds empires by devaluing and exploiting others. The Truth of God is a threat to the critical Parent and rebellious Child, because it exposes and condemns their deceptions.

Jesus characterized most of the Jewish religious leaders as hard ground. He, as the Truth, was a threat to their position of power. They neither valued God nor people. Their only concern was to exploit the faithful and maintain power over them. The critical Parent within the religious leaders searched for flaws in Jesus but found none. The religious leaders in the final analysis were unwilling to use their Adult faith function to assess God's truth. Doing away with Jesus, the source of truth, was the only way for them to avoid exposure. Ironically, the chief priests' prediction of the expediency of one man dying to preserve the nation turned out to serve God's purpose rather than theirs!*6*

People characterized as the *shallow ground* receive the light of truth into their Adult faith function for a short period of time. They enjoy listening to sermons and have a vague idea that the message is true. They "sort of" believe it for awhile, and have joyous experiences praising the Lord all over the place. The message, however, never really takes root within their Adult-Ego, nor does it remain long enough for their Adult function to assess and assimilate its truth and reality. They are not able to sustain their faith when things get tough for them. The presence of ridicule for professing faith in Christ crushes them, and they wither away to return to their old ways of life.*7*

Many early followers of Jesus turned away when His message and claims began to offend them and unveil their unbelief.*8* They had earlier told Jesus,

"Show us more miracles if you want us to believe you are the Messiah. Give us free bread every day, like our fathers had while they journeyed in the wilderness."*9* They were only interested in bread and circuses, not the substance of life being offered by Jesus.

The Adult-Ego within shallow people is dominated by data from their compliant Child, who expects magic and views the world through Disneyland eyes. The inner Child thrives on pleasant feelings and spends all of his time avoiding any pain. Shallow people expect to indulge every whim and provide an ideal environment. Many can be seen flitting from religious meeting to religious meeting, looking for a religious fix or high. Faith for them is often equated with feelings. Shallow people are easily deceived and will follow any religious or political guru who promises utopian life. These people are the Pinochios of the world, in search of pleasure. Barnum aptly described them as "the suckers who are born every minute."

Magicians and con men are successful, because they can appeal to magical instincts of the compliant Child within people. This Child wants to believe magic because the illusions of utopia produce momentarily pleasant feelings. Anyone who has ever watched a masterful magician is enthralled and spellbound by the illusions he weaves throughout his act. The audiences are awed by magicians and attribute god-like power to them.

Magic can be a source of great entertainment, when represented as such by the magician. One day on a local radio talk show, a magician who frequently performed in Las Vegas told of spending up to $40,000 to develop one of his two minute magical illusions. This man is so skillful that he invites people from the audience to stand within a foot of him while he performs his magic. He admits having the skill to fool people into believing illusions that don't exist. However, the danger of one skilled in the art of illusion and trickery comes when magicians turn into con men and exploit others for their ends and purposes.

Appearing on the national television program, "That's Incredible," James Hydrick awed the studio audience and nation by causing a needle enclosed in a glass case to turn around and around. He represented himself as having psychic powers and was successful in drawing national attention to himself. However, Danny Coren, a prominent and skilled magician himself, didn't believe Hydrick possessed psychic power. On April 24, 1983, James Hydrick and Danny Coren appeared on Channel 5-TV, Las Vegas, Nevada, together. During the program, Hydrick repeated the feat performed on "That's Incredible."

Coren carefully observed Hydrick while he performed and noticed that Hydrick could turn the needle only when he sat at one end of the glass case. After examining the glass case, Coren found that the bottom end of the case, where Hydrick sat, was not totally sealed, like the other three sides. There was a paper-thin opening at that end, through which Hydrick would blow a subtle puff of air to move the needle. After being exposed by Coren, Hydrick confessed. He told Coren he had trained himself, while in solitary confinement in prison, to breathe and blow without its being noticeable to others. Hydrick seemed relieved after being exposed and talked freely about his background.

While serving a year in the Los Angeles County Jail, he was hailed by the Chaplain and fellow inmates for his fervent witnessing for Christ. By using the needle trick and claiming it was power from God, he influenced many inmates to believe and accept Christ. Hydrick went on to tell of a sordid childhood, in which his father often beat his mother, and both parents often physically abused and beat him. According to Hydrick, the father confined James within a locked car till the age of nine. Hydrick never learned to read and conned teachers to read for him.

This young man admitted that he craved attention and had discovered that he was clever and could easily fool people. He was able to present himself as having supernatural powers and developed the needle trick to prove it. The real tragedy is that James Hydrick's cleverness was not put to better use. Behaviors of this type exemplify how the *shallow ground* prevents the truth of Christ from taking root within a person's Adult-faith faculty. Setbacks, or any form of stress, can easily crush and often embitter shallow people toward God for failing to live up to their magical expectations. These are the people who bitterly blame God for the sinful condition of the world and the horrendous tragedies perpetrated by mean and cussed human beings.

There are many people who were once faithful churchgoers, who have become disillusioned, because they feel God has let them down in some way, or that they have failed to measure up to their own expectations. Many shallow people become tragic figures and live out their lives as victims dwelling in self-pity. Typically they are not able to handle any form of rejection or disappointment. Eventually many of them resort to alcohol, drugs or sex to avoid the pain of living. Some of them end up in psychiatric wards.

There is another form of *shallow ground* where people perceive God as some kind of lifeguard, who exists for the sole purpose of bailing them out of a crisis.

Joyous emotions are natural and healthy expressions of intimacy with God. However, throughout church history, emotionalism has also been used to exploit and manipulate by unscrupulous religious leaders. Religious gurus emerge from shallow soil to exploit the magical characteristics of shallow people.

Rev. Jim Jones is a recent gruesome example. Jones was a man with a powerful personal charisma, who emerged from a family with unstable religious roots. He was able to draw a following from dependent kinds of people and sell himself as a god. Hundreds of his followers sold all of their worldly possessions and gave the proceeds to Jones in the belief that he would take care of them forever.

The founding of Jonestown is a monument to his persuasive and powerful leadership. The logistics and organization to lead and transport his followers from San Francisco to Jonestown was a staggering undertaking. It was almost like a replay of Moses leading Israel out of Egypt. Tragically Jones deluded himself into believing he was god. This developed into a full blown psychosis. The result is history. The massacre at Jonestown shocked the world. Jonestown is evidence of the potential danger of the overwhelming shallowness existing in the world, which is characteristic of contaminated First Order System.

Jesus explained to the disciples, "The thorny ground represents the hearts of people who listen to the Good News from God and receive it, but all too quickly the attraction of this world, the delights of wealth, the search for success and the lure of nice things, come in and crowd out God's message from their hearts, so that no crop is produced."10

171

Adult function in thorny people receives and recognizes the truth of God revealed in Jesus Christ but is totally dominated by data from the critical Parent, pressuring the compliant Child to measure up to his unattainable expectations. The Child is attracted to the superficialities of this world and values its tinsel-laden toys. The critical Parent values power and wants to be viewed as powerful and successful. An alliance is formed between the Parent and Child to gain control over the environment. This alliance is totally obsessed with wealth and maintaining power. Fear of not measuring up drives the anxious child to try harder. This obsessive and distracting data chokes and crowds out the truth before the Adult function can fully assess and process it.

Of the four kinds of soil described by Jesus, the *thorny ground* is the saddest of all. Many thorny people are sincere, hard working people. Some of them may be described as workaholics. They desire to be good people and are often the responsible ethical members of their communities and churches.

One day a rich young ruler sought out Jesus for counseling and asked, "What must I do to get to heaven?" Jesus named a number of the commandments and the young man told Him, "I've never once broken a single one of those laws." Jesus felt a genuine love for the young man as He looked at him and said, "You lack only one thing. Go and sell all you have and give the money to the poor, and you shall have treasure in heaven. And come, follow me."*11*

Jesus certainly recognized this young man's earnest desire for something more than he had. He was probably quite likable and warm. Jesus never discounted the young man's ethical values, only that He perceived the young man trusted his wealth more than God. This stunned the rich young ruler. As Jesus watched him sadly walk away, He turned to His disciples and with sadness in His voice, told them, "It is almost impossible for those who trust in riches to get into the Kingdom of God! It is easier for a camel to go through the eye of a needle than for a rich man to enter the Kingdom of God."*12*

Jesus was not discounting economic responsibilities in his comments to the disciples. He was not saying that rich people are banned from the Kingdom of God. Jesus knew well that ownership of wealth tends to oppress and bind people to their wealth. People all over the world are obsessed with the idea of acquiring and maintaining wealth for the purpose of insuring themselves a pain-free ideal life. It is this obsession that produces more pain and squeezes life out of people. Instead of setting people free to live and have the Image of God formed within them, possessions and maintenance of wealth restrict and immobilize people with fears and apprehensions.

This is exactly what prevented the fine young man from entering into the eternal and satisfying life he so diligently sought and desired. Sadly, he was entrapped by his wealth. When the way was offered, the pull and security of wealth in his contaminated Parent and Child deceptively overwhelmed his Adult-Ego. This contaminated data choked and crowded out the uncontaminated data from Jesus, who offered him life. Contaminated data that values security and personal merit over freedom and life were now the only data available to his Adult function. It is the entrenchment of this data in the Adult-Ego in all human beings that makes it easier for a camel to go through the eye of a needle than for a rich man to enter into the Kingdom of God.

However, it is not only the rich who seek after the fragile security of wealth and fabrication of a pain-free world. This is the basic desire of all people dominated by a contaminated PAC. The poor, the rich, the intelligentsia, the idealist, the political, the powerful, the weak, the religious—all people, regardless of race or national boundaries—are obsessed with acquiring the security of wealth and the development of a pain-free ideal utopia for themselves. All people remain blind to the truth when their Adult-Ego processes only myths. It isn't any wonder that the world doesn't take seriously what Jesus has to say about the myth of wealth and utopia, when this condition persists in all people. Jesus counsels His disciples and the world not to...

"...store up treasures here on earth where they can erode away or may be stolen. Store them in heaven where they will never lose their value and are safe from thieves. If your profits are in heaven, your heart will be there, too... You cannot serve two masters: God and money. For you will hate one and love the other, or else the other way around.

"So my counsel is, don't worry about things — food, drink and clothes. For you already have life and a body—and they are far more important than what to eat and wear. Look at the birds! They don't worry about what to eat. They don't need to sow or reap or store up food, for your heavenly Father feeds them. And you are more valuable to Him than they are.

"Will all your worries add a single moment to your life? And why worry about your clothes? Look at the field lilies! They don't worry about theirs. Yet King Solomon in all his glory was not clothed as beautifully as they. And if God cares so wonderfully for flowers that are here today and gone tomorrow, won't He more surely care for you? O men [and women] of little faith! Don't worry about having enough food or clothing. Why be like the heathen? For they take pride in all these things and are deeply concerned about them. But your heavenly Father already knows perfectly well that you need them, and He will give them to you if you give Him first place in your life and live as He wants you to. So don't be anxious about tomorrow. God will take care of you tomorrow, too. Live one day at a time."*13*

Kidnapping the rich has been reaching epidemic proportions. A recent television news segment was devoted to the growing security industry. Rich people are paying enormous sums, employing security agencies to protect every member of their families. Lloyd's of London is insuring an increasingly large number of rich people all over the world. They are paying huge premiums to insure themselves and their families in the event of kidnapping. From all these accounts, it seems ironic that for all their wealth and power, they are not free to enjoy a leisurely stroll through a supermarket without fear of kidnapping or violence.

The myth that wealth frees from pain and establishes an ideal utopia is the irony that oppresses thorny people throughout their lifetimes. The irony is that very word "utopia," as mentioned earlier, doesn't mean "ideal and free from pain," as most people suppose. Utopia just "never was."

In summation, the common denominators seen in the three infertile soil conditions are: (1) It chokes out seeds of truth. (2) It prevents the reality of God from penetrating and taking root in the Adult-Ego. (3) It prevents the human PAC from blooming into the Image of God.

Without truth, the Adult function only has myths and lies to process. Truth and the reality of God is available to everyone. Everyone's Adult-Ego communicates inwardly that the Gospel of Jesus is the truth and reality of God. The obstacles inherent within the infertile First Order System boil down to one thing: People have ears in their Adult function but don't hear; have eyes in their Adult function but don't see. The unproductive soil condition in the PAC of all members stuck within a First Order System prevents the seeds of Truth from taking root in their Adult function and blooming into the Image of God.

The disciples were flabbergasted when Jesus told them that a camel could go through the eye of a needle with more ease than a rich man entering the Kingdom of God. "Then who in the world can be saved?" they asked. Jesus looked at them intently and said, "Humanly speaking, no one. But with God, everything is possible."*14*

2. TRANSITION FROM INFERTILE SOIL CONDITION OF UNBELIEF TO FERTILE CONDITIONS OF BELIEF
"I believe. Help me in my unbelief!" — Mark 9:24

The truth of God staggers the imagination. It seems so very improbable to the human experience. Believing the truth is not as easy as it might sound or appear to be. Truth is unfamiliar to the eye of the Adult-Ego in all human beings. Only deception and distortions of truth are familiar and tend to dominate the evaluative processes of the Adult function. Glare from the shining light of truth shocks the Adult function. Light and truth are so overwhelming that the Adult-Ego is not immediately able to assess and process truthful data. There is a delayed reaction. Many people react incredulously to revelations of truth with such phrases as, "Unbelievable!" "I don't believe it!" and "How can it be?"

Jesus encountered this reaction on a number of occasions. One day a distraught father brought his young son to Jesus to be healed of seizures that caused the boy to roll uncontrollably on the ground, foaming at the mouth and grinding his teeth. After the disciples had failed to heal the boy, the father asked Jesus to have mercy on the boy. With a trace of doubt in his voice, he asked, "Do something—if you can." Jesus picked up the doubt in the father's voice, as if to say, "If I can?" and then assured him, "If you can believe anything is possible to those who believe and have faith." The father responded with a surge of faith: "I do believe and have faith!" But he was so overwhelmed and incredulous by this assurance, he cried out, "Help me in my unbelief!"*15*

In all probability the father had tried to get help from many sources. When the disciples failed to heal his boy, the Adult function within the father was also processing contaminated data of doubt from his Parent and Child. "Can this man heal my son, when his own disciples failed?" Jesus put the responsibility on the father by challenging him to use his Adult-faith function. The father's Adult-Ego in the presence of Jesus was able to glean a ray of possible hope. But he also recognized the presence of doubts from past failures to have his son healed. He could admit that what faith and belief he had of the truth was also clouded with doubts from contaminated data. This admission of the true condition within his Adult-Ego was the key that unlocked his faith. This recognition on his part allowed the healing power of life to flow out of Jesus into the boy and restore him to a sound mind. Not only did the father admit his doubt, but he asked for grace and power to overcome the tenacious pull of doubt within his contaminated Parent and Child.

Jesus, in essence, told His disciples, "Even a kernel of belief within the Adult-Ego, empowered by grace, overcomes doubts and releases the life and power of God to move mountains." *16* In contrast Jesus was not able to do much healing in His hometown. Most of His old acquaintances and relatives were contaminated with unbelief in their Adult function. There was not even doubt. Most of them just plain rejected Jesus, *17* whereas earlier in another community a woman who had been ill for years made her way, crawling through a crowd, in her desire to touch Jesus. Reaching out, she barely managed to brush the hem of His garment. Nevertheless, in that congested situation, Jesus felt a surge of power drain from Him and suddenly called out to the crowd, "Who has touched Me?" The astonished disciples replied, "Lord, what do you mean, who touched you? There is a mob of people touching you."

When the woman identified herself, Jesus told her, "Your faith has made you whole." Her Adult-faith function assessed the information she had about Jesus and became convinced that she would be healed. Even though she had to endure excruciating pain in her fight through an unconcerned crowd, she found renewed health and strength through contact with Jesus. *18*

When any person is born of God's Spirit, the light of the Holy Spirit establishes a foothold within that individual. One may experience a strange mixture of belief and unbelief as he progresses through his new life of faith. A continual tug of war goes on between the contaminated and uncontaminated data. His Adult function constantly assesses and processes to determine what is valid.

Some people experience moments when their faith looms strong and they are able to sing, "My heart is fixed, O God," but under cloudy skies during periods of stress, the song fades and doubts from the contaminated Parent and Child chill the Adult-Ego within. A person experiencing moments of doubt generally has feelings that something is wrong with himself, or that he has failed in some way. Many do not immediately realize that, as believers in Christ, two sets of conflicting data—the Truth and distortions left over from old life scripts—are present and being processed within their Adult-faith function.

The truth of God gains a foothold within the Adult-faith function through this continual process. God's Spirit moves relentlessly within, occupying and erasing the old sinful tapes that once dominated and controlled that individual. This occurs as a person grapples with the myriad stresses of his life experiences. He begins to see the bankruptcy of everything he has valued and trusted in the past. A realization that none of his little gods sustains him in time of need begins to dawn. In this way, he comes to himself, much like the prodigal, and is faced with making choices between the truth and deceptive lies. There can be no straddling of fences.

Jesus told His disciples, "If you are not for Me, you are against Me.*19* You cannot serve both God and the system of the world. You'll either love one and hate the other, or follow one and leave the other."*20* Jesus insisted that there can only be one God ruling the Adult-Ego of a person. He warned that people must be willing to relinquish all things that prevent and stand in the way of His truth totally prevailing within their Adult-faith function. In fact, He exhorts people to be quite radical, if necessary. "If your eye offends, pluck it out; if your hand offends, cut it off."*21* This is not a command for people to disfigure themselves, but to illustrate that we are not to let anything be an obstacle to the fullness of God's Image being formed within our PAC.

We see this process taking place within men and women in the Bible. Early in the great patriarch's life, we see Abraham palming off his wife as his sister so that he wouldn't incur the disfavor of an Egyptian ruler, who was drawn to Sarah's beauty.*22* However, his faith developed steadily throughout his life. Later Abraham was able to meet the zenith test of his faith when he demonstrated his willingness to sacrifice the greatest gift God had ever given him, the son of his old age. This was the promised son, through whose seed Jesus would emerge. No doubt, this seems like a staggering request from God. Only a man of experienced faith would be willing to carry it out and express the confidence that God would himself provide a sacrificial lamb.*23*

Over and over, we see growth and development of faith within the Adult-Ego of Biblical characters. The stumbling cowardly Peter was chosen by Jesus to feed His flock. We later see him preach a powerful sermon at Pentecost, where several thousand people responded and received the gift of life from God. St. Paul spent several years in obscurity, learning and having his faith developed from unbelief to a mature, undaunted faith that prepared him to minister and powerfully proclaim the Gospel in the face of hostility and adversity.*24*

St. Thomas was staggered when his fellow disciples told him Jesus was alive after the crucifixion. He told them, "Unless I can see the nail prints in His hands and place my fingers in them, I will not believe." When Jesus appeared to him, however, Thomas fell on his knees and cried out, "My Lord and My God." Thomas is accused of being a doubter. Actually, Thomas was a pragmatist. Resurrection from the dead is not within the realm of First Order logic. It can only be seen through the eyes of faith in Second Order Change. The Lord was gracious in giving Thomas the first hand evidence he needed. As a result, Thomas moved from incredulity to an all-consuming belief and faith.*25*

Maturity and development take place within a person during the transition from unbelief to belief. As the seed of uncontaminated data is sown in the Adult-faith function of a person, the Holy Spirit is at work, nurturing and cultivating those seeds. Like the seed of an oak tree planted in the soil, it eventually begins to emerge from the ground as a small bud. Over the years, it develops into the fullness of a beautiful oak tree that graces its environment. Anyone going through this transition needs to realize and see himself as clay in the Potter's hand. For the moment, he may be chipped and marred. But as he becomes pliable in the hands of the Potter, and teachable, his PAC is slowly being shaped into the Image of God. This frees him from the oppression of contamination. A person becomes a new creation in Christ: "Old things are passing away...all things are becoming new" as he goes daily through the metamorphosis from unbelief to belief.

Social relationships and structures can only be transformed and become healthy as group members undergo the metamorphosis of spiritual change that reflects the Image of God. This is what transforms a First Order System into a Second Order System.

3. HEALTHY SOIL CONDITION OF BELIEF IN SECOND ORDER CHANGE
"...and some fell on good ground." — Matthew 13:8

People characterized as being *good soil* by Jesus represent those who listen to the message of God, understand it and accept the truth. The seed of truth in the good ground produces a harvest for God, thirty to a hundred times more than was planted in their hearts.*26* The difference between good soil and the three unproductive soils is that the fertile soil receives and permits the seeds to penetrate and take root. Even if there are contaminating substances present, the strength and resources within the healthy soil are sufficient to ward off being dominated by contamination. The seed in the good soil is able to flourish and produce a crop far greater than the original implantation.

In contrast, the seed in *hard, contaminated soil* never penetrates to receive the benefits of the potentially nourishing qualities present in the soil. In *shallow ground,* the seed is unable to take root and establish itself before the hot sun withers it, or the winds blow it away. In *thorny ground,* foreign substances, such as weeds and thorns, crush and crowd out life within the seed before it can take root. People who are *good, fertile soil,* on the other hand, have pure hearts. They hunger and thirst for righteousness and readily receive the seeds of truth.

The prodigal son eventually became fertile soil when he reached the end of the line in the pigsty. While he had money, wine, women and freeloaders polluting him, the seeds of truth could never penetrate his Adult-faith function. Only as he came to himself did he experience the awful stench of the pigsty and realize the painful cost of his follies.

Pain and cost are the key factors that cultivate and prepare fertile soil to receive truth. When Jesus told the disciples it was easier for a camel to go through the eye of a needle, He also told them "with God all things are possible."*27*

By the mercy of God, contaminated soils are plowed up through pain and loss. This prepares and cultivates it into good healthy soil, which can receive the seeds of truth.

I remember vividly the pain of pastoring and preaching to a church full of hard, contaminated soil. From the hardened looks on their faces, I knew nothing was penetrating. After my first sermon, I retreated to the study to seek God's guidance. A passage in Jeremiah caught my eye and set the tone for my ministry: "Fallow the hardened ground; otherwise good seeds will be wasted among the thorns."*28* After several years of plowing, the hardened ground, dominated by First Order System thinking, gave way and became good productive soil. The seeds of truth began penetrating and rooting in softened hearts. Faith and love blossomed forth and transformed many lives who were formerly hardened ground.

The prodigal was humbled by the pigsty and became teachable. His Adult function was then able to assess that servants working for his father had far superior working conditions to his in the pigsty. After processing all this data, he took responsibility for himself and knew he deserved his fate. He expressed faith by getting out of the pigsty and returning home in the hope that his father would at least hire him as a lowly servant. Instead he was joyously received as a son.

One day as Jesus passed through Jericho, a man named Zacchaeus wanted to get a glimpse of Him. Zach was quite short of stature and couldn't see over the crowd, so he ran ahead and climbed a sycamore tree beside the road to watch. When Jesus walked by, He looked up and noticed Zacchaeus. Jesus called him by name, told him to come down from the tree, and invited Himself to be a dinner guest at Zach's house. An excited Zacchaeus quickly climbed down to take Jesus home. But the crowd became quite hostile toward Jesus for going to this notorious man's home.

Zacchaeus was an influential Jew, working for the Roman I.R.S. He lined his own pockets and became quite rich. His oppressive tax collecting tactics did not endear him to his fellow countrymen. However, Zacchaeus was quite moved by the attention he received from Jesus, for, in spite of his wealth, he was shunned and isolated. Unconditional acceptance by Jesus moved Zacchaeus to give half of his wealth to the poor, and he paid back four dollars for every dollar he overcharged in taxes. Jesus acknowledged Zacchaeus and told him that salvation had come to his home. Then, turning to the crowd, He said, "This man was one of the lost sons of Abraham; and I, the Messiah, have come to search for and save such souls as his."*29* Jesus characterized Zacchaeus as good soil. The Adult-faith function within Zacchaeus hungered and thirsted for truth and life. All the power and riches he had acquired by cheating left him empty and unloved. Anyone of good reputation would not be caught dead associating with him. Indeed, to dine with such a person was unthinkable in that day.

Mealtimes are times of fellowship and sharing. Jesus spent His last evening before the crucifixion sharing the Passover meal with the twelve disciples. After the resurrection, Jesus cooked breakfast for them and had an intimate talk with Peter. Jesus spent a lot of time being close to people He dined with.

In view of this, one can fully appreciate that Zacchaeus was joyous about Jesus inviting Himself to dinner. In all probability, Zacchaeus felt totally unworthy of Jesus' company, and by no stretch of his imagination could he conceive of Jesus accepting an invitation to dine with him. Yet the Son of God valued Zacchaeus by inviting Himself to share in an intimate time. This self-invitation by Jesus confronted Zacchaeus as he muddled in his gold-lined pigsty. His Adult-faith function not only recognized the truth but joyously received it into his fertile soil. Truth began rooting itself deeply, to establish the Image of God firmly within his PAC. He was moved to relinquish all contaminated data. He repented of all the pain and hurt he had inflicted and took responsibility for himself by making generous amends to those he had wronged.

Zacchaeus and the rich young ruler demonstrate a vivid contrast between good fertile soil and contaminated infertile soil. By worldly standards, Zacchaeus was a crook and cheat. He was totally despised and rejected. He was obnoxious. There was nothing likable about him. On the other hand, the rich young ruler was young and attractive, a highly ethical and respected man. He was a comer, who fit the image of the all-American boy. Anyone would be honored to have him accept an invitation to dine in his home. The common denominator for both men was their wealth, and Jesus loved and valued them as they were.

Their responses to Jesus and His invitation were in marked contrast, however. The young ruler valued his wealth and investments in hopes of becoming an utopian person. His Adult-Ego was dominated by contaminated data which prevented him from assessing and processing the truth and reality contained in the invitation from Jesus to sell all and follow Him. He remained blind to the contaminated, infertile condition within his PAC, and continued to be encumbered and dissatisfied.

For all his good works, Jesus told him, he still lacked eternal life. He expected approval and walked away, dejected by the realization that his efforts were worthless. Unlike the prodigal, the encumbrances of his wealth and deception of self-justification had not yet brought him out of his gold-lined pigsty. He had not come to himself, so his Adult-Ego could not assess with the light of truth the contaminated nature of his PAC.

Zacchaeus, on the other hand, had no illusions about himself. His Adult-faith function recognized that his contaminated PAC had led him into the gold-lined pigsty of life. He truly came to himself and was moved by the invitation from Jesus. His Adult-Ego was free to assess the worthlessness of his values and encumbrances of his wealth. None of this brought him a life of satisfaction—only pain and rejection. His Adult-faith function was fertile soil. The seeds of truth and life from God burst forth with astounding joy.

Zacchaeus was free as he disengaged from the oppression of his self-deception and relinquished the encumbrance of his wealth. Unlike the rich young ruler, he traded in the deadness of his wealth for joy and uncontaminated life. He was set free from all contaminated oppression. Zacchaeus believed unto eternal life. The rich young ruler disbelieved unto death. Zacchaeus chose the freedom and discovery of uncontaminated Second Order Change. The young ruler continued to be locked into the oppressive deadness of contaminated First Order System.

Remember, the healthy spiritual life within group members and social interactions is what distinguishes a Second Order System from a First Order System. Second Order System is fertile; First Order System is infertile. Christ, the agent of Second Order Change, is the source of life, nourishment and light that transforms group members, the social structures and interactions in a Second Order System.

POWER TO CHANGE

CHAPTER XI. AREAS OF HUMAN DISTORTED THINKING

1. A Look at Distorted and Undistorted Belief and Faith

2. Psychological and Religious Distortions That Effect Thinking

3. Distortions in Christian Thinking (That Inhibit the Salvation Process in Second Order Change)

1. A LOOK AT DISTORTED AND UNDISTORTED BELIEFS AND FAITH

"Examine yourselves, whether you are in the faith."
                                    —I Corin. 11:28

Most notions about faith are conceived within people's contaminated PAC. These notions have never been examined or processed by their Adult-Ego function, and thus they emerge as myths without substance. One of the essential properties of First Order System is that the contaminated Child is governed by deceptive feelings and prone to magical thinking. The appeal in the Garden was made to the Childish feelings of the first couple. They allowed themselves to be deceived by what seemed to sound logical and reasonable. They were seduced by what appeared to be "good." Most destructive decisions and behaviors result from people reacting to the pressures of life with their feelings, rather than to data. Any notion of faith based upon feelings is form without substance to back it up.

188

Many come to God, expecting magic to lift them out of the pain of living and to indulge their childish whims. Several ideas have been floating around in Christian circles which are, in fact, products of magical thinking. Positive affirmation and positive thinking are a couple of the more popular notions. There are kernels of truth in each of these notions, which sound attractive. Positive affirmation perpetuates the idea that a person can simply affirm a Biblical promise and that mandates God to do it. Positive thinking conveys the idea that by holding a positive image or thought, the image will be translated into a reality that will happen. When the prayer, affirmation or image does not seem to be answered or become a reality, these people often experience a sense of devastation and failure. They often conclude something is wrong with their faith; or others will tell them they do not have enough faith. People with this mindset rarely engage their Adult-faith function to search out the mind of God for themselves.

Faith never conjures up some quantity or energy or thought that will make something happen. Nor is faith a manipulation of God, or a mandate to God to perform our bidding. God is sovereign and cannot be manipulated or appeased.

What Is Faith? All people believe something and have faith or trust in something or someone, whether they admit it or consciously realize it. When any of us boards an airliner, we believe that the pilot knows how to fly the plane. We also believe that the airplane has been dutifully maintained by the airline and is in good condition to fly us safely to our destination. We generally have sufficient data to believe this to be true. Consequently we entrust ourselves to the skill of the pilot and the safety of the plane. *This kind of belief has*

189

confidence in the reliability of the data.

A person expresses faith, then, when he acts and entrusts himself to the one he believes in, or the data he believes in. This is faith in substance. Many people say that they believe this or that, but they never act upon or entrust themselves to what they say they believe. *Failure to act on what one believes is really doubt. Doubt is always the result of some question about the reliability of what one says he believes and/ or his unwillingness to take responsibility to act upon and test out the data and his belief.* When there is some question about the reliability of what one believes, it is certainly prudent not to act upon it.

Faith, then, really has to do with trusting the reliability of the data behind what we believe. Only when we are convinced that the data of what we believe is reliable and trustworthy, will any of us entrust ourselves to it and act upon it. Human nature, being universally contaminated, draws the vast majority of people to believe in magical myths and illusions. Many people entrust themselves to someone whose claims are unreliable and act upon beliefs that have no substance. The confusion and destructiveness we all witness about us in human affairs are a tragic monument to the sinfulness in human nature and the unreliability of what human beings believe and in whom they place their trust.

The most important and paramount question facing all of us is not just what we believe *about* something, but what we believe *in,* or whom we believe *in.* What are you trusting? Or more precisely, *to whom* do you entrust yourself? This is an assessment each of us must face in the process of daily living, for it has far-reaching implications and consequences. Hiding one's head in the sand and refusing to take responsibility always has dire consequences.

The reality is that whatever you trust or whomever you entrust yourself to becomes the god or gods that govern or control your life. It is of utmost urgency that everyone make an honest assessment of what or who governs and controls his or her life. This God or gods either sets one free or is the oppressive tyrant that squeezes out life. *The gods of this world are the fabrication of the contaminated Parent and Child processed by a faulty Adult-Ego. These fabricated gods dominate First Order System. All mythological gods and images of gods of all world religions reflect the distorted image of man's contaminated PAC.*

All human beings endeavor to be gods unto themselves and are determined to establish their own little kingdoms. This reflects the adversarial properties of the power struggles found in First Order System. Nothing changes, because life is locked into a perpetual struggle of surviving the onslaught of others. The condition of this world is the product of the power struggle of four to five billion little gods who not only fight among each other but also ally themselves with like political, national and religious gods to enlarge their power base.

Legalism and self-justification go hand in hand. When legalism prevails within any social group, the individuals within the group have no recourse, if they are to survive, but to engage in self-justification for not measuring up to unattainable legalistic standards. *Legalism produces social psychosis.* Self-justification ends up burying a person deeper in the pits of despair. An individual is damned, no matter what happens. Efforts at self-justification are always tainted with distortion and self-deception, in order to make a person look good in the eyes of others. To appear "OK," one must always mask his flaws. This always leads to games and mistrust. Intimacy can never be achieved with God or others when mistrust is present. Legalism and self-justification end up estranging us from God and from each other.

Only faith in Christ reproduces the image of God within the PAC and re-establishes intimacy with God and in turn with others. *Faith* justifies the person who relies not on his own efforts but reflects the Image of God, for he is governed by the Source of truth, which needs no justification.

The Image of God continues to be reflected in a person's human nature only as he continues to live by faith in the Source of truth (Christ). A mirror continues to reflect the image of the person standing in front of it, as long as the two remain in the same position in relation to one another. Self-justification is totally unnecessary and a waste of time for anyone living by faith and reflecting the Image of God.

The life of faith is a life of discovery and choice. Faith never attempts to make life fit into ideal notions or squeeze it into a mold. Truth is discovered by the eyes of faith as the Holy Spirit reveals and illuminates it within the Adult-Ego. Faith tests out truth in daily life by choosing to act on it.

Faith is unable to fathom or contain the awesomeness of God or to see Him clearly face to face. St. Paul told the Corinthian church:

"We can see and understand only a little about God now, as if we were peering at His reflection in a poor mirror, but some day we are going to see Him in His completeness, face to face. Now all that I

know is hazy and blurred, but then I will see everything clearly, just as clearly as God sees into my
heart right now."*1*

Our faith and choice is hampered by human vision
that is clouded and limited by contamination within our
PAC. Our sinful Adult-Ego remains dimly lit and out of
focus, viewing life around us and God through distorted
eyes. A contaminated PAC cannot co-exist in the
presence of God with uncontaminated PAC, any more
than water and oil can mix and blend. No one with a
contaminated human nature can stand in the presence
of the awesome glory of God without being totally
overwhelmed and annihilated. Moses stood on holy,
uncontaminated ground in the presence of God at
Midian.*2* He was instructed at Mt. Sinai to set boundaries and tell his people that they would die if they
passed over or even touched the boundaries.*3*

Undergoing the full metamorphosis of the salvation
process is the only way sinful human nature can be
brought into the full presence of God. This process
brings the eyes of the Adult-Ego into focus. It allows the
eyes of one's faith to see life and the truth of God with
clarity. Faith based upon clear vision empowers us to
make wise and decisive choices.

Faith peers into the infinity of the resurrected life
and discovers glimpses of light here and there. These
glimpses come into sharper focus as blinders are
continually being peeled away from our eyes, allowing
more light to shine. It is much like looking at an infinite
movie screen and seeing a bit of the picture, perhaps
a bottom corner, and then a bit in the center of the
screen, and a few more bits of the picture scattered in
different parts of the screen. Sometimes faith is like a
movie camera that zooms in for a close-up, and we see

clearly what is in the close-up. As the camera dollies back, we begin to see the larger picture. Or the reverse may be true: The movie, "Sound of Music," begins with a breathtaking panoramic view of the majestic Austrian Alps and then zooms in on Julie Andrews singing the theme song. Focus is essential to discover what faith is all about, and our Adult-faith faculty helps us do just that.

Faith sees thousands of pieces of an infinite jigsaw puzzle before it and discovers several pieces fit in one area and a few others fit together in another area of the enormous puzzle. Faith in this life never sees the complete picture of the infinite God. In Hebrews 11, the writer recognized that many of the promises given to men of faith pertained to events still far in the future, but they remained steadfast in faith.*4*

Faith stands in awe and reverence, as it begins to recognize that it has embarked on a journey with infinite possibilities. One is humbled as his faith realizes that he has only touched a grain of sand from the limitless sands in all the world's oceans. This is incomprehensible. God is making available His unlimited power and resources, which can only be discovered and known by Faith.

This awesomeness does not terrify faith. Rather, it causes a person to worship and praise, because of the certainty and stability God provides from his storehouse of infinite resources.

There is only one God worthy to be adored and loved. This is the God who sent His only begotten Son as the uncontaminated Sacrificial Lamb to set free all who wish to be liberated from their sinful nature. This God so loved [*agape*] the world that He gave His most precious, only Son to die, that we might receive His resurrected life as a gift without strings attached.*5* "No greater love has any man than this, to lay down his life for his friends; and you are my friends if you let me live my uncontaminated life within you."*6*

Faith sees with confidence that what we desire most of all is waiting for us, even though we cannot see it in completeness yet. Faith doesn't hope in a vague way; it knows the One in Whom it believes and has confidence in God's reliability and integrity to make it happen.*7* Throughout history many God-believing people acted on this kind of faith. Faith believes and knows that the world and the entire universe were made at God's command from things that cannot be seen.*8* Faith assures us that nothing can separate us from God's love and power.*9* Through the eyes of our faith, we know that in God's time, every knee shall bow and confess Him as Lord.*10*

Contrary to what people may suppose, faith is expressed in what is thought of as scientific thinking. The idea of science is to discover what is and what works. Much of what has been passed off as science has been preoccupied with finding causes and giving explanations. The assumption has been that we must know reasons why and causes before we can be scientific. Any attempts to give explanations and find out the "whys" and "causes" is a First Order Change endeavor and falls within the parameters of the four demonstrable properties. Any endeavor falling within these guidelines is not concerned with discovering truth or data that works, only what fits into the assumptions and proves a point.

A scientific endeavor cannot discover truth of "what is" when only selected data is considered. Only Second Order Change endeavors are scientific, because the

Adult-Ego is engaged to consider all data in its evaluation and decision-making. This process leads to discovery of "what is." Theories and hypotheses, along with observable facts, are data that can be considered by the Adult-Ego function. These are not necessarily provable, but can be observed to work and may be used as data.

Genuine science believes hypotheses and theories and acts on what it believes. Much of technology is a discovery of "what works," rather than "why it works." Many principles have been discovered about how it works, but no one has many explanations of why principles work as they do; and it really isn't that necessary to know why anyway. It wouldn't make any difference one way or another if we knew why, when we already know how it works.

All people make assumptions about many issues in life. Assumptions are basically ideas or views people have about anything they believe to be true. Therefore, assumptions are essentially beliefs. Unfortunately, most assumptions are speculative in nature, usually unsupported by data. Assumptions or speculations are often used to fill gaps with what appear to be plausible explanations. In most cases, confirming data is lacking, and after serious examination, wide gaps still exist and raise many more questions.

The idea that we must know the "why?" or "causes" before it can be established as scientific thinking is not supported by data and reality. Ninety percent of scientific knowledge and technological advances have been discovered in the last two hundred years. That is an overwhelming fund of knowledge about how a lot of things work in this world. Many recent discoveries have made earlier theories obsolete. Even with a great fund of data, workable hypotheses and theories, no one, including scientists, can provide provable data without gaps to establish the origin that causes these discoveries to work, or why things work as they do. However, we all observe that we can still use and benefit from these discoveries.

Most controversy and confusion about scientific thinking and faith are not about discovered data but about the speculations regarding the "causes" and explanations of the "whys." The problem occurs when speculative explanations are passed off as established data, to be accepted as truth. These attempts are deceptive, because these speculative explanations are really the beliefs and dogmas of the particular person or group espousing them. It is grossly dishonest to say anything to the contrary.

The Roman Catholic Church recently admitted that its long held theological views of the world were in error. The Church finally admitted that Galileo was correct after all. This admission only demonstrated the intractability of people, churches, and other opinionated groups. Many in the field of science make the same kind of assumptions about their explanations of causes and pass them off as scientific dogmas. This kind of so-called scientific thinking is as erroneous as many theological dogmas have proven to be.

The psalmist recognized God as sovereign ruler of His creation.11 Faith in God is not the product of commonly held views of legalistic or magical thinking. Faith, like genuine science, is based on the reliability of the data. Faith, like genuine science, tests its data and acts on the trustworthiness of it. Faith of Second Order System knows and entrusts itself to God and acts upon His revealed truth.

2. PSYCHOLOGICAL AND RELIGIOUS DISTORTIONS THAT EFFECT THINKING

"...as a man thinks, so is he." —*Proverbs 23:7*

"As a person thinks, so is he" is a simple and observable truth. *12* A person's ability to think clearly depends on the data that dominates his thinking. It either enables him to make wise decisions or produces confusion, often leading to disastrous decisions. St. Paul pointed out that deception and truth are present within us all at the same time. *13* The source of lies and distortions is the contaminated spirit of this world. The source of all Truth is God, as revealed in Christ and transmitted to all people by the Holy Spirit.

The writer of Proverbs observed, "There is a way that seems right unto man, but the end result is the way of destruction." *14* Contaminated data on the surface often appears to be light and truth. In fact, it can be a baldfaced lie. Most of us are vulnerable to the subtlety of deceptive data when it appears so right and logical. It takes a healthy Adult-Ego to sift through and sort out subtle distortions.

Humanistic philosophy and logic have the appeal of often sounding so right and profound. These emanate from the contaminated Child of the philosopher and logician. Philosophical data tends to be speculative in nature, as it attempts to search for answers and meaning to life. Logical data tend to make life issues fit within the limits of human reason.

In the seventeenth century, philosopher Rene Descartes, at one point in his life, was able to reason himself into doubting the actual existence of his own body as a possible illusion and dream. *15* Many generally agree that Descartes' *Discourse on Method* is a philosophical classic that radically influenced the trend

198

of modern philosophical thought. It introduced a new mentality and, of course, new problems for thinking. However, all the volumes written by humanistic philosophers and logicians have not been able to provide the world with meaning or answers to life. This is obvious, since the world remains in the clutches of First Order System.

Humanistic philosophy and logic really end up perpetuating and maintaining First Order System. The only thing people find as they search so diligently for meaning and answers to life is doubt and uncertainty. This leads to eventual despair, because nothing changes; nothing improves. Truth and life, found only in Second Order System of the resurrected life in Christ, is never discovered within the boundaries of First Order System.

The principal living religions of the world originated in three geographical areas:

India: Hinduism, Buddhism, Jainism, Sikhism
China and Japan: Confucianism, Taoism, Shintoism
Middle East: Judaism, Zoroastrianism, Christianity, Islam

Of these, Christianity, Islam, Hinduism, Buddhism and Judaism are the five major religions. Judaism, Christianity and Islam agree that human beings live only once on earth and have only one chance to obtain a happy after-life. Salvation is the survival of human personality in a happy existence in heaven. Judaism and Islam reject Christianity's Divine Savior. According to Hinduism and Buddhism, human beings are born and reborn, reincarnated indefinitely. Salvation is not survival but obliteration of the individual personality.

Each of these religions has what might be called a high register and a low register. High register is the level of intellectual, educated, sophisticated belief. It is high-minded, philosophical, and concerned with correct doctrine and the spiritual life. Low register is the level of widespread popular belief. It is far more down-to-earth and concerned with practical matters. The main concern at this level is to obtain the good things of life and ward off life's evil, suffering, poverty, disease, deprivation, and bad luck, in order to secure a more enjoyable physical life after death, or the next time around. Trouble is taken, at this level, to conciliate and win the favor of the supernatural powers, who are the holders and givers of the good things in life.

Popular religion believes polytheistically in many gods. However, in atheistic systems, such as Buddhism, there is a disbelief in any kind of god. Objects of reverence in various religions differ widely. They may be trees, forces sensed in the wind, rain, crops, dead or living human beings.

A sense of the sacred lies at the heart of religion—a feeling that there is another dimension of life besides the material and temporal everyday experiences. Behind and beyond the visible is a sense of reality, that arouses emotions of awe and reverence. Most religions believe that good is rewarded and wickedness punished. These religions also observe that in reality the good frequently suffer, while the wicked flourish. Unfairness in life raises an awkward problem for religion, since it suggests that divine powers are cruel and unjust. The solution found in all religions is a system of justice which extends beyond this life. The good are rewarded and the wicked punished in the life after death, or in the next life on earth.

Of all the religions in the world, only Christianity (faith in the Person of Christ) offers a way out of First Order System into Second Order System. All religions recognize that human nature is contaminated in some form and the prevalence of evil and injustice seems to prove it. The Islamic and Judaic solution is to earn salvation in this life, before death, by a series of good works and adhering to a strict religious legalistic code. Eastern religions believe there is no salvation for the contaminated nature of man—only obliteration. This is fatalistic and hopeless. There is no hope of deliverance or freedom from the oppressive contaminated nature of man, only eventual obliteration. Denial of the terrifying eventual obliteration of human personality is perpetuated and delayed indefinitely by a series of reincarnations.

Christianity is founded on Judaism. To the Christian, Jesus is the Christ, the fulfillment of the Old Testament, the promised Messiah and Savior to the nation of Israel. He is the seed of woman promised in the Garden, who would come and bruise the head of the father of all lies, Satan. His coming is prophesied throughout the Old Testament as coming through the seed of Abraham and the fulfillment of David's throne. However, Judaism rejects Jesus as the Messiah and still awaits a Messiah to come onto the scene. During Passover, an empty chair and place is set at the Seder dinner. The door remains open for an expected arrival of Elijah, the harbinger, announcing the coming of the Messiah. Faithful Jews all over the world have been expecting this harbinger for nearly two thousand years.

All four of these religions remain entrapped in the oppression and death of First Order System. The Judaic and Islamic religions offer salvation by works. Their salvation process is to try harder and measure up to the standards of a God characterized as a critical, controlling Parent, who can never be pleased. This form of salvation perpetuates the legalistic and adversarial properties of First Order System. The Adult-Ego function remains a prisoner to contaminated Parent and Child data. There is no way to redeem the sinful, contaminated human nature (PAC) from the clutches and death of First Order System. The strip in the Middle East, which has been dominated by the Islamic and Judaic religions, is a dramatic portrait of First Order System consequences.

Eastern religions are dominated by the contaminated Child within its followers. Through a series of infinite reincarnations, the contaminated Child within these Eastern religious adherents can magically deny the eventual terrifying obliteration of human personality (PAC). Reincarnation postpones the inevitable indefinitely. This magical denial characterizes the deceptive properties of First Order System. Reincarnation only perpetuates and hastens the individual's deterioration under the First Order System. Poverty, which devalues and impoverishes the human spirit, has been the legacy of cultures and societies dominated by First Order System in Eastern religions. The fatalistic hopelessness that perpetually postpones the threat of extinction has sapped the people's strength and will to survive and live creatively.

The purpose of all religious expressions is to make sense out of life that faces extinction. The need for certainty in an uncertain world is a basic human need. It drives human beings to find explanations and meanings for life. The contaminated Child must insure himself freedom from the threat of extinction. He cannot survive without having some value or meaning and power. The contaminated Child survives by forming an alliance with the powerful, controlling Parent and becomes a god unto himself, to control others who would threaten him. All human beings emerge as gods unto themselves, subject to the whim of the gods they form in the image of man. This instinct to make life fit and control others is another property of First Order System. Collision of five billion little gods and competing religions perpetuates the adversarial nature of all religious expressions locked into First Order System.

A fundamental concern of all religious expressions is to offer a way out of the threat of death and extinction. Only two ways are offered by non-Christian religions: A legalistic way of works that might gain favor and approval from God; or an illusive, magical scheme that indefinitely postpones and avoids the consequences of extinction. None of these religious schemes deal with the way *out of the sinful nature (PAC) of all human beings. None offers a way out of death from First Order System. There is no offer of an uncontaminated life of discovery, nor is there a door open to enter into the life found in Second Order System. All religions are dominated by contaminated data and properties of First Order System.*

As a result, all these religions continue to distort, rather than restore, the Image of God within people. Religions perpetuate the death and extinction of life in human nature, instead of being a channel breathing the life of God into the human spirit. *The legacy of all religions around the world is the perpetuation of First Order System, which devalues human life and God's Spirit.*

Only *uncontaminated* Christianity offers emancipation from human nature's sinfulness. It alone offers an exit from the threat of extinction perpetuated in First Order System. Uncontaminated Christianity does not waste time speculating about reincarnation, nor does it encumber anyone with legalism. A cross is offered instead, which opens the door into the resurrected life as a new creature in Christ. A new birth impregnates human nature, imparts life, and decontaminates PAC. It restores the Image of God within the individual's PAC.

Anyone can enter into a life of freedom and discovery found in the Second Order System. God provides the way out as a free gift to all who will receive it. There is no suggestion that you must deserve it by measuring up to unreachable standards, or that you must receive it with clean hands. One receives it so he may be cleansed and decontaminated from his PAC.

3. *DISTORTIONS IN CHRISTIAN THINKING (THAT INHIBIT THE SALVATION PROCESS IN SECOND ORDER CHANGE)*

Contaminated data from First Order PAC has tended to create confusion in Christian thinking and religious expression throughout its history of nearly two thousand years. Truth and life, as a result, have been impeded from saturating the hearts and minds of believers and have obscured its value from a world in need. The dangerous and chaotic condition of this world is a tragic testimony to this fact.

Since its inception, the enemies of God within and without the Christian church have vigorously attempted to contaminate and distort God's truth and prevent the spread of the Good News. The Gospel according to John was written to combat the early idea that strictly spiritualized Jesus and denied His humanity. St. Paul almost singlehandedly fought to keep the church and the Gospel from gravitating back into Jewish religious legalism. His writings and theology established the unique foundation that distinguishes and sets Christianity apart from all other religious expressions. The letters of St. Paul addressed issues and problems within the life and ministry of the early church. His single-mindedness firmly sorted out all the prevailing distortion that threatened to corrupt the Gospel and distort the truth revealed in Jesus Christ. Paul, a former Pharisee and persecutor of early Christians, clearly defined and established the uncontaminated data that is the bedrock and foundation of Christian theological truth. Salvation is the Good News that frees people from their contaminated PAC and is appropriated by faith alone in Jesus Christ.

As the Christian movement grew and developed, a number of church councils met over the years to define and maintain uncontaminated orthodox Christian doctrine. The doctrine of the Trinity was dogmatized to decontaminate polytheistic notions and establish the oneness of God. It affirmed the one God of Judaism and the only Christian God. By the fourth century the body of writing now known as the Bible was established as the source of the Word of God and His revelation of Himself in history. As the influence of the Gospel spread and gained acceptance throughout the Middle East and Western Europe, the church became more organized. The power of religious leaders grew as the Gospel was cast more and more into doctrines, dogmas and rituals. Instead of using his Adult-faith function, the faithful Christian became more of a contaminated Child, dependent upon the controlling Parentage of powerful religious leaders. Through the development of doctrines and dogmas, powerful religious leaders told people what to believe and not to think for themselves.

This movement increasingly isolated the faithful Christian from a personal faith and relationship with God. Christ became increasingly cast as a distant deity who was viewed as a critical Parent, ready to pass judgment for the minutest infractions. Doctrines and dogmas emerged, and were used to govern every aspect of human behavior. The end result was more of the same oppression that Christ died to free people from. The Christian church and its religious leaders were playing out the same script of First Order System found earlier in legalistic Judaism. The religious leaders were emerging as legalistic tyrants, cut in the same mold as the Jewish Pharisees. As religious power began to be concentrated in the hands of a few, a hierarchy of religious leadership developed with the faithful believer at the bottom of the totem pole. Emperors and kings came under the influence of the Church as it grew and became politically strong.

By the fifth century a full blown fusion of church and state had begun to dominate the thinking and political life of the Middle East and Western world. During this time, political power struggles were in the wind. The dominant power of the western Roman empire was eroding. As a result, the powerful Roman Catholic Church began losing its influence and hold over the Eastern Catholic Church. These churches never came under the influence of a dominant bishop or political regional force. They emerged as the Eastern Orthodox Churches, still tied in and fused with the political state of their national origin.

From the fifth century, the Roman Catholic Church dominated the political and religious life of Western Europe. Up until the thirteen century, the religious expression of the Roman Catholic Church was influenced by the mysticism of Augustine. During the thirteenth century when Western Europe began moving out of the Dark Ages into the Age of Reason, the Roman Catholic theology began to be influenced greatly by the Aristotelian theology of Thomas Aquinas. The logic of Thomasian theology forced the church to embrace the untenable doctrines of the infallibility of the Roman Catholic Pope and Mariology to accommodate its mystic elements.

A doctrine of Purgatory was developed to deal with the issue of extinction. Purgatory is sort of a holding tank for the dead that delays final judgment and extinction. This, of course, resulted in many abuses and oppressions that increased the wealth and power of the church and papacy over the political life of all Western Europe. Payoffs for indulgences and penances were imposed upon the lowly faithful. The character of religious expression gravitated further into the dark oppression of legalism and the magical superstition of mysticism. The church, with its legalistic, superstitious religious expression, oppressed and tyrannized emperors, kings and peasants alike.

The religious and political winds were ripe for the discovery of faith by Martin Luther in the early sixteenth century. Luther was a German monk tortured by a deep sense of sin and unworthiness. This was continually reinforced by legalistic church dogmas. Oppressive penances buried Luther still deeper in despair. His compliant Child never measured up to the contaminated controlling Parent of legalistic church doctrine. Luther was revolted by the extortions perpetrated by the doctrine of Purgatory, which played on the fears and superstitions of living relatives of the dead. Large sums of money were demanded by the Roman Catholic Church to extricate the dead in the limbo of Purgatory from the jaws of extinction. Luther was furious at the payoffs for easy indulgences to remit the consequences of sin. These abuses tended to keep the faithful in perpetual debt to the church. It turned out to be a powerful religious and political form of blackmail that kept the ruling class and peasants in line. Religious hypocrisy and cynicism toward the church and Christian doctrine became rampant.

The Bible at that time was written in Latin and only available to the clergy. Fortunately, Luther had been educated in his religious order and knew Latin. With a deep hunger for the truth, Luther searched Scriptures for answers. St. Paul's letter to the early church at Rome lit up the inner being of Luther's contaminated PAC. He read that no one can gain favor and justify himself with God by self-effort.

"No one can ever be made right in God's sight by doing what the law commands. For the more we know of God's laws, the clearer it becomes that we aren't obeying them. His laws serve only to make us see that we are sinners."*16*

St. Paul's declaration that human beings are only "justified" before God by "faith alone" blazed in his Adult-faith function, as Luther cried out, "*Solo fida!* — Faith alone!"*17*

This revelation freed the simple monk from the bondage of his contaminated PAC. It catapulted him to spark the Reformation movement, when he nailed his "ninety-five theses" to the door of All Saints' Church at Wittenberg on October 31, 1517. The movement opened up the Bible to the masses. Luther translated the Bible into German, and others followed by translating it into the vernacular of various languages in Europe. Political winds were anti-Rome; German princes allied themselves with Luther to emancipate themselves from the oppression of the Roman Catholic Church's legalism and superstition. Religious emancipation swept rapidly throughout Western Europe.

The Reformation movement took Western Europe further into a period of history known as the Renaissance. This period in its widest scope describes the transition from the medieval world (500-1500 A.D.) to the age of modern science (1700 A.D.). This was the beginning of modern society, the age of exploration, the discovery of the telescope, mariner's compass, and gunpowder. The invention of the printing press made the Bible and literature available in the vernacular of the people. As geographical discoveries were made, the rigid trade unions and guilds gave way to trade and commerce. The self-contained political districts, whose sole economic base depended upon agriculture and ownership of land, started giving way to trade in manufactured goods from other communities.

John Symonds, writing about the Renaissance in the nineteenth century, commented,

"It was the emancipation of the reason, in a race of men, intolerant of control, ready to criticize canons of conduct, enthusiastic of anticipated liberty, freshly awakened of beauty, and anxious above all things to secure for themselves free scope in spheres outside the region of authority. There was no problem they feared to face, no formula they were not eager to recast according to the new conception."*18*

The Renaissance contained a new concept of the universe in which religion consisted less in feeling dependence upon God and more in a faith in the possibility lying in mankind.*19* This era sowed the seeds of secular humanism.

During the late sixteenth and early seventeenth centuries, seeds for the Protestant Christian movement were sown, eventually blooming into various Protestant denominations of the current modern scientific age. "Protestant" was the word coined to characterize the religious protest against the dominance of the Roman Catholic Church.

The history of the church during the past three centuries has been characterized by the perennial ebb and flow in the relationship of faith and culture. Church history has also been strewn with tragic violence over doctrinal and dogmatic issues. This separated and established religious barriers rather than oneness in Christ. The life of the church is always shaped by two concurrent movements: the penetration and transformation of cultural life by faith in Christ, and the secularization of this culture. Secularization, unfortunately, has emerged as the dominant movement in the past three centuries.

The discovery of the truth that all human beings are justified by *"solo fida* — faith alone" emancipated the Adult-Ego of a German monk and ignited the Reformation movement. This set people free to think for themselves and discover the resurrected life of Second Order System, after nearly a thousand years of contaminated religious darkness. Ironically, the once emancipated Adult-Ego has since been contaminated and secularized, returning it to the dominance of First Order System. Humanism takes the truth of God, once it has permeated a culture, and attempts to disregard the God who is the source of that truth. This tension between the darkness of First Order System attempting to blot out the light of Second Order System has characterized all human history.

The tragic history of the Christian church has paralleled in many ways its predecessor, Judaism. Both were plagued and continue to be plagued with contaminated data that would make them indistinguishably part of the world of secular First Order System. Fortunately, God in His mercy continues to shed His light into darkness and emancipates the Adult-faith function of responsive multitudes. These individuals are the light of the world and lead the world to the source of truth, God as revealed in His Son Jesus Christ.

POWER TO CHANGE

CHAPTER XII. SOCIAL CRAZINESS IN THE SECULARIZATION OF FIRST ORDER SYSTEM
"You cannot serve two masters." — Matthew 6:34

Secularization of culture is the real enemy of all human beings. Rather than set people free, it oppresses society with its nitpicking regulation of life. First Order System properties of secularized humanism dominates the totalitarian and democratic world alike. Both are oppressed by the growing encroachment of Parental governments. Since World War II, the American government has grown to monstrous proportions. Its tentacles regulate every aspect of life. Life in the United States is dominated by legalisms of all kinds.

The legal profession, by its very nature, has played a dominant role in shaping the secularization of our society. Legalistic and adversarial properties of First Order System are the very heart and nature of the legal profession. Social issues that have had a horrendous impact on the life of this country have been shaped by the courts. Legalistic nitpicking under the guise of protecting individual rights have really eroded freedom. The simple and unobtrusive act of a moment of silent prayer is seen as an encroachment upon the concept of separation of church and state. Groups like the American Civil Liberties Union, which has courageously championed disenfranchised people, and even unpopular causes, in their fight to maintain freedom, seems to have been blindly drawn into this legalistic hysteria. These groups have no sense of history and totally ignore the fundamental historical data behind the struggle of separation of church and state. This struggle has always been between either the dominance of a powerfully organized church and its influential leaders dominating the state civil government, or a powerful totalitarian state totally dominating the church to inhibit any religious expressions. This has been characterized in history by the dominance of the Roman Catholic Church over the Western world for nearly a thousand years during the Middle Ages, or the dominance of the state establishing a state church over the religious life of people.

In England, prior to the Revolutionary War, the Anglican Church of England was under the wing and dominance of the English Crown. Taxes were used to maintain it, and other religious expressions or churches were not tolerated. The framers of the U. S. Constitution were addressing these two issues of not permitting any organized church to dominate the state politically and not allowing the government to support a politically powerful state church organization or group.

In Communist countries, the church is politically tolerated; and in Russia, the Eastern Orthodox Church is the officially accepted church. Other non-Orthodox churches are oppressively tolerated and monitored to insure that their teaching and preaching are not critical or threatening to the state. The Catholic Church in Poland has managed to remain free of state Communist dominance only because Catholic Christianity is so engrained in the Polish people's thinking.

The framers of the U.S. Constitution wished to prevent power from becoming concentrated in any one body or person. The government itself is structured to maintain a balance of power. The members of the Constitutional Congress certainly recognized Deity and the spiritual life as the bedrock of society. The intent has been for government and religious freedom to exist side by side, not as adversaries but as co-influences that maintain and regulate a healthy society.

The Biblical writings strongly support and recognize that civil governments are instituted by God. Governments are to be supported and obeyed by the faithful citizenry. All citizens are to take active interest and responsibility to shape and maintain government as a servant of the people, not as their master. The intent of the Constitution's designers was not to divorce government from the influence of spiritual concerns and Deity. The intent has always been for government to be responsive to the wisdom and grace of God as it discharges its responsibilities.

Benjamin Franklin, who was not known for deep piety, recognized this when the Constitutional Convention in 1787 was bogged down and struggling to draft the Constitution. He called that body to prayer for wisdom and guidance:

"Mr. President, The small progress we have made after four or five weeks' close attendance is, me thinks, a melancholy proof of the imperfection of human understanding. We indeed seem to feel our want of political wisdom, since we have been running about in search of it...In this situation, how has it happened, Sir, that we have not hitherto once thought of applying to the Father of Light to illumine our understanding? In the beginning of the contest with Great Britain, when we were sensible of danger, we had daily prayer in this room. Our prayers, Sir, were graciously answered...And have we now

214

forgotten that powerful Friend? Or do we imagine we no longer need His assistance?"*1*

The Preamble of the United States' Constitution recognizes itself as a nation under God. There is no reference to being under any certain church organization, doctrines or dogmas. The New Testament faith stresses the individual's responsibility in using his Adult-Ego faith function to assess all data and make choices. There is no call to blind religious allegiances. The Constitution guarantees people's right to believe whatever one chooses. It also guarantees the freedom to share these beliefs, be it on public or private property, without government interference, as long as it's done peacefully.

The secular movement is more concerned with eliminating God from human thinking than a valid separation of church and state. The movement has resorted to legalistic nitpicking. This legalism has had the dangerous effect of inhibiting and harassing the freedom of religious expression. Court judgments, since the Supreme Court decision to eliminate prayer in the schools, has had ludicrous and repressive repercussions. It has inhibited tax paying citizens from using public property and institutions to share and express religious belief and thought. As a result, the pursuit of truth in public institutions of learning is really inhibited and prevented. One tax paying citizen may prevent another tax paying citizen from sharing or expressing his religious belief, simply because the complaining tax payer may not share that belief and is offended by it. Over the past several years, it has become increasingly oppressive and ludicrously interpreted by public officials.

A news story told of a parent complaining to a

Florida high school principal about the inclusion of a picture of the Bible Club in the high school yearbook. The principal had this page removed from all the yearbooks before being distributed. However, on the back of this page was the picture of the Spanish Club. When the Spanish Club complained about omitting their picture, the principal profusely apologized to them, but no apology was given to the Bible Club. The principal justified his action on the grounds of his ludicrous interpretation of separation of church and state. Under this interpretation, students in the Spanish Club were of more value than the students of the Bible Club. Apparently the students in the Bible Club were not offended or oppressed. The tax-paying parents of Bible Club students were not of equal value as the tax paying parents of Spanish Club members, by this line of reasoning. Where, by any stretch of the imagination, is there a separation of church and state issue involved in a group of students forming a Bible Club, any more than in students forming a Spanish Club?

The whole point of education is to provide students with an environment for exploration and learning the truth. This would be an environment that encourages and permits the students to use their Adult-Ego function to assess and process all data. No education can ever really take place if public educators are wimpishly reacting to pressures of the vocal few who are not really oppressed but more concerned with nitpicking and inhibiting religious freedom of others. How, in this case, were the religious rights of the complaining parents violated or oppressed by a picture of the Bible Club appearing in the yearbook and meeting in a school facility, any more than the Spanish Club appearing in the yearbook and meeting in the school facility? The

Florida yearbook incident is not an isolated event. Unfortunately this kind of reaction from public officials is all too prevalent throughout this nation.

Gary Pierson received assurance from Georgia prison authorities that there were no outstanding warrants from North Carolina when he was paroled in the late 1970s. Prior to being imprisoned in Georgia, Pierson had escaped from a North Carolina prison two months before his prison term was to expire. A routine check in the summer of 1985 discovered that a warrant from North Carolina was indeed outstanding. Legal counsel to the Governor of North Carolina insisted that Pierson be extradited from Minnesota. Pierson had in the meantime married and established himself as a responsible citizen since his prison release. The North Carolina legal counsel was only concerned with maintaining a uniform policy in insisting on the extradition. The Associated Press quoted him as not wanting to take the time to evaluate the Pierson situation on its own merits and the consequences of extradition. The legal counsel seemed more concerned with the jot and tittle of the law than the mercy and justice of the law. He seemed unconcerned about the cost North Carolina and Minnesota tax payers would incur to carry out the extradition, not to mention the unnecessary emotional trauma for the Pierson family. He was apparently unable to see the value of Pierson's rehabilitation to society. Social craziness is often a product of this kind of legalistic nitpicking by people in power, who seem unable and/or unwilling to use discretion and reason in carrying out public responsibilities.*2*

Humanism and secular legalism are always attempting to make society fit into a mold. All its efforts are bent toward making a square peg fit into a round

217

hole. This inevitably produces social craziness and oppression. Jesus continually attacked religious legalistic nitpicking and exposed its ludicrous effects on society.

One day a man approached Jesus in the synagogue on the Sabbath, asking Him to heal his paralyzed hand. Many religious fault-finders lurked in the crowd, ready to pounce on Jesus if He dared heal on the Sabbath. Work was unlawful on the Sabbath, and healing was regarded as a form of work by their religious law. Jesus asked them if it was right to help or harm, to save a man's life or destroy it on the Sabbath.*3* As he gazed into the crowd's faces, He was at once angry and full of pity because of their blindness. He reminded them, "Anyone of you would pull out your sheep, if stuck in a hole on the Sabbath. A man is worth much more than a sheep!"*4*

Secularistic and humanistic efforts to eliminate God and the spiritual have fostered a pervasive cynicism throughout all societies and cultures. Paranoid nitpicking is the mood of the day. Everyone searches for the speck in his neighbor's eye, but fails to recognize the log jam in his own. This is reflected on every level of life. It can be seen in international and national affairs, as well as domestic affairs. A recent poll showed the public's distrust of the news media's tendency toward paranoid nitpicking. The impression has been that the news media seems more hell-bent on playing "I gotcha, you S.O.B.," than reporting factual news.

A number of years ago, a minister (a dear friend of mine) was accused and sued by a woman he had been counseling, on the grounds that he had made sexual advances toward her. The Los Angeles newspapers sensationalized this incident with banner headlines.

Television played it up on the six o'clock news. The judge threw the case out on the first day of the trial, because of lack of evidence; and he stated that the woman's intent was vindictive, solely to malign the minister's character. However, there was no mention of this the following day in any of the Los Angeles newspapers, nor was it on the six o'clock news. There are, no doubt, many responsible professionals of integrity in the news media; but unfortunately, there are also far too many incidents like the one just described to go unnoticed.

Literature and drama portray life with all its complex dimensions, from the full range of comedy to tragedy, without any reference to man's need for dependence upon God's grace or wisdom. Realistic faith and dependence on God are very rarely dramatized. Most portrayals of piety are caricaturizations and distortions, simply because the theme within the vast majority of literature and drama is humanistic. References to God are mainly cynical and hopeless in tone. The vast majority of literary writers and producers of drama are steeped in humanism, and blinded by their contaminated PAC. They simply have no idea or feeling for those whose lives are governed by faith. They are totally blind to the humor and drama experienced by those viewing life through the eyes of faith, and processed by a Spirit-emancipated Adult-Ego in Second Order System.

"Chariots of Fire" is an outstanding example of a financial and artistic success. It was produced on a relatively low budget, compared to current motion picture expenditures. The key to "Chariots'" success was that it captured in a very sensitive way the contrasting values and views of two young men who were competing in the 1924 Olympics. It powerfully and humorously contrasted a Christian athlete's spirit and values with those of a young man obsessed with the need and desire to win and be the fastest man alive. Both were outstanding young men of high standards. Both strove for excellence. There was a marked contrast, however, between the freedom of spirit in the Christian athlete who was governed by his faith and the fear and tension in the young man driven to win. He respected the Christian's running ability, but more than anything, he feared his indomitable spirit.

Secularism and humanism are products of the contaminated PAC of the vast majority of humanity. Legalistic nitpicking and adversarial human nature are at the very heart of First Order System. For all its pretenses, secular humanism and legalism devalue human beings and life. No matter how problems are dealt within this framework, multitudes of people are always devalued and get the short end of the stick. Secularism and humanism perpetuate the tragic craziness in this world. There will never be spiritual or mental health anywhere in this world as long as these two philosophies dominate individuals' and society's thinking.

POWER TO CHANGE

CHAPTER XIII. THE BIBLE IS THE WORD AND LIGHT
FOR CLEAR THINKING IN
SECOND ORDER SYSTEM OF GOD
"The Word of God is powerful and sharper than any two-edged sword." — Hebrews 4:12

Most homes in the Western world probably have a Bible. This is particularly true in the United States, where polls show that the vast majority have some belief in God and exposure to the Christian religion. However, the vast majority in our society are Biblically illiterate. Ironically this is true of many professing Christians and church leaders. Biblical illiteracy among political, business, labor, and professional people is quite astounding. This is probably a significant contributing factor in perpetuating the confusing First Order System in our society.

Unfortunately the Bible is the most misused book in the world. Over the years, scholars, theologians and lay people have used the Bible to develop and reinforce their particular doctrinal and dogmatic stances. Numerous denominations have emerged as each developed their particular doctrinal emphasis. This often confuses and perplexes the seekers of truth, as each group claims to be correct. The Bible, in these instances, is typically used as a legalistic document. Scriptural passages are often used out of context, as proof text to fit a particular doctrinal stance.

The Bible does not fit into any particular doctrinal or

dogmatic mold. One will always miss the truth the Bible expresses when read with a mind set of a particular doctrinal stance. The problem is not the doctrines. Many Christian doctrines and dogmas have a great deal of truth in them. *The problem lies in the mind set that is closed and blind to Christian truth and forces Biblical data into dead legalistic terms.*

Words written in Scripture are more than mere data. The words have life that penetrates and enlivens the human heart (PAC). The writer of Hebrews tells us this living Word...

"...is full of power and sharper than a two-edged sword. It cuts swiftly and deeply into our innermost thoughts and desires...Everything about us is bared and wide open to the all-seeing eye of the living God..."*1*

The Bible tells us the sum of the life and power within the written Word is focused in the One who reveals Himself as the "living Word in the flesh." St. John opens his Gospel account by stating that in the beginning, before anything else existed, there was the Word [*logos*]:

"This Word was Christ in God. He has always been alive and is Himself God. He created everything there is...nothing exists that He didn't make. This Word was made flesh and we beheld His glory [uncontaminated PAC]. Eternal life is in Him [Christ], and this life gives light to all mankind. His life [the Word made flesh] is the light that shines through darkness."*2* [Parentheses are mine.]

Christ is the living Word that emerges from the Bible. He is the One the Bible points to. St. Paul viewed Christ as the living Word and the sum and substance of the Word in the Bible.

"Christ is the exact likeness of the unseen God. He existed before God made anything at all, and in fact, Christ Himself is the Creator Who made everything in heaven and earth, the things we can see and the things we can't...He was before all else began, and it is His power that holds everything together."*3*

St. Paul warns his readers not to allow their faith to be spoiled by philosophies and shallow ideas of men that conform to contaminated First Order data. Christ alone has given the world uncontaminated Second Order data.

"For in Christ there is all of God in human body; so you have everything when you have Christ and are filled with God through your union with Christ. He is the highest ruler, with authority over every power."*4*

Martin Luther experienced a rebirth when he read the simple words, "*solo fida!*—faith alone!" in the Latin Bible. Blinders were removed, and he saw truth jump out at him from the printed Word. Light of truth set him free from the contaminated data that oppressed him throughout his life. Martin Luther discovered the truth of the Bible when he discarded all of his preconceived religious dogmas. He was then able to approach the Scriptures with an open mind in his Adult-Ego-faith function. Luther experienced the life and power of the living Word [Christ] pulsating within him.

To question the reliability of Biblical data is as legitimate as questioning the reliability of any writing or data. The Bible is divided into two periods of time. The Old Testament covers the period beginning with creation until about two hundred years prior to the arrival of Jesus. The New Testament covers the life, death and resurrection of Jesus; followed by a brief historical account of what transpired for a period of some fifty to ninety years after His death and resurrection. The word "Bible" comes from the Greek word *biblio,* meaning "book." The word "testament" means "covenant" or "agreement." The Old Testament is the covenant God made with man about his salvation before the arrival of Christ, whereas the New Testament is about salvation given through the work of Christ. The Old Testament gives a covenant of law, whereas the New Testament gives the covenant of grace through Jesus Christ. Law led into grace.*5*

The Old Testament begins with the origin of sin, which resulted in blemishing the Image of God within humankind and estranging all humanity from God. It goes on to tell about God selecting a people [Israel] to show forth His truth and preserve a record of Himself. The failure of the covenant law in the Old Testament to restore the Image of God in human nature is clearly obvious. St. Paul pointed out that "by the deeds of the law could no flesh be justified, for all have sinned."*6* The theme and purpose running through the Old Testament prepares the way for the coming of the Savior into the world. The New Testament records the life, death and resurrection of Christ, who frees from First Order System and establishes the uncontaminated life of God in the PAC of all human beings who respond to Him. He established the rule of *agape* love through Second Order Change. Christ does not set aside the Old Testament; He fulfills it.

As one studies the Biblical data, both a diversity and unity of data can be observed. It is impossible to reduce the Old and New Testaments to a flat uniformity in order to get them to say the same things. The unity of the Bible is dynamic, rather than static.

H. H. Rowley observed that the development of the Bible was not brought about by the unfolding of the human spirit through the mere passage of time:

"There is no automatic spiritual growth of mankind, and the Bible nowhere tells the story of such a growth. It records how men of God, acting under a directive which they believed to be of God, mediated ideas and principles to men. It does not tell how men, by the exercise of their minds, wrested the secrets of life and the universe from a reluctant Unknown but how God laid hold of them and revealed Himself through them. If there is any truth in this, then a unity of the Bible is to be expected. If God was revealing Himself, then there should be some unity about the revelation, since it was the same Being who was being revealed. There is still room for diversity, since God was revealing Himself to men of limited spiritual capacity, and could only reveal to each what he was capable of receiving. There are branches of higher Mathematics which no one could apprehend without a long and exacting process of preliminary teaching. Similarly, there are secrets of the spirit which could only be imparted to men in the measure of their spiritual capacity to receive them. Moreover, since God chose to reveal Himself not alone to men but through them, He was limited by the medium that He chose. *That is why the full revelation in human personality required the Incarnation.* The variety of the levels of the various parts of the Bible is then not surprising, and it doesn't spring from any variation in God but from the variety of the levels of the persons whom He used." *7*

St. Peter made the same observation: "No prophesy recorded in Scriptures was ever thought up by the prophet himself. It was the Holy Spirit within these men who gave them true messages from God."*8*

Many say the Bible doesn't lend itself to scientific study and typically invalidate people's beliefs. Those who study the Bible from what is called a scientific approach tend to limit and treat the study of the Bible only as a human story... They tacitly assume there is no validity in beliefs. However, if in fact human beings were genuinely moved by God, then the story under study cannot be fully understood if all factors, including beliefs, are not genuinely considered. Anyone who invalidates beliefs is not scientific at all. He is not willing to consider and examine all the data, including beliefs. Selectivity and refusal to consider all the data automatically limits any study to the processes of First Order System. To discount beliefs of other human beings is paradoxically a belief in itself.

Dr. Rowley points out that science...

"...seeks to trace results back to their causes and causes forward to their results, and any truly scientific study of the Bible *must ask for all the facts of a situation,* and not merely for a selection of them. If we merely study the message of the Bible in the light of the political and social circumstances out of which its books were born, we are just as guilty of a dogmatic approach as the theologian may be. For it's just as dogmatic to suppose that God is not a vital factor in human affairs as to suppose that He is."*9*

Sometimes the challenge is given to prove that God exists and is active in the world by applying abstract logic and mathematical reasoning as the only rigid acceptable proof. This kind of reasoning is totally irrational and leaves the one applying this reasoning with an arid agnosticism. It is a gross fallacy to conclude that belief in God is an unscientific dogma, because it cannot be proven by abstract reasoning. This kind of erroneous conclusion or assumption is the product of First Order System thinking. Any time a scientist endeavors to confine his investigation and research to the limits of his assumptions, he inevitably ends up with the same sort of erroneous conclusion Descartes made when he concluded he didn't exist.

Professor Rowley has always enjoyed a reputation as a sound Biblical scholar, and certainly he expressed an acute understanding of the scientific method when he wrote:

"Science is by no means limited to abstract reasoning, and it works with a great number of hypotheses for which it can advance no absolute proof. Yet they are not groundless hypotheses. There are many lines of evidence that point toward them and make them reasonable hypotheses, but they are not subject to rigid demonstration. *The scientist tests his hypotheses in every way he can, and the more they stand his tests the more faith he has in them,* even though he continues to recognize that they are theories, which are not susceptible to absolute proof. He is too scientific to profess the sort of agnosticism about them which leads him to ignore them. He relies on them and uses them, and they enable him to make the advances which have revolutionized modern life...*It is just as scientific in our sphere for us to test in every way we can the faith that the activity of God in human experience and personality is recorded in the Bible, treating this not as a dogma which must be accepted without question but as a faith to be examined and to ask whether it may be reasonably established and not whether it can be rigidly proved.* The scientific method must be appropriately applied to each separate discipline. But when applied, what survives may be trusted without disloyalty to the scientific spirit."*10*

Professor Rowley's description of the scientific method is in reality a picture of a person using his Adult-Ego faith function when he assesses and processes Biblical or any other data. This is when the Holy Spirit illuminates and reveals within the PAC of that person the intimate presence of God and His particular truth for him.

POWER TO CHANGE

CHAPTER XIV. VALUES-LOVE-EVIL
IN FIRST AND SECOND ORDER SYSTEMS
1. Moral Values and Beliefs That Shape Our Lives
2. Trashiness of First Order Values
3. Philio and Eros Views of Love in First Order System
4. Healthy Values and Agape Love in Second Order System
5. Problem of Evil in First Order System

"You shall love God...neighbor...self."—Luke 10:25-27

1. MORAL VALUES AND BELIEFS THAT SHAPE OUR LIVES

Moral values and beliefs shape our lives more than any other factor in the world and are also the source of most human pain and tragic consequences. Nothing can change unless value issues are addressed. Any thinking that discounts the need to deal with human values is ridiculous. The therapist, like the evangelist, precipitates change in human beings when he confronts the morals and values that bring about pain and loss.

Yet therapists trained from the various disciplines of the behavioral sciences are taught not to tamper with a person's values or beliefs. The usual rationale behind avoiding moral and value judgments is that not to do so would be a departure from so-called scientific inquiry. Psychiatrist Tom Harris points out that proponents of this kind of thinking overlook the fact that the scientific method itself is totally dependent upon moral values and the trustworthiness of the scientific observation.*1* Dr. Nathaniel Branden devoted a paper to this issue, lamenting the fact that values are often left out in dealing with client needs.*2*

All societies and cultures are made up of people with contaminated human natures. Power, control and materialism in First Order System are valued above God and life. Murder, exploitations, and devaluation of the human spirit are woven into the fiber of every strata of human life and culture around the world. Government, business, criminals and religion are some of the main culprits that oppress and devalue human life. Eastern religions value a sacred cow, for example, over the well being of human beings. Jesus also pointed out that this was true of the Jewish religious leaders of His day.*3* Legalistic religions oppress people with spiritual and psychological nitpicking. The six o'clock news is dominated by daily atrocities. The list could go on and on.

Every evangelist, every therapist, in fact, everyone concerned with bringing about change in the quality of human life, must bring into focus the fact that *the contaminated human nature and First Order System devalue human life and the human spirit. Wholesale devaluation and rejection devastates and destroys the human spirit. It is the source of all emotional, psychological and spiritual illness and leads to the death and eventual extinction of the human spirit.* Unless this realization begins to sink in and disturb everyone, all attempts of any kind to change are futile. Otherwise, whatever efforts are made to bring about change are really more of the same game of First Order System.

There may be changes in form, but not in substance.
Everything remains the same.

There are many people who discard or compromise what Christian values or beliefs they may have received in church or Sunday school. Uncontaminated values and love appear unworkable from a viewpoint locked into the world system. People generally discard their values and beliefs because they are in conflict with the First Order System and fear rejection or reprisal. These people have never experienced rebirth of their spirit or tasted of the uncontaminated life of God. Many people say they have tried love and found it doesn't work. They join the ranks of cynics and regard Christian love as idealistic and childishly naive notions. Bertrand Russell came to this conclusion when he rejected his Christian beliefs:

"Many adults, in their hearts, still believe all that they were taught in childhood and feel wicked when their lives do not conform to the maxims of the Sunday School. The harm done is not merely to introduce a division between the conscious reasonable personality [Adult] and the unconscious infantile personality [Child]; the harm lies also in the fact that the valid parts of conventional morality become discredited along with the invalid parts. This danger is inseparable from a system which teaches the young, en bloc, a number of beliefs that they are almost sure to discard when they become mature."*4* [Parenthetic material is mine.]

Of course, love never works when viewed through the eyes of the contaminated PAC and from within the framework of First Order System. Love only works when viewed through the eyes of the uncontaminated PAC and expressed from within the framework of the resurrected life

231

of Christ in Second Order System, which values all human beings. Love can never work within a view and system that does not value the human spirit.

However, love does shine into a system that does not love and value, to expose it for what it is. This is what the Holy Spirit does within the contaminated PAC. It illuminates, convicts, and convinces the Adult-thinking function of its sin-contaminated condition. The Holy Spirit then provides light and data to lead us out of the contaminated condition. This is the dynamic that takes place when genuine Christian love shines into the darkness of the world system. It exposes the system and shows the world an alternative uncontaminated system that leads to abundant life.

2. TRASHINESS OF FIRST ORDER VALUES

St. Paul was well born, from the pure blooded family of Benjamin. He had the best education of his time. As a very young man, he rose to one of the highest positions in the Jewish religious order. He was rigorous in keeping every religious rule and tradition. He was diligent in persecuting early Christians, to preserve the Jewish religious traditions. "But all these things that I once valued," he wrote later, "I've now thrown away so that I can put my trust and hope in Christ alone. Yes, everything else is worthless when compared with the priceless gain of knowing Christ Jesus, My Lord. I have put aside all else and do count them but dung, in order that I can have Christ."*5*

The Greek word translated as "dung" in the King James Version of the Bible comes closer to being the Greek street word for human excrement. I am not using this word as an expletive to shock anyone. I have discovered over many years of doing therapy and

232

working with human fatalities that this is a very thera-peutic metaphor. It grabs a person in the depths of his inner being (PAC). Moreover, this metaphor best illu-minates and most accurately describes and character-izes the worth of values in the sinful First Order world system. I have observed in my years of experience that a person changes and lets go of the old oppressive values only when he sees them as "dung," in contrast to the glorious freedom of discovering that God, in His *agape* love, values him "as is" and has provided a way out of the pigsty.

In fact, a person will not change until the impact grabs him that he is swimming in the toilet bowl of contaminated values of the world system. This is what happened to the prodigal son when he "came to himself." He was covered with excrement, but he was not dung. The street word St. Paul used must not be dismissed lightly because it is offensive, or doesn't sound "religious" and pious. Its offensiveness is in fact its therapeutic value.

The only real hope is for every human being to use his Adult-Ego to see the First Order world system for what it is—worthless corruption, based on lies and deception. When this is in focus, the truth from God becomes clear: The way out of the pigsty is to choose and receive the gifts of life found only in Jesus Christ, Who is the truth that sets men free.

3. PHILIO AND EROS VIEWS OF LOVE IN FIRST ORDER SYSTEM

Philio and *eros* are viewed as love in First Order System. *Philio* is a Greek word describing brotherly or family love. Part of the affection and loyalty extended stems from the fact that both parties belong to the same family or group. Labor unions and fraternal organizations view themselves as a brotherhood. The word "fraternal" has its roots in being a member of a family.

Eros is another Greek word that describes a love that has to do with the attractiveness of the object being loved. This is seen in sexual attraction. The value the love object has to the lover is that its attractiveness fulfills the desires for happiness within the lover. The attractiveness of a new car makes the purchaser happy. Romance is *eros*-love. *Eros* lovers put their best foot forward to be attractive and desirable to each other. It is really a con game made up of seductive deception. Couples are often dismayed after the marriage begins. The con game stops and the power struggle begins. Each spouse often feels deceived and betrayed.

Philio-love isn't extended to those perceived as not belonging to the family or group. This promotes alliances and factions that exclude non-members. Both *eros* and *philio* are conditional expressions of love from the contaminated PAC found within the framework of First Order system. Jesus told the disciples that the world system rejects and hates Him and them, because they are not part of the First Order System. This system only *eros* or *philio* loves those governed by their contaminated PAC.*6*

Philio and *eros* love are contaminated, because they devalue and reject human beings who do not measure up to certain standards of value. For all its pretenses, *philio*-love rejects and devalues when the object of love ceases to be a member of the group or of value to the system. *Eros*-love rejects when the love object loses its attractiveness and value to the lover. "I'm not in love with him/her," or "I don't love him/her anymore" are phrases heard often

234

in therapy. Both of these types of love use and exploit the love object. This rejection devastates the object of love and kills the life within it.

4. HEALTHY VALUES AND AGAPE LOVE

A healthy human nature reflects a basic view of life that perpetuates unconditional love and acceptance of all human beings. This view says, "I value me; I value you. I love me; I love you." Value of self and others is conveyed from the Adult-Ego of one person to the Adult-Ego of another. The source of these values and unconditional love is the reflection of the Image of God within the uncontaminated part of human nature. This is the *agape*-love talked about in the Bible.

Agape is an ancient Greek word rarely used in Greek literature. It characterizes God's love as being given unconditionally to someone who does not merit or deserve it. This word is used extensively in the New Testament to refer to God's love for His creation, and particularly for mankind, whom He created in His own Image. *Agape* is never used in reference to Greek mythological gods. The Bible tells us God is *agape*-love in Himself.*7*

One day Jesus was asked, "Which is the most important commandment?" He replied, "The Lord your God is one God. *Agape*-love the Lord God with all your heart, strength and mind. The second is similar: *Agape*-love your neighbor as much as you *agape*-love yourself. All other commandments stem from these two laws and are fulfilled if you obey them."*8*

Agape-love described by Jesus is three-tiered. It involves (1) loving God with your total being, (2) loving your fellow human beings, and (3) yourself unconditionally. All three dimensions go together, and you cannot have one without the other. A person is only

235

healthy when he has experienced *agape*-love from God and responded by giving *agape*-love to others and himself. Absence of any of these three areas of love is not love, but a rejection of all, and will result in sure death to the human spirit.

Anyone who fully *agape*-loves God with the decisions of his heart and choices of his will, with the complete energy of his body and clear thoughts from his mind, reflects the Image of God within his human nature. This person is saturated with the *agape*-love and uncontaminated life of God. It is the reflection of the Image of God within a person that *agape*-loves his neighbor and himself. This is the person who can say, "I value me; I value you. I love me; I love you."

This is the person who has plugged into the Source of healthy values and is being saturated with unconditional *agape*-love. This person and others have discovered how to make *agape*-love work within the framework of First Order System. They are the salt of the resurrected life of Christ, flavoring the First Order System of this world.

They are in the world but not of it. These folks are the light shining into the darkened world system and providing a guiding light to show the way out. Who knows? Bertrand Russell might have held onto his childhood beliefs and values, had he been exposed to the reality of this healthy view and values. Perhaps there has been and still is a shortage of salt in this world!

St. Paul learned to express *agape*-love within the crucible of conflict and rejection from the very ones for whom he endangered and sacrificed his life. What is commonly known in the Bible as the "Love Chapter" was written when St. Paul was an old man. He had been tempered by *agape*-love firsthand.

Agape-love described by Paul recognizes the clay feet and vulnerabilities of the one he loves. The *Agape* lover also recognizes his own clumsiness and vulnerability. This love has power and grace to be patient and deal kindly with someone who may be trying and difficult. *Agape*-love doesn't respond with irritability toward the never ending foibles of the one he loves, nor does it become touchy and hurt when the loved one is not grateful or appreciative. *Agape*-love hangs in with the loved one. He doesn't abandon but continues to be loyal, regardless of the cost.*9*

A healthy person knows he has value, whether he receives value and approval from others or not. This is not conceit but certainty that comes from having received *agape*-love from the source, God Himself. *Agape*-love endures the pain of rejection and isn't devastated by it. He so values himself that he has no need to be jealous or envious of those who seem to be getting a better shake in life. *Agape*-love has no need to bolster his value at the expense of others. He has no need to be noticed, nor does he try to control or manipulate others to get his own way. One who *agape* loves does not look for flaws in others. He doesn't rudely or critically reject by pointing out flaws under the guise of trying to be helpful.

Relationships become free of power struggles when *agape*-love governs human nature. A husband doesn't seek to find value in himself by dominating and devaluing his wife and family. Nor does a wife seek to devalue her spouse or put herself in a devalued position. Each spouse engages his or her Adult-Ego to value the other as each values him/herself. Both spouses take responsibility to deal openly with each other about conflicts and issues.

Agape-love is action, not merely words or feelings. It is something people do and give in fact and in deed. *Agape*-love is a gift freely given without strings attached. It is never earned or deserved. *Agape*-love is always a choice and supplies one with the power to choose. This notion of love is unfamiliar and a stumbling block to people. Most familiar notions of love have to do with deserving or having some good feeling of affection toward the love object.

5. PROBLEM OF EVIL IN FIRST ORDER SYSTEM

A colleague once asked Dr. Tom Harris, "If I'm OK, and you're OK, how come you're locking your car?" Harris reflected, "The problem of evil is also a reality in the world."*10*

St. Paul observed,

"We are not fighting against people made of flesh and blood, but against powers and principalities—the evil rulers of the unseen world—those mighty satanic beings and great evil princes of darkness who rule this world; and against huge numbers of wicked spirits in the spirit world."*11*

People who view this statement through the eyes of the First Order world system will lightly dismiss St. Paul's statement. It just doesn't appear sophisticated to those involved in a so-called civilized society. However, history demonstrates that cruelty within a society increases in proportion to how civilized and culturally sophisticated the society is becoming. A great deal of cruelty is to be found in all the highly civilized ancient societies of Rome, Greece, Asia, Aztec Mexico and Egypt, etc. Children and other human sacrifices were the bedrock of their religions. Temple prostitution was a common practice in all these religious societies.

Their mythical gods were cruel and deceptive rascals that reflected their worshippers' contaminated human nature. Totalitarianism exists in highly cultured, civilized countries. Slavery and exploitive child labor were the rule rather than the exception, two hundred years ago in the English speaking world.

Today satanic practices are on the increase. In fact, citizens of the United States, as one of the most civilized and democratic societies ever developed, are appalled by the ever increasing revelations of child abuse and sexual molestation. Experts report that one out of four children are sexually molested and abused in this country. That figure is estimated as conservative.

I would estimate that nearly one in three women I have seen in therapy over a twenty-five year period have been sexually molested by her father or some significant male as a child.

Case after case of child abuse and neglect are coming out of the closet in epidemic proportions. Staggering numbers of women have had abortions. Rape and homicide are on the increase. The rapist's purpose is never sexual satisfaction but power and control that devalues and humiliates his victims.

Evil becomes rampant as it is able to control and contaminate the human spirit (PAC). Its concern is for power and control. It is in conflict with the force of nature and God. To prove itself powerful, evil must defeat and ascend over God. To do this, evil devalues and hates what God *agape* loves and values. This is why the human spirit (PAC) is devalued.

The German people during World War II were a civilized, highly cultured, educated people. The Lutheran Church and Christian values were certainly interwoven within the fabric of German life. Even so, Hitler was able to deceive the people with his satanic appeal to being a superior race.

Throughout history, as societies have become more civilized and sophisticated, so have their moral values deteriorated. This pattern is quite evident in the United States. When this country was unsophisticated, faith in God and morals prevailed as the main influence over people's lives. The quality of life was more innocent and gracious, even though it was cruder socially and harsher physically.

As the nation becomes more sophisticated, God and moral values are discarded and replaced by degradation of the human spirit. Young people seem old at eighteen. The sophisticated are jaded with boredom. Suicide and homicide are on the increase. Let no one be deceived: Evil satanic forces are making a last ditch onslaught on the human spirit. The purpose is not to free but to control and grind it into extinction. The only way evil thinks it can prevail is to deceive and bypass the living God of Jesus Christ our Lord.

Good and evil are locked into a battle. It is the evil First Order System versus the resurrected life of Christ in the Second Order System. The lines are drawn! However, the Good News is that Jesus Christ died and absorbed all of sin and evil into Himself. Evil and the First Order System are doomed to extinction. And now all authority has been given to Jesus Christ as He lives and reigns as the resurrected Lord and Savior. He offers life to those in the pits of evil First Order System. Those who will receive Him are rescued from the pits and clothed with the new resurrection life of Christ in the Second Order System. All they need to do is stand in the victory that was accomplished two thousand years ago on the cross of Calvary. Praise the Lord!

Summary

It doesn't take a scientific investigation to see that the horrid contaminated condition of this world is a product of what is valued by it. It is obvious that sinful human nature (PAC) and First Order System devalues God and the human spirit. It considers them as trash. Power, money, lies, deception, legalism, and things are the flimsy foundation of the world's First Order evil values. This is self-evident in government, business, the media, and, in fact, permeates all areas of human life. *What a person values and loves, in fact, is a searching question that sears the conscience (PAC) and weighs it on the scales of eternal justice. Survival or extinction of the world rests on what it really believes, loves and values.*

POWER TO CHANGE

CHAPTER XV. JUDGMENT OF FIRST ORDER SYSTEM IS MEANT TO HEAL, NOT CONDEMN
"You have been weighed in God's balances..."
—Daniel 5:27

1. Judgment That Condemns the First Order System
2. Judgment Is Meant to Heal and Transform
3. Balancing the Scales of Judgment

1. JUDGMENT THAT CONDEMNS THE FIRST OR- DER SYSTEM

(a) Judgment is a scary word to all people engulfed in the First Order world system. All human effort and energy within the world system are bent on surviving or avoiding the doom of impending extinction. The per- plexing, paramount question is how to survive. The First Order world system has been wrestling with this question since the dawn of history. Religions attempt to resolve this dilemma by either avoiding or magically delaying the scale of justice or engaging in legalistic efforts of self-justification. The world of First Order System fears the words given to ancient King Belshazzar: "You have been weighed in God's bal- ances and found wanting; you failed the test."[1]

The Ten Commandments were given to Israel after its redemption from Egyptian slavery and were meant to separate them from the contaminated life of the surrounding people. Israel was chosen to reveal God and His salvation to the contaminated nations around them. Their religious laws and rites were intended to point toward and deal with their sinful PAC. The crux of worship revolved around the sacrifice of an unblemished lamb at Passover for the sins of the people. However, the people of Israel were as contaminated as their gentile neighbors. Commandments that were intended to instruct and free people to live the uncontaminated life of *agape* love gravitated into religious legalism. Jewish religious leaders developed a refined network of nitpicking religious rules and regulations that became ridiculously oppressive. They had the effect of a "damned if you do, damned if you don't" double-bind.

Jesus once pointed out, as an example, that according to Jewish religious laws, a man could divorce his wife for any trivial reason. (The woman was not accorded a like privilege.) The ex-wife who had never committed adultery would be considered an adulteress, and any man who married her an adulterer, according to the legalistic law. Jesus pointed out that the woman was placed in an untenable position of condemnation, regardless of whether she remarried or not. The only way a woman in that day could have any financial resources would be to marry or enter into prostitution.*2*

Jesus made it quite clear to His disciples that He did not come on the scene to cancel the laws of Moses (Ten Commandments) and the warning of the prophets. "No, I came to fulfill them and make them come true...But I warn you, unless your goodness exceeds that of the Pharisees and other Jewish leaders, you can't get into the kingdom of God."*3*

According to Jesus, nobody can balance the scales of God's judgment unless his righteousness exceeds the righteousness portrayed by the self-righteous religious leaders of His day.

Legalism and self-righteousness are primarily concerned with outward appearances and projecting favorable images. A person must always withhold or cover up unfavorable data about himself, if he is to project a favorable image. Withholding or covering up flaws is really a deception or distortion about who a person "really is." Lies and distortions are incompatible with truth and the kingdom of God and will always tip the scales of God to disfavor the liar. That is why Jesus warns that a person's righteousness must exceed the outward appearance of the religious leaders. Otherwise, his inward life and PAC remain contaminated and unchanged.

The purpose of salvation is three-fold: To illuminate and eliminate the sinful PAC within all human beings; to restore the Image and glory of God within human nature; and to reconcile all people back into intimacy with God. This is accomplished as God agape-loves and establishes His sovereign rule within the hearts and wills of those who receive Him. People who refuse to submit to the purposes of God's salvation and to accept His offer of reconciliation remain in their sinful condition and continue to be governed by their distorted PAC. The purpose of judgment is to weigh and determine whether the salvation process has been completed or is in progress within an individual's trinitarian nature. The criteria of God's judgment is whether He sees His Image and glory being reflected and continually enlarged within a person's PAC.

The world system views God as a critical Parent, sitting in heaven, delighting to find fault with people He created and then zapping them into extinction. The world confuses and places attributes of the contaminated god of this world system on the eternal God. A lot of people spend a lifetime denying the existence of God or trying to avoid and outwit Him.

(b) Sin Is Lack of Faith in Jesus

Jesus told His disciples it was imperative that He complete His mission on the cross. Otherwise, the Holy Spirit could not complete His work in the world. The Holy Spirit would come to

"...convince and convict the world of sin [contaminated PAC], and of the availability of God's goodness and righteousness, and of deliverance from judgment. The world's sin is unbelief in Me; there is righteousness available, because I go to the Father, and you shall see Me no more; here is deliverance from judgment, because the prince of this world has already been judged."*4*

Sin contaminated the trinitarian make-up of the entire human race when the first couple believed a lie, instead of the truth from God. This set in motion the First Order world system, which leads to extinction.*5*

St. Paul wrote, "This one man, Jesus Christ, brought forgiveness to many through God's mercy."*6* Adam caused many to be sinners because he disobeyed God; and Christ caused many to be accepted by God because He obeyed.*7* Whereas Jeremiah could find no one fair and honest enough to avert the judgment of God, Jesus provides deliverance and the way out of judgment. Through His death on the Cross, He who knew no sin (being the one righteous man) absorbed the sin-contaminated PAC into Himself for all human beings and condemned the father of lies and the world's First Order System.*8* Through

245

His resurrection, Christ makes His righteousness and uncontaminated life of Second Order System available to anyone who will receive it as a free, unmerited gift.

(c) Legalistic Self-Righteousness Won't Cut It

Many people try to impress God and their fellow human beings with their good deeds and impressive credentials of religious activities and accomplishments. Jesus told the story about two men praying in the temple. The self-righteous religious leader thanked God that he wasn't a sinner like the tax collector praying next to him. The corrupt tax collector, on the other hand, could not even lift his eyes to pray. He could only exclaim, "God, be merciful to me, a sinner." Jesus then concluded, "This sinner—not the righteous leader—returned home forgiven; for the proud shall be humbled, and the humble shall be honored."*9* All self-righteousness looks like filthy rags in the sight of God.*10* Jesus warned the disciples to follow only Him and His instructions.

"Those who do so are wise," He said. "They are like a man who builds his house on solid rock. Though the rain comes in torrents and the floods rise, and the storm winds beat against his house, it won't collapse, for it is built on a rock. [Jesus is that rock and solid foundation; see I Corin. 10:4; Ps. 18:2; 92:15] But those who hear my instructions and ignore them are foolish, like a man who builds his house on sand. For when the rains and floods come and storm winds beat against the house, it will fall with a mighty crash."*11*

The crowds were really amazed at what Jesus was saying to them. He was teaching them as One who had great authority, not like their Jewish religious leaders. Jesus warned people about following blind leaders into the pitfalls of First Order System.*12*

(d) Consequences of Failing to Agape-Love and Value Life

In the parable of separating the sheep from the goats, Jesus teaches that:

"the King remains unimpressed and says to those on His left, 'Away with you, you cursed ones, into the eternal fires prepared for the devil and his demons. For I was hungry and thirsty, and you wouldn't feed or give me anything to drink. I was a stranger and you refused me hospitality; naked and you wouldn't clothe me; sick and in prison, and you didn't visit me.'"*13*

These people will be astonished and ask, "Lord, when did we ever see You hungry or thirsty, or a stranger, or naked, or in prison and not help You?"*14* And the Lord will answer, "When you refused to help the least of these my brothers [and sisters], you were refusing to help me."*15*

All of this is tragic. Many of these people are the well intentioned and "good" people of society. But they are preoccupied with the pursuits of the trivial, rather than what is really important. They value the unimportant things of the world and are blind to the real and obvious needs about them. None of these people recognize that their own bankruptcy of self-righteousness and lack of *agape*-love is keeping them out of the Kingdom. They have been enamored with the contaminated life in the pigsty and have never hungered or thirsted for the true bread of life.

(e) Refusal of God's Salvation Process Is the Condemnation

Refusal to repent and get out of the pigsty is the judgment and condemnation all people face. St. Paul wrote that no human being who has ever lived or who is currently living has any excuse for refusing God's way out of his contaminated condition:

"The man who finds life will find it through trusting God. God shows His anger from heaven against all sinful evil men who push truth away from themselves. For truth about God is known instinctively. God has put this knowledge in their hearts...So they will have no excuse...when they stand before God on Judgment Day... Instead of believing what they know is the truth about God, they deliberately choose to believe lies. That is why God lets go of them and lets them do these evil things. It is when they give God up and won't even acknowledge Him that God gives them up to do everything their evil minds can think of."*16*

These people perpetuate and distort the Image of God within them, sometimes beyond recognition.

The severest judgment of God, in all probability, will come down on those in the enlightened Western world who have the luxurious life in the pigsty and value their trinkets and idols more than the living God. Jesus warned:

"Not all who sound religious are really godly people. They may refer to Me as Lord, but they still won't get into Heaven. For the decisive question is whether they obey My Father in Heaven. At the Judgment, many will tell Me, 'Lord, Lord, we told others about you and used your Name to cast out demons, and to do many other great miracles.' But I will reply, 'You have never known Me or been intimate with Me. Depart from Me, for your deeds are evil.'"*17*

The rich young ruler was loved by Jesus. But he

valued his riches more than the gift of life offered to him. Many people are like this young man—in love with their Mercedes or BMW, boats, houses and sundry toys and trinkets. Many are devoted churchgoers, going about doing all kinds of good things in the name of the Lord. These folks are concerned with the power, the show, and the attention they receive by being known as good people.

Someday these folks will be surprised to hear the Lord say, "I am the Good Shepherd and know My own sheep, and they know Me and My voice and follow Me,"*18* and "Depart from Me. I never have known you, and you have never known Me."*19*

In the modern vernacular, it might read something like this: "All these good things you are telling Me are trash in My sight, because you have never taken time to know Me, My heart, My mind, and My will for your life." [Paraphrase mine.]

2. JUDGMENT IS MEANT TO HEAL AND TRANS-FORM FIRST ORDER SYSTEM.
(a) Healing Purpose of Judgment

Judgment can only be rendered impartially and without bias by one who is himself without sin. He alone can clearly see the condition of a person's heart "as it is." That is the reason none of the men accusing the adulterous woman could carry out judgment against her. Jesus told them that if there were one among them without sin, he would be allowed to cast the first stone. They all dropped their stones and quietly peeled away, starting with the oldest of the bunch. None of them could cast a stone. Their accusations and judgments were colored and solely intended to destroy, rather than heal and correct. These men were critical flaw-finders, nitpickers trying to make themselves look good.*20*

No one in his right mind would submit himself for treatment to a physician who would harass and condemn him for seeking treatment. Yet a lot of people view God in this way. Judgment to them means primarily condemnation. Both Christians and non-Christians tend to hold this view. Preachers from within religious legalistic persuasions seem to delight in haranguing and condemning people into the fires of hell. This kind of preaching and legalistic expression is blind to the healing and reconciling purposes of God's judgment.

A physician or any healer is never condemning a patient when he reveals to him the true condition of his state of health. A person who is told by the physician that he has cancer or some other debilitating illness or injury certainly experiences pain, fear and anxiety. *There is a real element of judgment and condemnation for the person who learns the true condition of his health and remains in the debilitating condition of cancer.* The patient is reassured with hope, when the physician or healer prescribes a treatment that will free him from the consequences of his illness or injury and the threat of possible extinction. The purpose of the treatment is not only to deliver the patient from the consequences but to restore the patient to the best possible health. However, the patient will eventually experience the consequences and condemnation, if he refuses to believe the physician and submit to treatment. Many times the treatment hurts and a patient often experiences more intense pain during or after treatment than prior to it. The Second Order salvation process is a surgical process; it removes the unhealthy condition and replaces it with health.

Numerous Biblical passages are devoted to calling attention to the sinfulness of human nature for the same reasons a physician calls attention to his patient's illness. Jeremiah, the great prophet shed a lot of tears in writing about the deceitfulness and gross wickedness of the human heart (PAC).

No one but the Lord knows how contaminated it is. God searches everyone's heart and examines the deepest motives. Then He can read each person according to his deeds and condition.*21* The Bible describes the hardness, blindness, deceptiveness and just plain corruption of sinful human nature, and how all human beings reject God and go about attempting to be little gods unto themselves.*22*

God is always fair in His judgment, for He also prescribes the treatment provided in the salvation process. Condemnation results from refusal of God's provision of salvation. Those who refuse to listen to the warning and submit to God's treatment remain in a contaminated condition and will eventually experience the condemning consequences.

(b) Key Word In Judgment Is KNOW.

The key word that will judge us all is "know." Not only does God know you, but do you know Him? God already knows us better than we know ourselves. He knows the number of hairs on our heads.*23 The word "know" indicates intimate relationships. Only those who walk with Christ on the narrow road through hostile country of First Order System get to know Him as an intimate Companion.* These are the people whose spirit has been born of God's Spirit and are going through the metamorphosis of the resurrected life of the new creation. The Image of God in them is enlarged as the contaminated PAC continually diminishes.

People yoked with Christ are teachable and pliable and never pull their own strings. These people fellowship with Christ when they give a cup of cold water to a thirsty stranger and feed the hungry and the disenfranchised.

Jesus said that He will come as the Messiah and sit upon the throne of His glory. He will gather all nations before Him and separate people, as a shepherd separates the sheep from the goats. The sheep will be given a place of honor at His right hand, and the goats a place of dishonor at His left. Then, as King of Kings, He will say to those on His right hand,

"Come, blessed of My Father, into the kingdom prepared for you from the foundation of the world. For I was hungry and you fed Me. I was thirsty and you gave Me water. I was a stranger, and you invited Me into your home; naked and you clothed me; sick and in prison, and you visited me."*24*

These people will be so astonished, they will reply, "When did we do all of these things?" The King will tell them, "When you did it to the least of these who are My brothers, you were doing it unto Me."*25* The striking thing about the credentials of a person accepted by God into His Kingdom is his lack of awareness of having done anything great or deserving. His life really reflects the Image and *agape*-love of God. It reflects the gentle and harmless quality of an unblemished sheep. What he does is second nature. He is unlike those at the left who are characterized as goats.

(c) Intimacy With Christ Writes Name in the Book of Life

Those who are walking the narrow road in intimacy with Christ have their names written in the Book of Life. These people have the certainty of eternal, uncontaminated life and salvation. Many who profess to be Christians do not seem to have the certainty of the uncontaminated life and salvation. They are like a woman who became upset with another lady who testified in a Sunday school class about her certainty in knowing Christ as her Lord and Savior. The upset woman thought it was presumptuous to have that kind of certainty.

3. BALANCING THE SCALES OF JUDGMENT
(a) Twofold Judgment of God

Judgment of God is twofold. First, it depends on what people value. People who devalue God do not value His gift of life and *agape* love. They value the dead life of their contaminated PAC over the eternal life found in their uncontaminated PAC. Worship is rendered to that which is dead and putrid.

Jesus said a person must hate the dead life of his contaminated PAC.*26* He must be willing to lose it, in order that he may find and replace it with the eternal resurrected life in his uncontaminated PAC.*27*Death is not permitted into the Kingdom—only life. Jesus tells us He came that we might receive His abundant, uncontaminated life.*28* The life of Christ within the uncontaminated PAC is the passport into the Kingdom. All others are excluded. However, there is another step in the judgment of God.

Once a person receives the gift of life and has embarked on the road of life, he must continue and endure to its completion.29 He must continually be on guard and recognize his vulnerability to the pull of the dying, contaminated PAC. He must continue to value the gift of life from God by investing and developing his gifts to the fullest potential. Jesus told the story about the two men who were praised and rewarded for

253

multiplying their gifts. One was given five talents and multiplied it fivefold. Another multiplied his two talents twofold. However, the fellow with one talent hid his gift and failed to multiply it. He was governed by fear, rather than faith. This fellow was reprimanded and had his one talent taken away.*30* The latter is a picture of many people who view God as a contaminated Parent and are fearful that they will never measure up. Instead of venturing forth in faith, they put their heads in the sand, failing to grow and develop into the Image of God.

The older brother of the prodigal seemed to view his father as a contaminated Parent. Anger flushed across his face when he was told that his father was throwing a party for his wayward younger brother. He was the "good kid" who stayed home and was a dutiful son. Instead of accepting his father's invitation to join the party, the older brother bitterly criticized his parent and brother. He pointed out how hard he had worked and how dutiful and obedient he had been all the while his younger brother had been squandering the family fortune.

"That son of yours doesn't deserve it," he cuttingly reminded his father, "and you have never thrown a party for me and my buddies." The father gently chided the older son and reminded him, "You and I are close, and everything I have is yours. It's right to celebrate. Your brother was dead and has come back to life. He was lost and now is found."*31* The attitude of the older brother is not unlike the legalism of many religious and non-religious people. He was certainly compliant, but sadly never knew his father's heart and mind. Everything his father had was his, but he never had enjoyed any of it, nor did he have intimacy with his father. His condemnation and judgment came from a contaminated, bitter spirit that alienated him from his father and brother.

(b) Contrasting Attitudes at the Cross

Calvary was the scene of two contrasting attitudes toward Christ. Two hardened criminals, crucified on either side of Him, knew where the First Order world system had brought them. One angrily attacked Jesus, "If you are the Messiah, prove it by saving yourself and us." The other criminal chided his accomplice, "Don't you even fear God when you are dying? We deserve to die for our evil deeds, but this man hasn't done anything wrong." Then, turning to Jesus, he said, "Remember me when you come into your kingdom." Jesus replied, "Today you will be with Me in Paradise. This is a solemn promise."**32**

That first criminal reflected the hostile attitude of the world system, even in the face of death. He never evaluated the condition of his life, nor took responsibility for it. All he wanted was to escape from the consequences and return to his old life of crime. There was no desire to change; indeed, in himself he could not. Blinded by corruption, he could not recognize the One who is the truth because his Adult-Ego function had become so darkened. This attitude is still prevalent today.

The repentant man was humbled in the face of death and recognized his condition. His Adult-Ego made an accurate assessment and took responsibility for his sin. Instead of trying to avoid the consequences, he asked to be remembered by this Man Jesus. He wanted change, even at that midnight hour of his life. Because of his expression of faith, Christ issued him a passport to exit from the clutches of death in the First Order System and to enter into the resurrected life of

Christ in the heavenly Second Order System.

The truth of the cross and resurrection of Christ stands in judgment of the world's First Order System, bringing condemnation to those who are dominated and governed by the hostile attitude of the one criminal. Condemnation and judgment are always the result of refusing the gift of life and intimate fellowship with the Source of truth.

However, no condemnation or judgment passes on those governed by the same attitude expressed by the penitent thief. He gratefully and humbly received the undeserved gift and took the other criminal to task for his blindness and stupidity. In the face of truth, he recognized his sinfulness and was emptied of all his hostility and pride. The penitent criminal was privileged to die alongside the sacrificial Lamb of God, who extended him mercy and absorbed his sinful PAC. Without hesitation, Jesus gladly granted him his heart's desire for a new life in Paradise. This is *agape*-love in action.

(c) God's Universal Invitation

In the Biblical parable, everyone was invited, but the vast majority insulted the king by refusing to accept his invitation to the wedding banquet for his son. They laughed off his invitation and went about their business. The king's messengers were treated with contempt, and some were even killed. Those who refused his invitation were declared unworthy by an infuriated king. Other servants were sent out to scour the highways and byways, inviting multitudes on the social fringe to attend. Some guests arrived not wearing the prescribed wedding apparel provided by the king for his guests. The angry king banned the guest for being improperly attired at the feast.

Those who initially refused are a picture of the religious people of Israel and the world today, who continually rebel and devalue God's graciousness toward them. The extention of the invitation to others is a picture of God inviting every person in the world into His kingdom and feast of life. The wedding guest who failed to put on the wedding garments is a picture of someone trying to crash a dinner party in blue jeans. Obviously this person was out of place in a formal setting.

He is a picture of a person trying to enter the Kingdom of God with the contaminated garments of his sinful PAC. *The wedding garment worn at the wedding feast in the Kingdom depicts a person's uncontaminated PAC that reflects the Image of God.* Jesus said many are called to the feast but few are chosen. *The vast majority are not permitted to enter, as long as their PAC continues to be improperly attired with sin-contamination.* This is a picture of the vast majority of people who have not taken the time to clothe themselves with the righteousness of an uncontaminated PAC. Contamination is not permitted in the society of God's Kingdom. Contamination and uncontamination cannot mix any more than oil and water. This is why God sent His Son as the unblemished Sacrificial Lamb to take away the contaminated PAC. Only those who have entered into the death and resurrection of Christ, emerging as the new creation in Christ with an uncontaminated PAC, are permitted to take citizenship in the Kingdom. These are the folks attired in the proper garb. The Kingdom of God can only be populated by those who reflect the Image of God within them. This is a holy, healthy society, without any physical, emotional, psychological or spiritual illness. Those who live in this society reside in new resurrected bodies.*33*

(d) Jesus Christ Balances the Scales of God's Judgment

A few years ago, ABC-TV presented the movie, "The Day After," a drama depicting the reaction and effect of a nuclear holocaust on Lawrence, Kansas. The absence of any expression of faith in the film was conspicuous. The characters seemed to thrash about without much hope or faith. What references were made to God were caricaturized pronouncements by an hysterical preacher on doom and judgment.

After the movie, ABC-TV presented a lengthy panel discussion about the implications of nuclear war. The panel was comprised of many distinguished people from all walks of life, including a former Secretary of State, Secretary of Defense, a military leader, a renowned conservative columnist, a Jewish philosopher-theologian, and others. In spite of the expertise and views expressed, no one seemed to have a clue how to prevent a holocaust or if the world could survive and recover from such devastation. They all presented what appeared to be First Order System solutions in terms of politics, military, economics, etc. None of them mentioned or talked much about the human equation. When the Jewish philosopher-theologian suggested that human nature and spirit needed a change and rebirth, the panel members blithely glossed over it and went on rehashing old ideas.

The ABC-TV panel missed the point in its discussion and deliberations. How sad to see and hear these brilliant people bogged down with the irrelevant. They were attempting to solve a dilemma that was part of an unchanging, destructive system. Lots of motion and activity, but no change, so the threat of destruction still remained. This only highlights human blindness and their refusal to get out of the nine dot solution. The panel failed to recognize the obvious fact that human beings and their contaminated natures perpetuate the destructive pattern.

Those who viewed the movie, "War Games," will recall how a teenage computer genius becomes bored with video games on his home computer and unknowingly plugs into the North American Defense Command Missile Warning System, in his quest for more challenging games. Innocently he sets in motion a nuclear confrontation between the United States and Russia. Located as the culprit by the F.B.I., he cooperates in a suspenseful effort to abort the delivery of missiles by both countries. The computer resists attempts to abort the mission, and although the actual delivery of missiles is averted, the sign on the giant computer screen flashes a foreboding message at the precise moment when both countries' missiles would have reached their destinations: "Game Over—No One Wins—All Destroyed." Only by introducing new game rules was the teenager actually able to avoid annihilation of the world.

"War Games" poignantly dramatizes the eventual fate of the world's First Order System. Life within this world system is not a harmless video game but is locked into playing itself out to its destructive end. There is no way out for the players locked into First Order System. Only the cross and resurrection of Christ provide an exit from First Order System and entrance into the Second Order System, which is programmed not to play itself out to extinction but to perpetuate eternal life. Through the rules of *agape* love, life and valuing [not hostility, death and devaluation] are set in motion.

The scales of God's judgment weigh whether a person knows God and has received His Son Jesus Christ and is living by faith in Him. A person can only escape judgment when his PAC becomes decontaminated and reflects the Image of God and His glory. Biblical data tells us that whoever has the Son [Christ] living within him has His eternal life. Those without the Son living within are already dead and condemned by their own refusal to accept God's gift of life. The joyous Good News is that God loved the world so much that He gave His only Son to set free anyone who chooses to trust in Him [by using their emancipated Adult-Ego] from the inevitable extinction of the First Order world system. "God did not send His Son into the world to condemn it but to save it,"*34* to rescue it from perishing and to give us eternal life.

Christ came to usher in the Kingdom of God in the hearts, minds and wills of all people, on earth as it is in heaven. Social structures at all levels can only be transformed from a First Order System to Second Order System as the rule of God's Spirit is established and maintained within the hearts, minds and wills of all social group members. Those who resist and refuse to be transformed perish in the death grip of First Order System societies. Those who are being transformed are ushering in the Kingdom of God's Second Order System and society on earth as it is in heaven.

POWER TO CHANGE

CHAPTER XVI. THE GOOD NEWS
*"God so loved the world that He gave
His only begotten Son." —John 3:16*

The Good News is that God sent His Son, not to condemn, but to save the world from extinction of First Order System. People need not remain in the oppressive double-bind Paul found himself in. The tyranny of the sinful PAC has been weighed, along with the father of lies, in the scales of God's justice, and has been condemned out of existence. The cross of Christ offers the only exit from death-producing First Order world system and the entrance into the uncontaminated resurrection life of truth in the Second Order System. *All of this is tantamount to ushering in the Kingdom of God on earth as it is in heaven.*

God cancelled out the old Jewish religious legalism and instituted a new plan—the resurrected life of the Second Order System.*1*

"He sent His own Son in a human body like ours, except that ours is sinful—and destroyed sin's control [First Order System] over us by giving Himself as a sacrifice for our sins [contaminated PAC]. Now we can obey God's law [Commandments] if we follow after the Holy Spirit [in the Second Order System], and no longer obey the old evil lies and legalistic nature [contaminated PAC].*2* So there is now no condemnation awaiting those who are in Christ Jesus and belong to Him, for the power of the life-giving Spirit—and this power is mine through Jesus Christ—has freed me from the vicious circle of sin and death."*3*

The power of God and His truth will crush the evil deeds of contaminated PAC when anyone allows the truth of the Holy Spirit to prevail. This opens the floodgates of God's uncontaminated life and Spirit to saturate one's PAC.*4* The Adult-Ego is set free to evaluate the difference between truth and distortions and endows one with power to choose truth rather than lies.

Only those who are governed by the Spirit of God become members of His family. Members of His family need not be a cringing, fearful lot. Any of us who have been adopted and born into the very bosom of God's family can have confidence. We can truly call God "our heavenly Father." The Holy Spirit speaks deep into our heart [uncontaminated PAC] and verifies to our human spirit that we are God's children. We share God's treasure as members of His family. All that God gives to His Son Jesus Christ is now also ours.*5* Moreover, we have the Holy Spirit within us as a foretaste of future glory. However, we will experience the same kind of opposition given to Christ during His lifetime. St. Paul certainly knew it still hurt to live in this hostile world, and it also hurts us in this generation, as we continue to journey and anticipate the day we will be given new bodies and be restored to full rights as God's children.*6*

"What we suffer now is nothing compared to the glory we shall receive when we reach our destination of heavenly glory... All creation is waiting patiently for the day when God will resurrect His children. On that day, thorns and thistles, sins, death and decay...will all disappear in the glorious freedom from sin which God's children enjoy."**7**

Think of it! There will be no more spiritual, emotional or psychological illness—only spiritual and mental health with no contamination whatsoever. We are being saved as we continue the journey and entrust ourselves to the intimate Companion. Trusting means we are looking forward to reaching our destination and receiving the full reward we do not yet have. The journey is only an appetizer. Hope and trust teach us to travel on the journey patiently and confidently. Many times the traveler may be perplexed and bewildered. A weary traveler does not always know what to pray for, or even how to pray. He discovers that the Holy Spirit helps him with his daily problems and prayers. In fact, the Holy Spirit prays within us and for us, with such feelings that it cannot be expressed in words. The Father, who knows all hearts [PAC] also knows what the Spirit is saying as He pleads for the traveler. Thus we become more intimate with our road Companion as we grow in confidence. After awhile we recognize that everything in our journey is working for our good and fits into God's ultimate plan for our lives.

What is even more breathtaking about this Good News is that God did not send His Son as an emergency measure. Salvation is not a hastily instituted plan that God devised from the top of His head! St. Paul verifies that,

> "Long ago, even before He made the world, God chose us to be His very own, through what Christ would do for us. He decided then to make us holy [healthy, without contamination] in His eyes, without a single fault—we who stand before Him covered with His agape love. His unchanging plan has always been to adopt us into His own family by

263

sending Jesus Christ to die for us. And He did this because He wanted to!"*8*

God choosing us to be His very own, before He even created the world is mind-boggling. God created people in His image to carry on an intimate *agape*-love relationship with Him. This kind of *agape*-love is inconceivable and incomprehensible to a contaminated mind (PAC) shackled within the lies and dark limits of the First Order world system. *Agape*-love is always a choice and is maintained by choice. When choice is removed, there is no truth of *agape*-love. *Eros* and *philio*-love found in the world's system is never based on choice, because there are lies and strings attached to this form of love. *Agape*-love is not only a choice but also a gift, given at a cost to the giver. The receiver of *agape*-love chooses to receive it, knowing that he or she does not deserve it. God chose to give His *agape*-love, with the foreknowledge that the recipients would be contaminated and living in the pigsty. His *agape*-love is so immeasurable that He knew He would be offering His most precious uncontaminated Son as an unblemished Sacrificial Lamb to redeem the contaminated and unjust from the pigsty.

Before creation He decided to make those who receive this gift holy [healthy and without contamination or flaws]. God sees and knows the Image of Himself that has been impregnated into the contaminated PAC. It is the Image (PAC) that is holy [healthy] and without fault [uncontaminated]. This is what God sees and values within us. This Image is going to be the finished product within us. The contaminated PAC is dying as we stand before Him, covered totally by His *agape*-love. It is the *agape*-love within the PAC that produces the metamorphosis and birth of the new, resurrected life in the Second Order System, as the old dead creation [contaminated PAC] is shed forever. God's plan has never been altered or changed. It is and always has been His plan to adopt those who choose to receive the gift of life into His own uncontaminated family by sending Jesus Christ to die for every lost person in the pigsty. He did this simply because He wanted to, out of *agape*-love. In fact, *agape*-love could do no other.

SUMMARY
"You shall know the truth and the truth shall set you free." —John 8:32

We have come full circle. Hopefully by shedding light and providing answers to the five basic issues raised in the Introduction, the trinitarian psychological functions are seen to be one and the same as the spiritual trinitarian functions reflecting the Image of God within human nature.

We have seen that the distorted Image of God [contaminated PAC] within human nature makes all human beings emotionally, psychologically and spiritually unhealthy. We have also seen that human nature is locked into the four properties of First Order System and maintains the PAC in a contaminated condition.

The trinitarian human nature was initially contaminated and distorted when the first male and female in the Garden failed to use their Adult-Ego faith faculty to assess lies and distortions and process them out from truth. They called God, the Source of truth, a liar and alienated themselves from intimacy with Him. This alienation distorted God's Image within them and the human nature of all subsequent generations. This

265

infection brought about the contaminated First Order System that governs and perpetuates the sickness of human nature and human relationships.

No one has the inner resources to restore himself to emotional, psychological and spiritual health. Restoration is the reconciling work of God focused in the death and resurrection of His uncontaminated Son [Christ]. This brings about the rebirth of the human spirit that emancipates the Adult-Ego so it can sort out truth from lies and distortions. A continual response of faith permits truth to decontaminate the PAC and restore the Image of God within human nature. The restoration of the trinitarian Image of God within human nature is the end product of salvation and results in making a person healthy emotionally, psychologically and spiritually.

While pursuing the task of shedding light and clarifying answers to these questions, we have observed that the common denominator in the make-up of Governor Pilate and St. Paul is their sin-contaminated PAC and that both men held this in common with all human beings. Both men had contact with the same Source of truth. However, St. Paul came to see and know the Source of truth, while Pilate remained blind and estranged from the truth. St. Paul went through the metamorphosis of becoming a new creation in Christ, whereas Pilate did not.

A metamorphosis occurs when the four contaminated properties of a person's PAC and the First Order world system have been swallowed up within the resurrected life of Second Order System.

1. In the first property, the common denominator of human nature in the world, is the sin-contaminated PAC. This is the universal distortion of the trinitarian

Image of God in human nature. In the resurrected life of the Second Order System, the common denominator of human nature is transformed into the undistorted trinitarian Image of God [uncontaminated PAC].

2. The identity member of the second property that perpetuates the contaminated system and distorts human nature is lies and deception; whereas in the resurrected life of Second Order System, truth becomes the identity member.

3. The rules of the third property within the contaminated human nature and First Order System are conditional love, rejection, hate, power and control. The rule within a healthy human make-up reflecting the Image of God and the uncontaminated Second Order System is unconditional *agape*-love, life and acceptance.

4. The reciprocals of the fourth property of the contaminated First Order System are adversarial, because the human make-up is a distortion of the Image of God. The game is to win. The game is played out to the bitter end. There is no winner in this game, only losers. This game leads to death and extinction. The reciprocals of uncontaminated Second Order System are complementary, because human make-up reflects an undistorted Image of God. This is *agape*-love in action.

Complementary relationships produce oneness with God and others. Life is born and nurtured within the complementary reciprocals. First Order reciprocals are discordant and deadly. Second Order reciprocals are harmonious and life-producing.

Simon Greenleaf was a prominent Jewish professor of law at Harvard University. He held credentials to practice before the Supreme Court of the United States.

Much of the Rules of Evidence used in courts of law were developed and written by this brilliant man. One day a student challenged him to examine the New Testament in the light of the Old Testament and subject it to the same Rules of Evidence he used in courts of law.

Mr. Greenleaf accepted the challenge and spent better than a year studying and subjecting the New Testament claims in light of the Old Testament to the Rules of Evidence. When Mr. Greenleaf finished his studies, he wrote an open letter to all members of the Bar Association across the United States in his day, outlining the challenge given to him by one of his students, and the conclusions he reached.

His conclusions were that the claims within the New Testament, particularly the resurrection, are of such preposterous magnitude that the human mind is incapable of perpetrating a hoax of that magnitude. Upon careful examination, over the period of a year, he found the evidence revealed in the New Testament would withstand the test of the Rules of Evidence and would be admissible in any court of law. Mr. Greenleaf put his reputation on the line and told his colleagues that he had accepted Jesus as the Messiah and had become a Christian. He challenged his colleagues to examine the data as he had and subject it to the Rules of Evidence. He expressed confidence that they would come to the same conclusion. 1

The evidence is available for the world to examine and act upon. The resurrection of Christ is the crux of history. Is it fact or fiction? God has given each person an Adult-Ego faculty and the presence of the Holy Spirit to examine the data. Failure to take this seriously and examine the evidence has condemning consequences. Examine the data and discover the Good News. God has cancelled the lies of the contaminated First Order System and replaced the system with a far healthier one in the truth of the resurrected life of Second Order System.*2* Christ is alive; death is indeed swallowed up in victory.

"O death, where then is your victory? Where then is your sting? For sin [contaminated PAC]—the sting that causes death—will all be gone and the law which reveals our sins will no longer be our judge. How we thank God for all this! It is He who makes us victorious through Jesus Christ our Lord!"*3*

St. Paul challenges everyone to "present and give your bodies to God. Let them be a living sacrifice, holy [healthy, uncontaminated], the kind He can accept. When you think of what God has done for you, is this too much to ask? Don't copy the behavior and customs of this world [First Order System], but be a new and liberated person with a totally fresh, uncontaminated PAC to make you truly alive in all you do and think. From your own experience you can come to know how His ways will really satisfy you."*4* [Paraphrases mine.] The writer of John's Gospel writes that "all who received Him [Christ], He gives the right to become children of God."*5*

In fact, as you are reading this, Jesus is saying to you: "I have been standing at the door of your heart [PAC], and I am constantly knocking. Hear Me calling you and open the door. I will come in and fellowship and be intimate with you, and you with Me...and we will walk the road together."*6*

This is Christ's invitation to the banquet of life. Feast or famine: Which will it be?

Choose Christ this day. He alone can give you the **power to change.** Let Him live out His healthy life within you!

Footnotes

Chapter I.
1 John 18:35-37
2 John 18:38
3 Romans 7:15-35
4 Romans 7:18b
5 John 18:38
6 Romans 7:24
7 Romans 7:25
8 Acts 9:1-22
9 John 8:32

Chapter II.
1 Shakespeare, William. *As You Like It,* Act II, Sc. 7.
2 Watzlawick, Paul; Weakland, John H.; and Fisch, Richard, M.D. *Change: Principles of Problems Formation and Problem Resolution* (New York: W.W. Norton, 1974), pp. 1-5. [Hereinafter referred to as Watzlawick.] Used by permission of W.W. Norton & Company, Inc.

Chapter III.
1 Romans 7:14-23 [Paraphrase is mine.]
2 Watzlawick, *op. cit.,* pp. 1-12.
3 *Ibid.*
4 Whitehead, Alfred North and Russell, Bertrand, *Principia Mathematica,* 2nd Edition (Cambridge: Cambridge University Press, 1910-1913), Vol. 3, p. 37.
5 Watzlawick, op. cit., pp. 110-115.
6 *Ibid.*
7. *Ibid.*

Chapter IV.
1 Harris, Thomas A., M.D., *I'm OK-You're OK.* (New York: Avon Books, 1973), p. 21. [Hereinafter referred to as Harris.] Used by permission of Harper Collins Publishers, Inc.
2 *Ibid.*
3 Berne, Eric, M.D., *Transactional Analysis of Psychotherapy* (New York: Grove Press, 1961), p. 24. [Hereinafter referred to as Berne, *T.A.*] Used by permission of Random House, Inc.
4 Berne, Eric, M.D., *Games People Play* (New York: Grove Press, 1961), p. 129. [Hereinafter referred to as Berne, *Games.*]
5 Harris, *op. cit.,* p. 40.
6 James, Muriel, and Jongeward, Dorothy, *Born To Win* (New York: Signet Classics, The New American Library, Inc., 1971), p. 26. Reprinted by permission of Addison-Wesley Publishing Company, Inc., Reading, Massachusetts.

7   Harris, *op. cit.*, p. 66.

8   *Ibid.*, p. 74.

9   Penfield, Wilder, *Memory Mechanism, AMA* (Archives of Neurology and Psychiatry, Vol. 67, 1957), pp. 178-198. [Hereinafter referred to as Penfield.]

10   *Ibid.*

11   Harris, *op. cit.*, pp. 123-124.

12   Genesis 1:1.

13   Genesis 1:27.

14   Genesis 1:1-27.

15   Henry, Matthew, *Commentary On The Whole Bible,* Vol. 1 (Old Tappan, New Jersey: Fleming H. Revell Co., 1952), p. 2. Available through World Bible Publishers, Inc.

16   Genesis 2:16-17.

17   Genesis 1:28-30.

18   *Ibid.*

19   Romans 8:22.

20   John 15:26.

21   John 8:44.

22   Romans 7:19.

23   Romans 3:23.

24   Harris, *op. cit.*, p. 259.

25   *Ibid.,* pp. 259-260.

26   Romans 3:23.

27   *Ibid.*

Chapter V.

1   Ellis, Albert; Harper, Robert, *A Guide To Rational Living* (North Hollywood, California: Melvin Power Wilshire Book Co., 1978).

2   Matthew 7:1-5.

3   Berne, *Games, op. cit.*

4   Hebrews 9:27; cf. Job 19:25-29.

5   Ross, Elisabeth Kubler, M.D., *On Death And Dying* (New York: Macmillan Publishing Co., 1962), p. 2. Used by permission of Macmillan Publishing Co., Inc.

6   *Ibid.,* pp. 34-121.

7   Glasser, William, M.D., *Reality Therapy: A New Approach To Psycho-therapy* (New York: Perennial Library, Harper & Row, 1965).

Chapter VI.

1   Harris, *op, cit.,* pp. 83-85.

2   Matthew 5:6.

3   Matthew 5:8.

4   Matthew 5:20.

5   Genesis 37:3.

6   Luke 15:11-24.

7   *Ibid.*

271

Chapter VII.

1   Watzlawick, *op. cit.*, pp. 82-83.
2   *Ibid.*, p. 84
3   Wittgenstein, Ludwig, *Philosophical Investigation,* 2nd Ed., translation by G.E.M. Anscomb (New York: Macmillan Publishing Co., Inc., 1958), p. 93. Used by permission of Macmillan Publishing Co., Inc.
4   *Ibid.*, p. 134.
5   Wittgenstein, Ludwig, *Tractatus Logico-Philosophicus* (New York: Humanities Press, 1951), p. 189. Used by permission of Macmillan Publishing Co., Inc.
6   Watzlawick, *op. cit.*, p. 88.
7   *Ibid.*, p. 84.
8   Exodus 17:3.
9   Numbers 13:28-30.
10 Exodus 32:9; 33:3, 5.
11 Matthew 12:43-45.
12 John 3:16.
13 II Corinthians 5:19.
14 Hebrews 2:9-10, 18.
15 Hebrews 1:16-18.
16 Hebrews 4:15.
17 John 8:1-11. [Paraphrase is mine.]
18 Matthew 4:1-11.
19 John 8:58.
20 Luke 22:39-53.
21 Genesis 21:1-7.
22 Genesis 21:1-19. [Paraphrase is mine.]
23 II Chronicles 20:7; James 2:3.
24 John 19:4.
25 Luke 23:39-43.
26 II Corinthians 5:21.
27 Philippians 2:5-8.
28 Hebrews 2:14-15.
29 II Corinthians 5:21.
30 Hebrews 2:9b-10.
31 Mark 15:33-34; Matthew 27:45-46.
32 II Corinthians 5:19.
33 John 20:24-31.
34 *Ibid.*
35 I Corinthians 15:12-20.
36 Acts 9:2-6.
37 Luke 1:1-4.
38 Acts 1:1-3.
39 Acts 1:4.

Chapter VIII.
1   John 3:1-3.
2   John 3:4-8.
3   John 3:9-17.
4   John 3:11-12. [Paraphrase is mine.]
5   John 3:8.
6   Romans 7:25.
7   Romans 8:1-2.
8   II Corinthians 5:17.
9   I Corinthians 15:55.
10 Galatians 2:20.
11 I Corinthians 15:55.
12 *Confessions of St. Augustine,* translated by Edward B. Pusey, D.D. (New York: Pocket Books, Inc., 1951).
13 II Corinthians 5:21; John 1:29; I Peter 2:22-24; Galatians 3:13.
14 John 12:23-24.
15 I Corinthians 15:54b.
16 Mark 10:15; Luke 18:17.
17 Jung, C.G., *Modern Man In Search Of His Soul,* translated by W.S. Dell and Cary F. Baynes (New York:A Harvest House Book, Harcourt, Brace & World, Inc., first published in 1933), p. 122.
18 Matthew 5:3-11; 6:33.
19 John 15:5.
20 Hebrews 5:12-14.
21 Genesis 12:10-20.
22 John 3:8.
23 Genesis 1:1; John 3:6.
24 Genesis 2:7.
25 John 15:26.
26 John 1:12.
27 Matthew 12:44-45.
28 I Corinthians 12:13.

Chapter IX.
1   John 8:32.
2   John 18:37.
3   John 18:38.
4   John 14:4-7.
5   John 14:10-11.
6   John 6:5b-13.
7   John 19:8-11.
8   Romans 7:21.
9   Matthew 27:24.
10 Matthew 27:25.
11 John 14:6.

12 John 8:58.
13 John 8:32.
14 John 16:7.
15 John 16:13-15.
16 John 15:26.
17 John 17:2-5.
18 John 17:23a.
19 John 17:22.
20 John 17:23.
21 John 17:4-25.
22 John 14:26.
23 John 16:33.
24 John 17:24.
25 John 17:4.
26 John 14:8-10; 18:38.
27 John 16:5-11.
28 Thomas, Lewis, M.D., "Diagnosing The Doctor," *Reader's Digest* (Pleasantville, New York: November 1983), pp. 185-188.

Chapter X
1   Matthew 8:10.
2   Isaiah 6:9-10.
3   Mark 4:3-9; Matthew 13:4-9.
4   Matthew 13:10-17.
5   Matthew 13:18-23; Mark 4:14-21.
6   John 18:14.
7   Matthew 13:20-21.
8   John 6:66.
9   John 6:30-31.
10 Mark 4:18-19.
11 Mark 10:18-25.
12 Matthew 19:16-23.
13 Matthew 6:19-34.
14 Matthew 19:25-26.
15 Mark 9:17-24.
16 Matthew 17:20; Luke 17:6.
17 Matthew 13:53-58.
18 Mark 5:24-34, Luke 8:44.
19 Matthew 12:30.
20 Matthew 6:24.
21 Matthew 18:8-9; Mark 9:43-47.
22 Genesis 12:10-16.
23 Genesis 22:1-18.
24 Galatians 1:13; 2:3-5.
25 John 20:24-31.

26 Mark 4:20; Matthew 13:22.
27 Matthew 19:23-26; Mark 10:27; Luke 18:24-27.
28 Jeremiah 4:3.
29 Luke 19:1-10.

Chapter XI.
1   I Corinthians 13:12.
2   Exodus 3:5; Acts 7:33.
3   Exodus 19:12.
4   Hebrews 11:1.
5   John 3:16.
6   John 15:13.
7   Hebrews 11:1-2.
8   Hebrews 11:3.
9   Romans 8:35.
10 Romans 14:11; Philippians 2:10; Isaiah 45:23.
11 Psalms 8:1-9; 104:1-22.
12 Proverbs 23:7, KJV.
13 Romans 7:22.
14 Proverbs 14:12; 16:25.
15 Descartes, Rene, "Discourse On Method," *Encyclopaedia Britannica,*
Macropaedia (Chicago, Illinois), Vol. 5, p. 601.
16 Romans 3:20.
17 Romans 1:17.
18 Symonds, John Addington, *Renaissance In Italy: Revival Of Letters*
(London, 1877).
19 Lindsay, T.M., *History Of The Reformation,* Vol. 1 (Edinburgh: T&T Clark;
New York: Charles Scribner's Sons, latest reprint, 1959), p. 45.

Chapter XII.
1   Franklin, Benjamin, Addressing the Constitutional Convention, 1787.
2   Matthew 12:10-12.
3   *Ibid.*
4   *Ibid.*

Chapter XIII.
1   Hebrews 4:12.
2   John 1:1-5.
3   Colossians 1:15-23.
4   Colossians 2:8-10.
5   Galatians 3:17-25.
6   Romans 3:20-23.
7   Rowley, H.H., *The Unity Of The Bible* (New York: Living Ages Books,
published by Meridian Books, 1957), pp. 19-20. [Hereinafter referred to as Rowley.]
Used by permission of Lutterworth Press, Cambridge, England.
8   II Peter 1:21-22.

9   Rowley, *op. cit.,* p. 20.

10   *Ibid.,* pp. 22

Chapter XIV.

1   Harris, *op. cit.,* p. 248.

2   Branden, Nathaniel, "Psychotherapy And The Objectivist Ethics,"
delivered before the Psychiatric Division of the San Mateo County Medical Society,
January 24, 1966.

3   Luke 14:5.

4   Russell, Bertrand, *Why I Am Not A Christian* (New York: Simon &
Schuster, 1957), pp. 169-170. Used by permission of Simon & Schuster.

5   Philippians 3:7-8.

6   John 15:18; I John 3:13.

7   I John 4:16.

8   Matthew 22:37-39.

9   I Corinthians 13:4-7.

10   Harris, *op. cit.,* p. 257.

11   Ephesians 6:12.

Chapter XV

1   Daniel 5:27.

2   Matthew 5:31-32.

3   Matthew 5:17-20.

4   John 16:9-11.

5   Romans 5:12-15a.

6   Romans 5:15b.

7   Romans 5:19.

8   II Corinthians 5:21.

9   Luke 18:9-14.

10   Isaiah 64:6; Psalm 14:31; 53:3.

11   Matthew 7:24-27.

12   Matthew 7:28-29.

13   Matthew 25:41-43.

14   Matthew 25:44.

15   Matthew 25:45.

16   Romans 1:17b-26.

17   Matthew 7:21-23.

18   John 10:14.

19   Matthew 7:23.

20   John 8:4-11.

21   Jeremiah 17:9-10.

22   Jeremiah 5:1-3.

23   Matthew 10:30; Luke 12:7.

24   Matthew 25:31-34a.

25   Matthew 25:34-36.

26   John 7:7; Luke 14:25-27.

27 Luke 14:27.
28 Matthew 16:25; Mark 8:35; Luke 9:24.
29 John 10:27-28; Matthew 10:22; 24:12-13.
30 Matthew 25:14-28.
31 Matthew 21:28-32; Luke 15:11-32.
32 Luke 23:39-43.
33 Philippians 2:5; I Corinthians 4:20; 15:42-58; II Corinthians 5:1; 10:5.
34 John 3:16-17.

Chapter XVI.
1 Hebrews 10:9; Ephesians 2:14-15.
2 Romans 8:3-4.
3 Romans 8:1-2.
4 Romans 8:13.
5 Romans 8:14-17.
6 Romans 8:22-23.
7 Romans 8:18-28.
8 Ephesians 1:4-5.

SUMMARY
1 Greenleaf, Simon, *Testimony of the Evangelists Examinated by the Rules of Evidence in Courts of Justice,* 1847, public domain. [Reprinted from 1847 edition by Baker Book House, Grand Rapids, Michigan: 1965, pp. 191-192. Also found in *Evidence That Demands A Verdict: Historical Evidence for the Christian Faith* (revised edition, compiled by John McDonnell, San Bernardino, California 92402: Here's Life Publications, Inc.)]
2 Hebrews 10:9.
3 I Corinthians 15:54-57.
4 Romans 12:1-2. [Paraphrase mine.]
5 John 1:12.
6 Revelation 3:20.

BIBLIOGRAPHY

Augsburger, David. *Caring Enough Not to Forgive.* Ventura, California: Regal Books, Div. of Gospel Light Publications, 1981.

Berne, Eric, M.D. *Games People Play.* New York: Grove Press, 1964.

Berne, Eric, M.D. *Transactional Analysis in Psychotherapy.* New York: Grove Press, 1961.

Brand, Dr. Paul, and Yancy, Paul. "A Surgeon's View of Divine Healing," *Christianity Today,* November 25, 1983.

Branden, Nathaniel, "Psychotheraphy and the Objecitivist Ethics," delivered before the Psychiatric Division of the San Mateo County Medical Society, January 24, 1966.

Confessions of St. Augustine, translated by Edward B. Pusey, D.D. New York: Pocket Books, Inc., 1951.

"Descartes, Rene–Discourse on Method," *Encyclopaedia Britannica Macropaedia,* Vol. 5, Chicago, Illinois, 1976.

Diary of George Mueller, compiled by A.J. Randle Short. Grand Rapids, Michigan: Zondervan Publishing House, 1972.

Dostoevski, Fedor Mikhailovich. *Brothers Karamozov.* New York: Modern Library, 1950.

Franklin, Benjamin. Addressing the Constitutional Convention in Philadelpia, 1787.

Glasser, William, M.D. *Reality Therapy: A New Approach to Psychiatry.* New York: Perennial Library, Harper & Row, 1965.

Graham, Billy, *The Holy Spirit.* Waco, Texas: Word Books Publishers, 1980.

Greenleaf, Simon. *Testimony of the Evangelists Examined by the Rules of Evidence Administered in Courts of Justice,* 1847. [Reprinted by Baker Book House, Grand Rapids, Michigan: 1965. Also available in *Evidence That Demands A Verdict: Historical Evidence for the Christian Faith* (revised edition), compiled by John McDonnell, San Bernardino, California: Here's Life Publications, Inc.]

Harris, Thomas A., M.D. *I'm OK - You're OK.* New York: Avon Books, 1973. [First published by Harper & Row, Inc., New York, 1967.]

Henry, Matthew. *Commentary on the Whole Bible,* Vol. 1. Old Tappan, New Jersey: Fleming H. Revell Co., 1952. Available from World Bible Publishers, Inc.

Herklots, H.G.G. *How Our Bible Came To Us.* New York: Galaxy Books, Oxford University Press, 1957.

James, Muriel, and Jongeward, Dorothy. *Born to Win.* New York: Signet Classics, The New American Library, Inc., 1971. Available from Addison-Wesley Publishing Company, Inc., Reading, Massachusetts.

Jung, C.G. *Modern Man in Search of His Soul,* Translated by W.S. Dell and Cary F. Baynes. New York: A Harvest House Book, Harcourt, Brace & World, Inc., 1933.

Kubler-Ross, Elisabeth, M.D. *On Death and Dying.* New York: Macmillan Publishing Co., 1962.

Las Vegas Review Journal, Sunday, September 15, 1985.

Lindsay, T.M. *History of the Reformation,* Vol. 1. Edinburgh: T&T Clark. New York: Charles Scribner's Sons, 1959.

The Living Bible, Paraphrased. Wheaton, Illinois: Tyndale House Publishers, 1972.

Penfield, Wilder. *Memory Mechanism, AMA.* Archives of Neurology and Psychiatry, 67 (1952).

Phillips, J.B. *Your God Is Too Small.* New York: The Macmillan Co., 1961.

Rohrer, Norman B. "A Visit with Joni," *The Christian Reader.* Wheaton, Illinois: Tyndale House, May-June 1982.

Rowley, H.H. *The Unity of the Bible.* New York: Meridian Books (Living Age Books), 1957.

Russell, Bertrand. *Why I Am Not A Christian.* New York: Simon & Schuster, 1957.

Steere, David. "Freud and Gallows Transactions," *Transactional Analysis Bulletin,* Vol. 9, No. 1 (January 1970).

Steiner, Claude. *Games Alcoholics Play: The Analysis of Life Scripts.* New York: Grove Press, 1971.

Symonds, John Addington. *Renaissance in Italy: Revival of Letters.* London: 1877. Currently published by Peter Smith Publisher, 6 Lexington Ave., Magnolia, MA 09130.

"War Games," 1984 release.

Watzlawick, Paul; Weakland, John H.; and Fisch, Richard, M.D. Change: *Principles of Problem Formation and Problem Resolution.* New York: W.W. Norton, 1974.

Whitehead, Alfred North, and Russell, Bertrand. *Principia Mathematica,* 2nd Ed., Vol. 3. Cambridge: Cambridge University Press, 1910-13.

Williams, Albert N. *What Archeology Says About the Bible.* New York: Association Press, 1957.

Wittgenstein, Ludwig. *Philosophical Investigation,* 2nd Ed. Translated by G.E.M. Anscomb, New York: Macmillan Publishing Co., 1958.

Wittgenstein, Ludwig. *Tractatus Logico-Philosophicus.* New York: Humanities Press, 1951.

Woollams, Stan, and Brown, Michael. *TA: The Total Handbook of Transactional Analysis.* Englewood Cliffs, New Jersery: Prentice Hall, Inc., 1979.

OTHER BOOKS NOW AVAILABLE FROM EDEN PUBLISHING, 8635, W. Sahara Ave., Ste. 459, The Lakes, NV 89117. Simply copy and fill out the form below and mail with your check or money order to EDEN PUBLISHING. Larger orders may be sent via FAX to (702) 796-0282 along with a VISA credit card number.

READERS AND DOES OF THE WORD... THE FUN WAY
by Fern A. Ritchey

365 days of Bible-related crafts and activities for families, daycare, VBS, Sunday School, junior church, and teen programs.
ISBN 1-884898-02-5 • *Trade Paperback $12.95*

BIBLE PUZZLES, QUIZZES & WORD SEARCH
by Fern A. Ritchey

Use with children, teens, men's and women's Bible studies, shut-ins, the church's calling program, on vacations, at parties and in family devotions.
ISBN 1-884898-03-3 • 64 pp. • *Paperback $3.95*

POWER TO CHANGE
by John Dan, M.A., M.Div.,

Widely acclaimed breakthrough book by John Dan, Christian Marriage & Family Therapist. *It will transform your relationships!*
ISBN 1-884898-00-9 • *Hardback Edition $24.95*
ISBN 1-884898-01-7 • *Trade Paperback $19.95*

ORDER NOW—TODAY!
FROM EDEN PUBLISHING, 8635 W. Sahara Ave., Ste. 459, The Lakes, NV 89117. Check enclosed. Please rush the following order to:

Name: _____ Phone: ( ) _____
(please print clearly)

Address: _____

City _____ State _____ Zip _____

Quantity Ordered	Book Title and ISBN #	Unit Price	Extended Price
	READERS AND DOERS OF THE WORD ISBN 1-884898-02-5 (Fern Ritchey)	$12.95	
	BIBLE PUZZLES, QUIZZES & WORD SEARCH ISBN 1-884898-03-3 (Fern Ritchey)	$3.95	
	POWER TO CHANGE (Trade Paperback) ISBN 1-884898-01-7 (John Dan)	$19.95	
	POWER TO CHANGE (HARDBOUND EDITION) ISBN 1-884898-00-9 (John Dan)	$24.95	
	TEACHING TRANSPARENCIES from POWER TO CHANGE $6.00		

TOTAL COST OF BOOKS .... $ _____
Add $2.00 for shipping and handling per book. .... $2.00 ea. ..... $ _____
(Orders of 3 or more of any individual title will be shipped free.)
Nevada Residents add 7% State Sales Tax .... 7% .... $ _____
ENCLOSED IS MY CHECK/MONEY ORDER FOR .... $ _____
Feel free to contact us about discounts for larger quantities.
Fax orders with Credit Card (VISA plus Expiration Date) to (702) 796-0282.
Also send information about the above books to:
Name: _____ Phone: ( ) _____
Address: _____
City _____ State _____ Zip _____